Folk Music in School

Edited by

ROBERT LEACH
Lecturer, Department of Drama and Theatre Arts
University of Birmingham
and

ROY PALMER
Headmaster, Dame Elizabeth Cadbury School
Birmingham

CAMBRIDGE UNIVERSITY PRESS
CAMBRIDGE
LONDON · NEW YORK · MELBOURNE

THE RESOURCES OF MUSIC SERIES
General Editors: *Wilfred Mellers, John Paynter*

THE RESOURCES OF MUSIC *by Wilfrid Mellers*
SOUND AND SILENCE *by John Paynter and Peter Aston*
SOMETHING TO PLAY *by Geoffrey Brace*
MUSIC DRAMA IN SCHOOLS *edited by Malcolm John*
THE PAINFUL PLOUGH *by Roy Palmer*
THE VALIANT SAILOR *by Roy Palmer*
TROUBADOURS *by Brian Sargent*
MINSTRELS *by Brian Sargent*
POVERTY KNOCK *by Roy Palmer*
JAZZ *by Graham Collier*
JAZZ LECTURE CONCERT (Record and booklet) *by Graham Collier*
RIGS OF THE FAIR *by Roy Palmer and Jon Raven*
POP MUSIC IN SCHOOL *edited by Graham Vulliamy and Ed Lee*
FOLK MUSIC IN SCHOOL *edited by Robert Leach and Roy Palmer*
VIBRATIONS *by David Sawyer*

Published by the Syndics of the Cambridge University Press
The Pitt Building, Trumpington Street, Cambridge CB2 1RP
Bentley House, 200 Euston Road, London NW1 2DB
32 East 57th Street, New York, NY 20011, USA
296 Beaconsfield Parade, Middle Park, Melbourne 3206, Australia

© Cambridge University Press 1978

First published 1978

Printed in Great Britain at the University Press, Cambridge

Library of Congress Cataloguing in Publication Data
Main entry under title:
Folk music in school.

(The resources of music series)

Includes index.

1. School music – Instruction and study. 2. Folk
music – Addresses, essays, lectures. I. Leach, Robert.
II. Palmer, Roy, fl. 1971–   III. Series.
MT1.F65   77-10560
ISBN 0 521 21595 1 hard covers
ISBN 0 521 29206 9 paperback

Contents

The contributors

A.L. LLOYD has an international reputation as a folklorist and ethnomusicologist and is the doyen of folk-music scholars in this country. His best-known book is *Folk Song in England* (Lawrence and Wishart, 1967; Panther, 1969; Paladin, 1975). As well as being a singer himself he has produced many records of field singers for Topic Records, of which he is artistic director. He is a frequent broadcaster.

PETER COOKE has well over twenty years' experience as a teacher of music in schools, colleges and universities. At present, as head of the music section at the School of Scottish Studies, Edinburgh University, he is concerned with research into all aspects of traditional music culture in Scotland and with the supervision of post-graduate students in ethnomusicology.

MICHAEL POLLARD taught in primary schools for ten years, where he discovered folk music through using it in the classroom. Now a full-time writer, mainly on educational topics, he has published a number of books, including *Ballads and Broadsides* (Pergamon, 1969), a collection for school use.

PAT PALMER teaches at present at King's Heath Junior School, Birmingham. Her experience includes work in both primary and secondary schools together with a good deal of amateur music-making. She has contributed articles to *The Times Educational Supplement*, *The Music Teacher* and *The Observer Colour Supplement*.

JACK DOBBS is Director of Musical Studies at Dartington College of Arts in Devon. As well as teaching in schools he has been county music adviser, university lecturer, and director of music in a Malaysian college. He is the current chairman both of the UK Council for Music Education and of the Schools Council Music Committee. He has edited a music course for primary schools, *Ears and Eyes* (Oxford University Press, forthcoming).

GEOFFREY BRACE has taught for over twenty years in secondary schools of all types: grammar, modern and comprehensive. His present post is Director of Music at the Grammar School, Ottery St Mary. He is widely known for his series of school songbooks, *Something to Sing* (Cambridge University Press, 1963–5).

iv

AILIE MUNRO graduated in Arts at Edinburgh University; after piano study and teacher training she worked in primary and secondary schools in Edinburgh, London and Glasgow, eventually specialising in music-teaching. She went on to take a B.Mus. degree, and her musical education was continued by her daughter, by her son and by the folk-music revival. Since 1968 she has been a lecturer in the music section of the School of Scottish Studies, Edinburgh University.

GEOFFREY SUMMERFIELD currently teaches English at the University of York. He is editor of *Voices* (Penguin, 1970) and other anthologies, and co-editor of John Clare's collected poetry. His own poems have been published in various collections in this country, the USA and the antipodes.

ROY PALMER has taught for twenty years in grammar and comprehensive schools. At present headmaster of the Dame Elizabeth Cadbury School, Birmingham, he has done considerable research into folk music and allied song and has written and lectured extensively on the subject. He has contributed a number of books to the Cambridge University Press Resources of Music series. His other publications include *A Touch on the Times* (1974) and *The Rambling Soldier* (1977) (both Penguin).

ROBERT LEACH has been Head of English at a large comprehensive school and Director of Education Services at the Midlands Arts Centre, and is currently Lecturer in Drama and Theatre Arts at the University of Birmingham. His play for young people *The Wellesbourne Tree* (Blackie, 1975) explores the use of folk music in drama. He has also written a handbook for teachers, *How to Make a Documentary Play* (Blackie, 1975), and has edited a collection of folk plays for secondary schools and an accompanying workbook, *The World of the Folk Play* (Harrap, forthcoming).

SANDRA KERR is a singer, instrumentalist, song-writer and qualified teacher. She frequently lectures on song-writing and folk music and has made several records (mostly with the Critics' Group) and taken part in many radio programmes for schools. She has also helped to provide the music for such television programmes as 'Bagpuss' and 'Combine'.

MICHAEL GROSVENOR MYER graduated from Cambridge in English and has taught for nearly twenty years. At present Head of Upper School in a comprehensive, he is also a freelance journalist, and contributes to *The Times Educational Supplement*, *The Guardian* and *Folk Review*. He regularly sings in folk-song clubs and has appeared on radio and television.

Acknowledgements

Thanks are due to the following for permission to use copyright material: cover photograph, Peter Baker; Plates 1, 8, by courtesy of Birmingham Public Libraries, Local Studies Department; 2, 3, Bodleian Library; 4, 5, 6, British Library; 7, University of London Broadside Collection; 10, Cirencester Newspaper Company; 11, 12, 13, 14, Brian Shuel.

Introduction

Folk song and the allied arts of street ballad and local anthem have been for centuries embedded in the national consciousness; indeed, they helped to create it. They were made for, and largely by, the common people, though they had a very wide appeal.

It is perhaps true to say that today more people than ever before are becoming aware of folk song, which is widely disseminated through books and records, though relatively little on radio and television. Yet less than a century ago, according to Cecil Sharp, 'it was only by a very few people that folk songs were known to exist in this country . . . It was generally assumed that we had no folk songs of our own' (*English Folk Song: Some Conclusions*, 1965 edn, p. xix).

The work of Cecil Sharp, and other pioneer collectors like Lucy Broadwood, Sabine Baring-Gould and Frank Kidson, led to the introduction of English folk songs into the curricula of both primary and secondary schools. Anyone at school in the 1920s, 30s and even 40s will remember 'Strawberry Fair', 'Gossip Joan', 'My Boy Billy', 'Admiral Benbow' and the like. It is fashionable to deride this movement now: the texts were often bowdlerised and the songs banged out to a universal piano accompaniment, and they were presented with a curious detachment, as though they had no connection with life. Nevertheless the tunes were often splendid, the stories exhilarating, and the idiom genuinely vernacular. A more serious reservation is that the material was almost exclusively rural; but at that time most of the urban and industrial songs which we now know still awaited discovery, or rediscovery.

This was one of the achievements of the post-war revival, which started in the 1950s and is still under way. In the last decade, schools have been experiencing the effects of a second wave of folk music. Now, there is greater freedom with texts and subject matter. As well as classic folk song, the repertoires of the street balladeer and the music-hall artist have begun to be explored. Regional, urban and industrial songs have been used, together with contemporary songs in a traditional idiom. Field-recordings of singers have helped to bring about a more authentic delivery. Guitars, concertinas, mouth organs, fiddles and a variety of more exotic instruments have been used, as well as the piano. The concern has often been largely with the song as communication; hence, it has been used by teachers of history, religious education, geography, and above all English, as much as or more than by music

1

teachers, though it is difficult to see why, logically, this should be so. After all, much of the music is in an idiom readily accessible to the ordinary pupil. At primary level particularly it has close affinities with playground song. Folk music can be studied in the classroom as the basis for musical training, though it by no means excludes other forms of music.

This book sets out to illustrate work done with folk music by teachers in a variety of fields. It is therefore mainly taken up with discussion of activities in particular subjects — English, drama, history and music — and with particular age-groups; but we have felt it worth while to set these practical statements in a wider framework. Thus, the chapters by A.L. Lloyd and Peter Cooke raise implications which teachers may care to ponder. We have felt it valuable, too, to suggest ways of bringing folk music and song into the classroom, either through the use of books and records or live by the teacher. Deliberately, most contributors to this book have restricted their comments and illustrations to the British — and in many cases the English — tradition. Nevertheless, we feel that a similar exploration of the folk music of other cultures would be a logical development of the suggestions made here.

Folk art, like the art of Shakespeare, exists and has validity whether or not it is used in schools. Nevertheless, like Shakespeare, it constitutes an invaluable resource for education, if properly employed. We would not suggest that it is a panacea, but we do believe that it can provide an extra dimension which is of real value. Folk music as a core element in an integrated curriculum is a very real possibility. Certainly, it already provides opportunities for much inter-disciplinary work, as several of the chapters on specific subjects suggest. And beyond the school timetable, folk music is often an exciting part of the school's wider social and cultural life, through assemblies, concerts, school plays and special events — harvest festivals, Christmas, Easter and so on. However, it should be added that no teacher needs to feel that he is obliged to become a fanatic in order to succeed with this resource. He can draw on it sparingly or heavily, occasionally or regularly, as seems appropriate. This book is intended to help him when he decides it will be useful.

Language is today commonly seen as central to the educational process, and one respect in which folk song is particularly important is that it uses vernacular language is a unique way. Vernacular is 'the language of slaves' — that is, now, the language of the common people — and any teacher ignoring it may be doing his pupils a considerable disservice. The folk song and ballad provide one key to an understanding of vernacular, because they demonstrate this kind of language at its finest.

For the common people, speech — the oral language — has always been a particularly keen tool, yet one whose keenness is essentially different from the keenness of the literary language. Some of the speech recorded by Ewan MacColl, Peggy Seeger and Charles Parker in their Radio Ballads shows the vernacular at its most potent:

I was taught at a very early age that it was like hitting out with the hammer of hate on the anvil of bitterness . . .
(John Williams, miner, on *The Big Hewer*)

Railways went through the back of your spine like Blackpool went through rock . . .
(Jim Howarth, train driver, on *The Ballad of John Axon*)

These folk will exist till the end o' time, and they'll never, ever change their ways, and you'll never get rid o' tinkers. They'll be there till Doomsday in the afternoon . . .
(Belle Stewart, tinker, on *The Travelling People*)

The vitality of the vernacular comes from the fact that it is the language of non-literate (not necessarily illiterate) people — people who store most of their wisdom and experience in their heads and not on pieces of paper, and whose need for a vivid spoken language is therefore paramount. Few of our pupils may rise to the heights of poetic utterance which John Williams, Jim Howarth and Belle Stewart achieve here — but it is from within this linguistic context that most of them operate orally. Folk song can teach us to recognise not just the validity of this context, but also its extraordinary versatility, potential and power.

Moreover, an understanding of folk song can shed new light on the nature of children's creativity. In the first place, folk art at its best is both improvisatory and ritualistic, involving constant reinterpretation of familiar material according to the situation, the audience, the artist's mood, and so on; it is never a once-for-all fixed and finished piece. And secondly, folk art expresses particularly powerfully shared experience as against individual experience. This is not to say that it cannot express an individual experience, merely that it is often most exciting when voicing a communal attitude or experience. 'Railways went through the back of your spine like Blackpool went through rock' is an individual expression of an attitude probably shared by most railwaymen. It specifically relates to railwaymen's experience of their work and their life, but few would want to deny that the use of language is genuinely creative. Similarly, the song 'Admiral Benbow' voices the shared feelings of Benbow's men during the battle, not an individual's experience of it. Folk art, in other words, is a binding, inclusive kind of art, one which expresses solidarity amongst people who have things in common. In our often divisive society, this may be of some consequence. We think of the dying Johnnie Armstrong saying in his 'Last Goodnight':

> . . . Fight on, my merry men all,
>   And see that none of you be ta'en;
> For I will stand by and bleed but a while,
>   And then I will come and fight again.

Or the agricultural labourers joining together to sing, 'Oh, the prop of the land is the hard-working man . . .'

Children are, of course, some of the non-literate members of our society, and they have preserved for themselves a huge store of language, song and custom. It should be remembered that folk song is not a solitary phenomenon, but part of a continuum of folk culture which includes language (sayings, idioms, turns of phrase, aphorisms), lore (proverbs, beliefs, superstitions), ritual (dance, drama, ceremony, custom), and material art (artefacts, and even houses and landscapes). Perhaps because folk culture is so clearly akin to children's culture — indeed children's culture is a form of folk culture — we find that it has a strong appeal to young people. This is particularly true of folk song, which is often able to encapsulate an experience in an unusually direct and concrete manner. The directness makes for immediate communication. Whatever the subject of the song — and there is hardly an area of life which is not celebrated in folk song — the primacy of communicating is usually there, and young people undoubtedly find such honesty refreshing.

It often seems that there is today a growing interest in the past, an increasingly important search for roots. This may help to explain the renewed vigour of the folk-song revival, the growing interest in mumming plays, the popularity of traditional events of all kinds. Certainly, there seems to be a reversal of the trend which was observable from the time of the Industrial Revolution right into the present century, that of breaking with the past, particularly in its traditional elements. The new tendency to conserve and build on the past is surely a healthy one. Folk culture, perhaps particularly folk music, has an integral part to play in the new processes of rebuilding.

1 *The meaning of folk music*

A. L. LLOYD

It has long been understood that folk song is a special kind of artistic creation. (See particularly P.G. Bogatyrev and R. Jakobson, 'Die Folklore als eine besondere Form des Schaffens' in *Donum natalicum Schrijnen* (Nijmegen–Utrecht, 1929), 900–13.) It differs from formal literature and music in the way it's made and transmitted, and it differs in function too. In its natural state, folk song is an oral art, not a written one. Formal poetry or music is objectified: that is, you can handle it, you pick up a book and there it is on the page, in the form in which the author or composer intended it to be read or performed. Folk song is subjectified; it has no fixed form, it is there in the singer's head and it only exists while it is actually being uttered, and the next performer who comes along may utter it differently. The path of formal literature is from page to reader. The path of folk song is from performer to performer. Behind each individual folk song is an amorphous mass of ancestors of the same piece; ahead of it, if the tradition is alive, stretches an unpredictable line of descendants. Folk song proper is an art of variation, and it is an art with its own history, just as surely as the fine arts have theirs. And if each folk song has no fixed identity, existing simply as a bundle of variants under constant change, well, the folk themselves — whoever the 'folk' may be — are likewise undergoing transformation all the time. Societies change, and their songs change with them.

Allow me to offer a picture that is admittedly crude, idealised, over-systematic but, I believe, in rough outline as true as average. The classic type of tribal or clan society is intensely communal. Culturally the group is more or less all of a piece without much distinction between 'high' and 'low'. The land is likely to be collectively owned, worked in gangs for the common good. The great virtues are those that hold the community together: courage, loyalty, solidarity; private sentiments count for little (a modern Albanian folklorist reports that when he asked a mountaineer for love songs, the singer replied: 'Such songs are not fit for heroes'). The everyday songs of such societies are likely to be collective in character, with plenty of refrains for the mob to join in, and if the texts carry a message (and quite often they are wordless, or wildly redundant) the subject matter is likely to be of general concern to all rather than the expression of an individual's state of mind. Such, we stress, are the typical *everyday* songs of such societies. For diversion or encouragement, they are likely to have a number of hero epics and praise songs of substantial length.

5

With the 'folk' of post-feudal times, the situation is otherwise. Over most of Europe at least, the peasant smallholder, the family farmer in an underdog position, is the typical representative of the social order whose cultural horizon is bounded by folklore — individualistic, segregated ('This bit of land is mine and nobody else's'), proud of the privacy of his little family within the seclusion of their four walls. Such a person would in most cases be not unneighbourly, but for him the great virtues would be those that reinforce his individuality — independence, self-reliance, a dogged sense of his personal rights. Private feelings count for much, and it shows in the songs. For instance, the love song, of little weight in classic tribal societies, predominates among the post-feudal bearers of folk song. For them, the characteristic song is not collective, choral; rather they favour the solo song of personal emotion. In such communities, the sung tales, equivalent of the epic of earlier societies, become short novelistic ballads.

The 'folk' of industrial societies are different again. In a sense their outlook and their home-made culture synthesise the views and the lore of both the former societies sketched above, but on a quite different level. It is well known that the coming of industrialisation broke up many of the old rural communities; it is not always realised that the growth of industry brought about a new group awareness. The solidarity of mining communities is proverbial; also, quite clearly in the Industrial Revolution the establishment of large factories employing hundreds of spinners or weavers under one roof meant an enlargement of communal feeling among textile workers. Subsequently this tendency among the new working class was strengthened by the growth of trade unions with their firm emphasis on common action. For the makers and bearers of industrial folklore, the great virtues are a combination of solidarity and independence, at once a sense of class pride and personal pride, a strong feeling for the homely kin but also for the working community. The workers' folk songs — those created from within the industries on behalf of the community of 'insiders' — reflect this synthesis. They are predominantly collective, not necessarily in form (though chorus-songs abound) but notably in content. In the repertory of industrial song, works of private emotion — love lyrics and such — are rare and belong mainly to the early stages of the tradition. More characteristic are the songs of communal concern, strike songs, disaster songs, songs of craft pride, everyday comedies and dramas affecting the crowd.

Do not imagine that in offering this simplified picture of the society and folklore of the remote past, yesterday and today, I am suggesting a linear evolution with each phase having its tidy beginning and end. Not at all. Such developments are quite uneven. The habits and notions of former societies linger on here and there long after one might have expected them to fade. European feudal society had many features that it inherited from the ancient world: European capitalism is cluttered with feudal relics. So too the song styles and indeed the actual songs of various anterior societies are co-existent in present-day Britain. In current jargon they are at once diachronic and synchronic, coming one after another in time yet living side by side. What? elements of tribal song still with us? We need only recall that in parts of Scotland, for instance, the clan system was predominant till the mid eighteenth century, and strong vestiges of its culture have not only coloured the folk song of later times, but also survived almost intact, well into the twentieth century, in fringe territories such as the Hebrides. The famous waulking songs, sung to accompany the fulling of tweed, are still fresh in the mouths of many island women, and they are prime examples of a kind of collective song whose form has remained constant not merely through centuries but through millennia. Our example, from the island of Lewis, was recorded in 1955.

He mandu, 's truagh nach di-geadh, He mandu, siodh 'gham iar - raidh,
He mandu, gil-le's li-tir, Hi ri o - ro each is diol-laid, He man-du, hi ri o - ro Ho ro hu o.

> *He mandu*
> 's truagh nach digeadh
> *He mandu*
> siodh 'gham iarraidh
> *He mandu*
> gille 's litir
> *Hi ri oro*
> each is diollaid
> *He mandu*
> *Hi ri oro*
> *Ho ro hu o.*

(Transcribed from a Tangent recording, *Scottish Tradition II, Music from the Western Isles* (TNGM 110), side 1, band 1)

(Apart from the refrain-vocables, the text of this song, as often, consists of phrases drawn more or less piecemeal from other songs, without much regard to continuity or even logic. The words of this first 'strophe' run: 'Alas, that these don't come to fetch me — a messenger and a letter, a horse and saddle.')

It is the post-feudal folk song, the product of segregated small family farmers — many of whom were becoming part of a rural proletariat of farm labourers in England by the eighteenth century — that forms the most characteristic part of the British traditional lyric, the kind of lyric we most immediately recognise as folk song. As we have mentioned, the general tendency of these songs is towards an expression of personal emotion. The 'I' song is uppermost. We offer as typical a piece that has been recorded in innumerable variants during the twentieth century in many parts of England, Scotland and Ireland. It is one of nine versions collected by Cecil Sharp.

Oh, when that I saw my love in the church stand,
With the ring on her finger and the glove in her hand,
I jumped in betwixt them and kissed the false bride,
Saying: 'Adieu to false loves for ever.'

Oh, when that I saw my love out the church go,
With the bridesmen and bridesmaids they made a fine show,
Then I followed after with my heart full of woe,
For I was the man that ought to had her.

Oh, when I saw my love sat down to meat,
I sat myself by her but no thing could eat.
I thought her sweet company better than wine,
Although she was tied to some other.

Go dig me a grave both long, wide and deep,
And strew it all over with flowers so sweet,
That I may lay down there and take my long sleep,
And that's the best way to forget her.

(From R. Vaughan Williams and A.L. Lloyd, *The Penguin Book of English Folk Songs* (1959), p. 37)

Where modern industrial societies are concerned, the typical home-made songs are again collective, communal, in text content at least if not always in form, whether they treat of strike or disaster, union exhortation or craft pride, like the following song from the Clyde shipyards concerning the building of the liner *Queen Elizabeth II*, a song that acquired new force a few years back with the dramatic work-in at the UCS yards. It is called 'The Ballad of the Q4', and was recorded on 19 March 1971 in the Burnside Hotel, Glasgow. The singer was Matt McGinn.

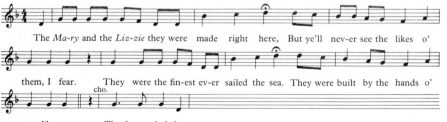

The *Ma-ry* and the *Liz-zie* they were made right here, But ye'll nev-er see the likes o' them, I fear.   They were the fin-est ev-er sailed the sea. They were built by the hands o' men like me.   *Thank you, dad, for* etc.

(Chorus) Thank you, dad, for all your skill,
          But the Clyde is a river that'll no stand still.
          Ye did gey well, but we'll do more;
          Make way for the finest of 'em all — Q4!

The *Mary* and the *Lizzie* they were made right here,
But ye'll never see the likes o' them, I fear.
They were the finest ever sailed the sea.
They were built by the hands o' men like me.
(Chorus) Thank you, dad, etc.

We have an order we'll fulfil
With a touch of the master an' a bit more skill.
Now, the backroom boys are on their way,
An' their pens ull be runnin' till the launchin' day.
(Chorus) Thank you, dad, etc.

There's big Tom O'Hara wi' his burnin' gear,
The plumber an' the painter an' the engineer.
There's young Willie Wylie wi' his weldin' rod.
They'll be waitin' at the ready for the backroom nod.
(Chorus) Thank you, dad, etc.

We'll burn an' cut an' shape an' bend.
We'll be weldin' an' rivettin' an' in the end,
When the painter puts his final coat,
We'll be launchin' the finest ever shot the lot.
(Chorus) Thank you, dad, etc.

We've worked an' sweated an' toiled, an' now
See the expert's hand from stern to bow.
She's ready for the turn and so to sea,
She's a credit to the Clyde an' you an' me.
(Chorus) Thank you, dad, etc.

What are we to understand by 'folk'? In the minds of traditional folklorists, the 'folk' comprise the lower layers of society as they developed in the period between the latter days of feudalism and the days of mass industry. For such traditionalists, the term is attached in the main to country people — smallholders, farm workers, small craftsmen, artisans and have-nots, the inhabitants of farmsteads, villages, perhaps the outskirts of provincial towns relatively isolated from more progressive urban centres. The stage of society contained by this view has been much romanticised by scholars with a sentiment for the quaint, the antiquarian. Folklorists such as Cecil Sharp, landing in the hayfields from the outer space of bourgeois Hampstead, saw their country singers as a kind of noble savages, unlettered, innocent, free from the pestilence of the sinful city. 'Rousseau lives!' might well have been the slogan of many folk-song enthusiasts of the early twentieth century, who looked for ancient idylls (old is good, new can't be), and whose work — valuable if narrow in scope — was inspired by their longing for an idealised past rather than by observation of life as it really is.

The modern view of the 'folk' goes far beyond the traditionalists' rural utopianism (which sometimes, as with Bartók, took the form of a romantic anti-capitalism). I would suggest that nowadays by 'folk' we understand groups of people united by shared experience and common attitudes, skills, interests and aims. These shared attributes become elaborated, sanctioned, stabilised by the group over a period of time. Any such group, with communally shaped cultural traits arising 'from below' and fashioned by 'insiders', might be a suitable subject for folklore studies. Some of these groups may be rich in oral folklore (anecdotes, speechways, etc.) but deficient in songs; others may be specially notable for superstitions and customs. Perhaps for English society the most clearly defined of such groups are those attached to various basic industries: for example, miners with their special attitudes, customs, lore and language, song culture and such. But it will be seen that my suggestion does not rule out the possibility of regarding hitherto unexplored fields, such as the realms of students, actors, bank clerks, paratroopers, hospital nurses, as suitable territory for the folklorist to survey.

The present-day folklorist, who views the problem in its social entirety, and extends his researches into the process by which traditional folklore becomes adapted to the conditions of modern industrial life, has to consider the classic 'peasant' traditions as being but a part — the lower limit, if you like — of a process by which folklore becomes an urban popular affair. Indeed, as far as song is concerned, that is the present stage of folklore development: nowadays there is far greater use of the folk-song repertory and of folkloric forms of creation in our industrial towns than in the countryside.

In a sense, the situation is not so novel as some pretend: the process by which folklore becomes an urban affair has been going on for centuries. From the time when capitalism began to emerge towards the end of the Middle Ages, with the expansion of urban marketing and the practice of paying money wages for labour, the folkloric idiom of the peasantry was coming into amiable collision with the popular idiom of townsfolk. The contact was made mostly in the market places, in the inns and on fairgrounds, and it increased as the smallholders came to have more and more surplus produce to sell in the trading centres. From this contact arose a somewhat altered — one could call it hybrid — kind of folklore that in the course of centuries of development eventually took on forms typical of modern industrial society.

An early product of this process is the lyrical ballad, the most prestigious form of folk song in the view of Eng. Lit. professors, with its neat strophic verse form, its message-laden content, its rounded songlike tune. The features of the ballad contrast strongly with those of the more autarchic folk compositions such as the songs made to accompany work tasks, which are often non-strophic (as far as text is concerned), sung to single- or two-lined tunes instead of the four-lined ones usual in English-language ballads, with texts that are generally scrappy and loaded with repetitive refrains, as with the hauling shanties of nineteenth-century clippermen. Compared with the more basic kind of shanty, the classic folk ballad shows that it owes quite a lot to cultivated poetry and melody of past urban fashions, particularly where the form of verse and tune is concerned. To take a standard ballad of which Bertrand

Bronson (in his *Traditional Tunes of the Child Ballads* (Princeton, N.J., 1966), vol. III, pp. 278—9) prints some sixty variant tunes, mostly collected in the twentieth century, here is 'Geordie' (or 'Georgie') as sung by the Norfolk farm worker Harry Cox in the 1950s.

As I walked o - ver _ Lon-don _ Bridge One mid - sum-mer's morn - ing ear - ly, And there I be - held a fair la-dy La - ment- ing for her Geor - gie.

As I walked over London Bridge
One midsummer's morning early,
And there I beheld a fair lady
Lamenting for her Georgie.

'I pray can you send me a little boy
Who can go on an errand swiftly?
Who can go ten miles in one hour
With a letter for a lady.

'So come saddle me my best black horse,
Come saddle it quite swiftly,
So I may ride to the King's Castle Gaol
And beg for the life of me Georgie.'

So when she got to the castle door
The prisoners stood many:
They all stood around with their caps in their hands
Excepting her bonny bonny Georgie.

'My Georgie never stole neither horse nor cow
Nor done any harm to any;
He stole sixteen of the king's fat deers
Which grieved me most of any.°

'Now six pretty babes that are born by him,
The seventh lay at my bosom;
I would freely part with six of them
To spare the life of me Georgie.'

Now the judge he looked over his left shoulder.
He seemed so very hard-hearted.
He said: 'Fair lady, you are too late,
Your Georgie is condemned already.'

'Now me Georgie shall be hanged in the chains of gold,
Such gold as they don't hang many,
Because he come of the royal blood
And courted a very rich lady.'

(To be heard on a Topic record, *The Folk Songs of Britain*, vol. 5: *The Child Ballads II* (12T 161) side 1, band 9)

Some versions have: 'And sold them in Bohemy'.

A modern theory suggests that the lyrical folk ballad as we know it first showed itself in late medieval France at the turn of the thirteenth and fourteenth centuries, and spread out in ripples from the centre. The territories nearest the centre, such as England, Germany and North Italy, received the ballad in its classic form. Those further off, such as Spain and Portugal, Bohemia, Scotland and Scandinavia, received it too, but in more attenuated form that allowed shaggier or more epic—heroic pre-occupations — magical, militaristic and such — to mingle with that graceful novelistic utterance that, according to this theory, is proper to the original West European lyrical folk ballad. Arising from this comes the novel suggestion that the ballads of magical content, generally thought to represent the oldest stratum, may often in fact be later developments of quite realistic song-tales that became infused with spooky bits as the ballad flowed up into the Northern mists.

Presenting this plausible if unproven hypothesis, Lajos Vargyas suggests that the ballad evolved when and where it did on account of a change in the life of the people that brought about a change in their taste and their demands on poetry (*Researches into the Medieval History of the Folk Ballad* (Budapest, 1967)). It was a time when the new system of ground rent appeared, in which money gradually replaced what the peasant had formerly paid his landlord in labour and kind. To keep pace with rising demands, more intensive cultivation was required, hence the three-crop system, improvements in the plough, here and there the substitution of the more efficient scythe for the sickle. The peasant's need for money meant the increased marketing of his agricultural surplus in the towns, and thus his closer contact with urban culture, whose relative graces and general lyricism were congenial to the new spirit among the bearers of folklore. Indeed, some scholars will have it that the beginning of folk song proper, folk song as we understand the term, dates from this time. Thus the German Lutz Mackensen suggests that in earlier times, if knight and peasant differed in social standing, they resembled each other in culture, or lack of it: their view of the world was similar, their music too. The picture only changed when an urban merchant patriciate evolved, which not only created new usages but also participated in education, which till then had been the professional privilege of the clergy. So began the evolution that split the community, and the 'people', for-merly to a large degree internally united, became divided into two classes, the 'cul-tured' and the 'uncultured'. Thus the gap began to form between the high arts and the folk arts. Says Mackensen, 'folk song as we understand it can only be imagined when the spiritual unity of a nation gives way to class stratification'. The argument requires a more subtle dialectic, for the same factors that were making for class division and cultural gap were also, in Western Europe at least, facilitating the peasant's contact with urban popular music and poetry.

Lofty spirits have maintained that the 'uncultured' classes are incapable of creat-ing works of art for themselves, that folk song is merely a comedown version of a kind of lyric evolved in former times by educated people and now passed out of fashion in its original circle. Others, particularly nineteenth-century romantics, have held the opposite view, that the noble rustic savage created his own poetical and musical repertory without reference to cosmopolitan high culture, and from this notion arose the idea, not far from chauvinism, that folk song is 'national song', somehow enshrining the soul of the race.

We have to realise that much of our balladry, and a good deal of shorter lyrical folk song too, far from being an exclusively national product and possession, is broadly and firmly international. Of the first hundred pieces (i.e. the older stratum) in Child's *English and Scottish Popular Ballads*, approximately three-quarters have their close parallels in foreign balladry, and in many cases the ballad is shared by a large number of continental countries ranging from Portugal to Greece, from Sweden to Sicily.

Let one example stand for many. Child's no. 4, called 'Lady Isabel and the Elf Knight' (it has many other titles, including 'May Colvin' and 'The Outlandish Knight', also 'Take off, take off them silken stays') shows itself to be one of the most persistent ballads among English-speaking singers. Bronson alone prints 143 variant tunes and texts, and many others have come to light. Seemingly it is based on a turbulent epic tale of considerable antiquity (a Siberian gold relief of the third century B.C. in the Leningrad Hermitage appears to present a scene from the story) that became widely current in Europe and at some stage was versified and spread as a ballad as far westward as Portugal, as far eastward at least as Poland and Romania. Exactly when the tale was lyricised is unclear, but the ballad was already printed on a Nuremberg broadside of 1550 (more than 270 German-language variants of the ballad have been reported). For the sake of comparison we offer one of several French versions, called 'Renaud, tueur des femmes' ('Renaud the woman-killer'):

Renaud a de si grands appas
Qu'il a charmé la fille au roi.
L'a bien emmenée à sept lieues
Sans qu'il lui dît un mot ou deux.

Quand sont venus à mi-chemin,
'Mon Dieu, Renaud, que j'ai grand faim!'
'Mangez, la belle, votre main,
Car plus ne mangerez de pain.'

Quand sont venus au bord du bois,
'Mon Dieu, Renaud, que j'ai grand soif!
'Buvez, la belle, votre sang,
Car plus ne boirez de vin blanc.

Il y a là-bas un vivier
Où treize dames sont noyées.
Treize dames y sont noyées;
La quatorzième vous serez.'

Quand sont venus près du vivier,
Lui dit de se déshabiller.
'N'est pas affaire aux chevaliers
De voir dames se déshabiller.

Mets ton épée dessous tes pieds
Et ton manteau devant ton nez.'
Mit son épée dessous ses pieds
Et son manteau devant son nez.

La belle l'a pris, embrassé.
Dans le vivier elle l'a jeté.
'Venez, anguilles, venez, poissons,
Manger la chair de ce larron.'

Renaud voulut se rattraper
A une branche de laurier.
La belle tire son épée,
Coupe la branche de laurier.

'Belle, prêtez-moi votre main.
Je vous épouserez demain!'
'Va-t'en, Renaud, va-t'en au fond,
Epouser les dames qui y sont!'

'Belle, qui vous ramenera
Si vous me laissez dans ce lieu-là?'
'Ce sera ton cheval grison
Qui suit fort bien le postillon.'

'Belle, que diront vos parents
Quand vous verront sans votre amant?'
'Leur dirai que j'ai fait de toi
Ce que voulais faire de moi.'

'Belle, donnez-moi votre main blanche.
Je vous épouserez dimanche.'
'Epouse, Renaud, épouse, poisson,
Les treize dames qui sont au fond.'

(From Henri Davenson, *Le livre des chansons* (Neuchâtel, 1946), pp. 192–5)

(Renaud has such great charm that he has enchanted the king's daughter. He's carried her off some seven leagues without saying more than a word or two.//When they have gone halfway, 'My God, Renaud, but I'm hungry!' 'Eat your hand, my handsome, for you'll not eat bread again.'//When they came to the edge of the wood, 'My God, Renaud, but I'm thirsty!' 'Drink your blood, my handsome, for you'll not drink white wine again.//There is a pond down there where thirteen ladies are drowned. Thirteen ladies are drowned in it; the fourteenth you shall be.'//When they come near the pond he tells her to undress. 'It's no business of knights to see ladies undressing.//Put your sword beneath your feet and your cloak before your nose.' He puts his sword beneath his feet and his cloak before his nose.//The fair one has taken him, embraced him. Into the pond she's cast him. 'Come, eels, come, fish, eat this scoundrel's flesh.'//Renaud tries to take hold of a branch of a laurel tree. The fair one takes his sword, cuts the branch of the laurel tree.//'My handsome, lend me your hand. I'll marry you tomorrow!' 'Away, Renaud, down to the bottom. Marry the ladies who are there!'//'Who will take you back, my handsome, if you leave me in this place?' 'It'll be your dapple horse, that follows the postillion well.' //'My handsome, what will your parents say, when they see you without your lover?' 'I'll tell them that I've done with you what you wanted to do with me.'// 'My handsome, give me your white hand. I'll marry you on Sunday.' 'Marry, Renaud, marry, you fish, the thirteen ladies down at the bottom.')

The same story, practically without alteration, spread to Italy and England, and, with some changes, to the Lowlands, the German territories, and beyond (for instance, more than fifty versions are reported from Hungary). An English version recorded in 1974 from the Shropshire farm worker Fred Jordan follows the course of the French story closely enough, with the traditional element, usual in English and Scottish versions, of the artful talking bird, once magical, now rationalised into a parrot.

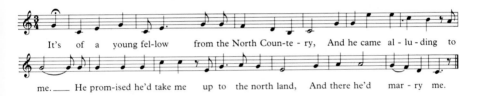

It's of a young fellow from the North Country,
And he came alluding to me.
He promised he'd take me up to the north land,
And there he'd marry me.

'Come bring to me your father's gold,
Your mother's wealth', said he,
'And the two best horses that stands in the stall,
Where there stands thirty and three.'

She brought him out her father's gold,
And her mother's wealth got she,
And the two best horses that stood in the stall
Where there stood thirty and three.

She mounted on a milk-white steed,
Him on a dapple-grey.
Many miles they rode till they reached the sea
So long before it's day.

'Alight, alight from off your steed.
Deliver him now unto me.
Six pretty fair maids I have drowned here.
The seventh one you shall be.

'Come strip me off your fine silken blouse
And all of your jewels', said he,
'For better I sell them for what they are worth
Than they rot with you under the sea.'

'Oh stay, oh stay, you false-hearted man,
And turn your visage', said she,
'For not fitting it is that a ruffian like you
A naked lady should see.'

So he turned his head while she undressed,
To where the leaves grow green.
She caught him by the small of the waist
And she flung him into the sea.

He plungèd high and he plungèd low,
And at last the side reached he.
'Oh, save my life, my pretty fair maid,
And my bride you shall be.'

'Lie there, lie there, you false-hearted man.
Lie there instead of me;
For if six pretty maids you have drownèd here,
The seventh has drownèd thee.'

So she mounted on her milk-white steed;
She led his dapple-grey;
And fast she rode till she reached her own home
Just as it was breaking the day.

Now the parrot that was in the window so high
Looked down as he saw her ride by.
'Where has thou been, thou wilful child?
Some ruffian has led thee astray.'

'Don't prittle, don't prattle, my pretty Polly,
Oh, and tell no tales on me,
And thy cage shall be made of the glittering gold,
The door of the best ivory.'

'Why shouted so loud my pretty Polly,
So loud and so early?' quoth he.
'Oh, the cat has climbed up in the window so high,
And I fear that he will have me.'

'Well done, well done, my pretty Polly.
For you've changed your tale well for me.
So thy cage shall be made of the glittering gold,
And its door of the best ivory.'

(Transcribed from a Topic record, *When the Frost Is on the Pumpkin* (12TS 233), side 1, band 1)

If indeed this relatively graceful kind of poetry and melody — applied as it was to a ferocious story from the shaggy heroic past — reflects a certain lyrical expansion of the peasant horizon, we need to recall that while the conversion of the peasant's surplus produce into cash gave the prospect of more tolerable living conditions, the acquisition of personal property, a growing self-confidence on the part of the under-dog, the economic changes were also a source of tension and unrest, reflected in the countless local rebellions like the French Jacquerie of 1358 or the English rising of 1381, or (more rarely) full-scale civil wars such as the war of the Catalan *remensas* in the fifteenth century, or the German peasant war at the beginning of the sixteenth. (These and other popular subversive movements of the late Middle Ages are well discussed in Rodney Hilton's *Bond Men Made Free* (M.T. Smith, 1973).) In parts of England and Scotland, the woods were haunted by rebels and outlaws on the run from authority and conducting guerrilla warfare against seigneurial power. The common people viewed these outlaws as champions, and celebrated them as *their* heroes in the ballads of Robin Hood, Hughie Graeme, Johnny Cock and the like.

If the 'classic' kind of romantic novelistic ballad of amorous or domestic situation represented one branch of folk song, the outlaw ballads represented another branch, specifically realistic and subversive, leading to the kind of protesting songs of rootless men — beggars, sailors, itinerant labourers — that ultimately formed a bridge between the old rural folk lyric and the home-made songs of the industrial towns (that bridging role is seen most clearly in the so-called 'bothy songs' of Scottish seasonal farm workers).

Among the surviving ballads of early outlaws is the sung tale of Johnny Cock, also known as Johnny of Braidislie or Johnny the Brime, whose territory is vaguely put as somewhere in Northumbria or Dumfriesshire, and whose era is more shadowy still. The redoubtable Jean Robertson recorded this exemplary version for the BBC Archive in 1953. (The BBC Library number of the recording is 21091.) The tale unfolds somewhat like an incident in a Western movie.

John-ny he rase one May morn-in', Cold wa-ter to wash his hands: Roar-in', 'Bring to me my twa grey-hounds That are bound in i- ron bands, bands, That are bound in i- ron bands.'

Johnny he rase one May mornin',
Cold water to wash his hands:
Roarin', 'Bring to me my twa greyhounds
That are bound in iron bands.'

His old wife she wrung her hands:
'To the greenwoods dinnae gang,
All for the sake of the venison
To the greenwoods dinnae gang.'

But Johnny went up in Monymusk
And down on through some scrogs,°
And it was there he spied a dandy leap,°
Lyin' in a bush of sprogs.°

The first arrow he fired at her,
For he wounded her on the side,
And between the water and the wood,
Oh, his greyhounds laid her pride.

Johnny he ate of the venison
And the dogs drunk of her blood,
Till Johnny and his twa greyhounds
Fell a-sleepin' in the woods.

But by came a silly old man,
And an ill death may he dee!
He went up and tellt the first forester,
And he tellt what he did see.

'If that is Johnny frae Brimie's land,
We better leave him a-be.
If that is Johnny frae Brimie's land,
We better leave him a-be.'

He went up and tellt the seven foresters.
He was Johnny's sister's son.
'If that is young Johnny the Brime,
Tae the greenwoods we will gang.'

The first arrow they fired at him,
For they wounded him on the thee,°
And the second arrow they fired at him,
His hairt's blood blind his e'e.

But Johnny rose up wi' an angry growl,
For an angry man was he.
'I will kill all you six foresters,
And break the seventh one's back in three!'

He put his foot upon a stone
And his back against a tree,
And he killed all the six foresters
And broke the seventh one's back in three.

Johnny broke his back in three,
And he broke his collar-bone,
And he tied him on his grey mare's back
For to carry the tidin's home.

scrogs underwood
dandy leap dun deer asleep
sprogs blackthorn
thee thigh

Other versions have memorable moments such as Johnny's apostrophe to the foresters and to his bow and hand, after his assailants have wounded him while sleeping:

'The wildest wolf in aw this wood
Wad not ha' done so by me;

> She's ha' wet her foot i' the wan water,
> And sprinkled it o'er my brae,°
> And if that wad not ha' wakened me
> She'd ha' gone and let me be.
>
> O bows of yew, if ye be true,
> In London where ye were bought,
> Fingers five, get up belive,
> Manhood shall fail me nought.'

brae brow

The talking bird (starling or parrot) appears towards the end of some versions of this ballad too, reminding Johnny's mother or his men that the outlaw is long returning. In at least one version, reminiscent of some epic hero-ballads of the ancient world, his men, warned by a bird at the window, find the runagate dying, and bear his body home on a bier made of hazel and sloe-thorn rods.

Indeed, the wide air of ancient hero-epic still blew through many of the lyrical ballads, even if the blast was tempered to suit the manners and outlook of the newer, less rude societies. But where the most classic type is concerned, in the view of such an experienced scholar as Lajos Vargyas, 'the ballad is a medieval genre: what we are witnessing today is merely its final expiry, in which we cannot recognise its once flourishing life' (op. cit., p. 7).

Too pessimistic, that view? We must realise that, in folk song, varying degrees of folkishness are involved. The tradition of deep folklore, once clearly separate from the tradition of fine art, has tended over the centuries to move closer towards urban popular culture, towards a music and poetry showing ever fewer divergences from the conventions of the arts of the 'establishment'. In the course of that passage, lower-class music and poetry have become increasingly susceptible of being turned into commodity goods. For instance, folk song has been adapted in various ways as 'performance' song, sung 'for listening to', and directed to audiences that may well be total strangers to the singer, outsiders, not an in-group. Thus we find folk song as street song, fairground song, pleasure-garden song, ballad-opera song, etc., all kinds that have deeply affected the repertory of the bearers of traditional lyric, just as in recent times the repertories of quite remote communities in the Balkans, Black Africa or the Siberian tundra have been affected by phonograph and radio.

Particularly in Western Europe the process began long ago with the wider dissemination of print, with the spread of popular education (at however rudimentary a level), with the encroachment of factory goods into the world of the home-made, with the improvement in communication routes, and such. A typical product of this process is the broadside ballad, produced specifically for sale and intended for the widest possible distribution.

The broadsides have been exerting their power on traditional singers since before Shakespeare's time, and they still do on that dwindling band of surviving country performers, though the last broadside house of any weight in England closed its shutters before the First World War. The broadside ballad is similar to the 'classic' folk ballad in form, but less folkloric in content — less fantastic, more rationalising, less concerned with real passions, more given to a deliberate exploitation of pathos and sensationalism — like some popular Sunday newspapers — in the hope of commercial success. A good specimen of that kind is the widespread and frequently published ballad known variously as 'The Prentice Boy', 'The Butcher Boy', 'The Wexford Girl', 'The Oxford Girl', 'Hanged I Shall Be'. It derives somewhat from a broadside of 1650 describing a Hereford murder, combined with a later crime ballad concerning John Mauge of Wytham, hanged in 1744 — a song called 'The Wittam Miller' that affected several nineteenth-century broadsides. A characteristic version was recorded in 1969 from a well-known gypsy singer, Phoebe Smith, of Woodbridge, Suffolk. She calls it 'The Wexport Girl'.

I fell in love with a Wexport girl,
She had dark and rolling eyes,
And I feeled too shamed of marrying her,
Her being a young-a maid.

I went down to her sister's house
About eight o'clock one night,
And to ast her if she would take a walk
Through the fields and meadows gay.

And there we'd walk and we'd sit awhile,
And we'd fix our wedding day,
And the answer what she gave to me,
It lay so far away.

I caught fast hold of her lily-white hand,
And I kissed both cheek and chin,
And I had no thoughts of murdering her,
And yet no evil ways.

As I pulled the stake out from the hedge
And I cracked her on the crown,
And the blood from that poor innocent girl
Come trickling through the ground.

I cotched holt of her curly curly locks,
And I drags her through the fields
Until I came to a deep riverside,
I gently splunged her in.

Look how she goes, look how she flows,
She's a-floating by the tide,
And instead of her having a watery grave
She ought to been my bride.

I went down to my master's house
About twelve o'clock that night,
And I asted him for a candle
To light me up to bed.

He asked me and he questioned me
What stained my hands with blood,
And the answer that I gave to him,
I'd been bleeding from the nose.

It was about three weeks after then
When that pretty maid were found,
Come floating down by her own mother's door,
A place called Wexport town.

The judges and the jurymen
On me they did all agree:
For the murdering of that Wexport girl
It's hanged I must be.

(Transcribed from Topic 12T 193, *Once I Had a True Love*, side 2, band 5)

The air of the towns, especially of the back streets, is strong in songs like that. It is stronger still in some later nineteenth-century broadsides, that are full of a kind of false pathos that comes near to the emotionality of such tear-jerking stage pieces as 'The Poor Little Match Girl' or 'Underneath the Gaslight's Glitter' ('Won't you buy my pretty flowers?'). Students of folk song tend to overlook the effect of middle-class condescension on parts of the traditional repertory; some of the latter-day folk songs particularly display enervating illusions about the plight of the working class. Phoebe Smith, on the same record that contains her performance of 'The Wexport Girl', sings with great conviction a prime example of this banal sentimental balladry, the song of a foundling, called 'The Dear Little Maiden'.

The towns show their influence on home-made song in other ways. Notably towards the end of the eighteenth century, the relatively sluggish flow of elements from the educated world, from the written arts, quickened, and during the nineteenth century it had reached a fair intensity, so that by the opening years of the twentieth, the song repertory of the English and Scottish villages (at least) was a very heterogeneous affair. The country singers possessed a ragbag of lyrical bits — sentimental patriotic and parlour ballads, standard hymns, music-hall pieces — and such folk songs as they still retained were mainly the kind of short lyrical compositions whose face was turned towards the towns, towards the conventional sources of music and poetry. That is, the musical repertory showed a dwindling of modal character in favour of the 'standard' major—minor system, waltz rhythm tended to intrude, rhythms were becoming more and more conventionalised ($\frac{5}{4}$s

transformed into ⁶⁄₈s, etc.); likewise, in the words of the songs, high-flown, if sometimes half-understood, elements drawn from nineteenth-century book poetry made
an increasingly frequent appearance, especially in Scotland where literary Edinburgh
was far more benevolent towards the country arts than literary London ever was.
Lizzie Higgins, a housewife of traveller ancestry (daughter of the renowned Jean
Robertson) has recorded a typical example, 'Bogieside' (on a Topic record, *Back o'
Benachie* (12T 180), side 1, band 2), that combines an evocation of love and landscape in a way that seems to have one foot in folklore and the other in a book. In
the song, Lizzie's fluctuating use of dialect reflects the dichotomy.

Assist me, O ye Muses, your downcast spirits raise,
And join me in full chorus to sing brave Huntly's praise,
For the girl I left behind me, whose charms were all my pride,
When I said farewell tae Huntly toon on bonny Bogieside.

For it's doon the road tae Huntly Lodge where pleasant steps I drove,
Almost inspired with rapture the sweet girl that I love,
Who joined me in my rambles and choosed me for her guide
To walk upon the Deveron's banks on bonny Bogieside.

Farewell ye lads o' Huntly toon, tae you I'll bid adieu.
The pleasures of our evenin's walk I'll share nae mair wi' you.
The sky was clear and bonny when on an eventide
I'd lay me doon an' rest awhile upon the Deveronside.

May the Powers above protect this girl, so young and fair and fine,
And save her from all dangers, who has this heart of mine,
Until my hairt forgets to beat, and death does us divide,
For I'll return to Huntly toon on bonny Bogieside.

Alongside the somewhat high-flown lyrical stream with its conventionalised
meditations, another stream flowed vigorously. Earlier, in considering the outlaw
ballads, we referred to a current of songs of uprooted and homeless men, reflecting
quite different preoccupations from those of settled, more or less stable peasants
and country workers in the bosom of their families. Not only in their poetry but to
a certain extent in melody too, this dissident, shiftless kind of song forms a powerful part of the traditional repertory throughout Europe. Central European scholars
sometimes refer to this type as the Morris—allemande—outlaw cycle, with emphatic

melodies characterised by heavy crotchets and a double- or triple-stamp ending, and by texts of raffish, dissentient, even downright subversive drift. In England perhaps the most characteristic songs of this cycle are found in the repertory of seafarers (such as 'The Rambling Sailor', with its devil-may-care lyric wedded to a bold hornpipe tune). In Scotland, it is perhaps the songs concerning beggars and 'travellers' — for example, the celebrated 'Tinkler's Wedding', whose fine tune later carried the ribald text of 'The day we went to Rothesay-o' — that make the core of this genre. A striking body of such songs would appear to belong to the itinerant Scottish farm servants, contracted at local feeing markets for a season or a period, and serving on properties large or small, particularly in the north-eastern Lowlands, as horsemen, cattlemen, shepherds, labourers, ploughmen, harvesters and such. Such men were commonly housed in 'bothies' — rough bare shelters of stone or brick, usually accommodating six men at a time (in three beds), without table or chairs (each man had a chest for his clothes, which served as a seat with his knees for table). The harvesters in particular came from a number of sources, often from the ranks of rural tradesmen — blacksmiths, carpenters, shoemakers, weavers — often poor crofters, even seamen. Working conditions were commonly as rough as the living conditions, and particularly during the period 1870–1912 when the system was operating fully, the songs produced and sung in the bothies tended to be sharp and critical. Ian Manuel, brought up on a dour north-eastern farm, sings an example in point, with a sharp-toothed text set to a fine striding Re-mode (Dorian) tune. It is called 'The Scranky Black Farmer', and can be heard on Topic 12TS 220, *The Frosty Ploughshare*, side 2, band 2.

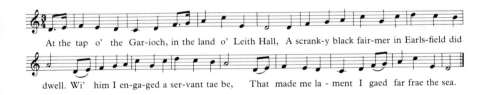

At the tap o' the Garioch, in the land o' Leith Hall, A scranky black fairmer in Earlsfield did dwell. Wi' him I engaged a servant tae be, That made me lament I gaed far frae the sea.

At the tap o' the Garioch, in the land o' Leith Hall,
A scranky black fairmer in Earlsfield did dwell.
Wi' him I engagèd a servant tae be,
That made me lament I gaed far frae the sea.

I engaged wi' this fairmer tae drive cairt an' ploo.
Hard fortune convenit an ill-fated crew;
Me yin o' that number, it causes me rue
That e'er I attempted the country tae view.

(In the head o' the Garioch we all did appear,
From various counties, some far and some near,
From the parish of Kinnethmont, Kilmarnock and Keith,
From Aberlour, Rothiemay and Fordyce.

The harvest in our country is both early and late,
And all kinds of drudgery of course we do get;
Our usage is rough and our ale is but pale.
It's the brown bree o' molasses that we get for ale.)

For it's early in the mornin' we rise tae the yoke.
The storm an' the tempest will ne'er mak' us stop;
For the wind it does beat an' the rain it does pour,
Ay, an' aye yon black fairmer on us he does glower.

Ah, the time is expirin' an' the day it'll come,
Tae various counties we a' must gan hame.
Bonny Bawbee must traivel, bonny Jeannie also
Back tae the beyont o' Montgomery must go.

So it's fare ye weel, Rhynie, an' adieu tae ye, Clatt,
For I hae been wi' ye baith early an' late.
Baith early an' late, baith empty an' fu';
An' fare ye weel, Rhynie, an' I bid ye adieu.

Oh, an' fare ye weel, Bawbee, an' adieu tae ye a',
Likewise yon black fairmer that lives at Leigh Ha';
For tae serve yon black fairmer I'm sure it's nae sport,
An' I must be gaun tae my bonny seaport.

(The verses within brackets are quoted from John Ord, *Bothy Songs and Ballads*
(Paisley, 1930 and J. Donald, 1973))

The relatively short-lived, albeit powerful, tradition of the bothy ballads was the product of a critical time when, in the Scottish Lowlands, the pre-capitalist mode of production of the farm family employing short-term seasonal labour was increasingly at a disadvantage vis-à-vis the capitalist methods of farmers oriented towards cash-crop production with heavy investment in machinery and property-improvement. Capitalist farming meant new crops, new techniques, new implements; it also meant that labour was used more consistently throughout the year, with less demand for casual workers and a notably flatter peak at harvest time, now that reaping machines were replacing sickle and scythe. The feeing fair, where casual labour once was hired, ceased to be important, and the old social relations between farmer and servant, centred not so much on wages as on reputations, declined.

We have suggested that it is such critical songs as the bothy ballads, with their sharp complaints about conditions, that make a bridge between classic 'peasant' folklore and the modern type of industrial songs such as the one recorded by A.E. Green in 1965 from a Batley weaver and subsequently sung on a commercial record by Roy Harris (Topic 12TS 212, *The Bitter and the Sweet*, side 2, band 1). The refrain 'poverty knock' is said to be inspired by the characteristic clatter of the old Dobbie loom.

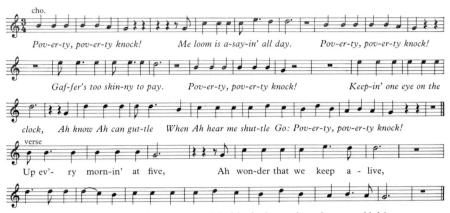

cho.

Pov-er-ty, pov-er-ty knock! Me loom is a-say-in' all day. Pov-er-ty, pov-er-ty knock!

Gaf-fer's too skin-ny to pay. Pov-er-ty, pov-er-ty knock! Keep-in' one eye on the

clock, Ah know Ah can gut-tle When Ah hear me shut-tle Go: Pov-er-ty, pov-er-ty knock!

verse

Up ev'- ry morn-in' at five, Ah won-der that we keep a - live,

Ti - red an' yawn - in' In the cold morn-in', It's back to the drear-y old drive.

(Refrain) Poverty, poverty knock!
Me loom is a-sayin' all day.
Poverty, poverty knock!
Gaffer's too skinny to pay.
Poverty, poverty knock!
Keepin' one eye on the clock.
Ah know Ah can guttle°
When Ah hear me shuttle
Go: Poverty, poverty knock!

Up ev'ry mornin' at five.
Ah wonder that we keep alive.
Tired an' yawnin' in the cold mornin',
It's back to the dreary old drive.
(Refrain) Poverty, poverty knock! etc.

Oh dear, we're goin' to be late.
Gaffer is stood at the gate.
We're out o' pocket, our wages they're docket;
We'll a' to buy grub on the slate.
(Refrain) Poverty, poverty knock! etc.

An' when our wages they'll bring,
We're often short of a string.°
While we are fratchin'° wi' gaffer for snatchin',
We know to his brass he will cling.
(Refrain) Poverty, poverty knock! etc.

We've got to wet our own yarn
By dippin' it into the tarn.
It's wet an' soggy an' makes us feel groggy,
An' there's mice in that dirty old barn.
(Refrain) Poverty, poverty knock! etc.

Oh dear, me poor 'ead it sings.
Ah should have woven three strings,°
But threads are breakin' and my back is achin'.
Oh dear, Ah wish Ah had wings.
(Refrain) Poverty, poverty knock! etc.

Sometimes a shuttle flies out,
Gives some poor woman a clout.
There she lies bleedin', but nobody's 'eedin'.
Who's goin' t' carry her out?
(Refrain) Poverty, poverty knock! etc.

Tuner° should tackle me loom.
'E'd rather sit on his bum.
'E's far too busy a-courtin' our Lizzie,
An' Ah cannat get 'im to come.
(Refrain) Poverty, poverty knock! etc.

Lizzie is so easy led.
Ah think that 'e teks her to bed.
She allus was skinny, now look at her pinny.
It's just about time they were wed.
(Refrain) Poverty, poverty knock! etc.

guttle eat
string length of cloth
fratchin' quarrelling
Tuner loom-maintenance man

It is characteristic of industrial folk song that the texts are directed to the 'in'
community of workers, reflecting their common plight as it is conditioned by their
calling. Such songs may be at once broadly communal and intensely intimate. On
the page, their depth doesn't really show, but sung by an informal group of, say,
miners and their womenfolk gathered in a pit-village kitchen or a club meeting-room,
their emotional force and their power to bind the community together become
movingly manifest. Such a song is the relatively recently composed but already
widespread anthem called 'Ee aye, Aa could hew', made by Ed Pigford, son of a Co.
Durham miner, about the plight of his father, once a strong coal-face worker, but
now incapacitated through pneumoconiosis. As given here, the song is transcribed
from a tape-recorded rendering in the Three Tuns public house, Birtley, Co. Durham,
in March 1971.

When Aa was young an' in me prime, Ee aye, Aa could hew, Why, Aa was hew-in'
aal the time.   Now me hew-in' days are through, through, Now me hew-in' days are through.

When Aa was young an' in me prime,
   Ee aye, Aa could hew,
Wey, Aa was hewin' aal the time.
   Now me hewin' days are through, through,
   Now me hewin' days are through.

At the face the dust did flee,
   Ee aye, Aa could hew,
But now that dust is killin' me,
   Now me hewin' days are through, through,
   Now me hewin' days are through.

Aa've lain doon flat an' shovelled coals,
   Ee aye, Aa could hew;
Me eyes did smart in the dust-filled holes.
   Now me hewin' days are through, through,
   Now me hewin' days are through.

Aa've worked wi' marras,° an' they were men,
   Ee aye, Aa could hew,
Aye, they were men an' sons o' men.
   Now me hewin' days are through, through,
   Now me hewin' days are through.

It's doon that pit ne mair Aa'll see,
   Ee aye, Aa could hew,
But Aa'll carry it round inside o' me,
   Now me hewin' days are through, through,
   Now me hewin' days are through.

marras mates

Finally we come to a kind of composition that represents a drastic expansion of the conventional frame of folk song. Indeed, some would say it falls right out of that frame, but it is nonetheless a community song originating from below, destined for a tightly knit audience, and based on a traditional pattern, particularly where the verse-form is concerned. First, the model from which the poem derives: it is a children's street song of derisive character, particularly common in the back alleys and tenement courtyards of Glasgow:

I married me a wife, amen, amen,
I married me a wife, amen.
I married me a wife, she's the plague o' my life,
Ah, the world must be comin' tae an end, amen.

I sent her for butter, amen, amen,
I sent her for butter, amen.
I sent her for butter, an' she dropped it in the gutter,
Ah, the world must be comin' tae an end, amen.

And so on through a litany of domestic disasters, to the catastrophic Judgement Day. Using that lyric form (and nowadays no creations are more deeply folkloric than the self-made street and playground songs of city children) the 'bard of the Clydeside working class', Matt McGinn, made a song whose natural concert hall is the smoke-filled room of a workers' meeting. The song ranges far beyond the domestic horizon that hitherto seemed to us characteristic, and even a *sine qua non*, of folk song. But the working class *has* a wider horizon nowadays, and perhaps this kind of composition is symptomatic of the process by which home-made song, emerging from below, owing little to the establishment culture of the entertainment corporations but much to that unofficial culture of which folk song is a component, begins to move towards a new style, a broader ambience, a more ample perspective. The song, 'With fire and with sword', is here given as transcribed from the singing during a mass meeting of shipyard workers in Glasgow in March 1971. Vietnam and Kent State were in the mind then, but the song reflects an ever-present care, particularly with men whose yards find it easier to get war contracts than peaceful ones. Not folk song? As the folk change, their songs change: it's a truism.

With fire an' with sword, amen, amen,
With fire an' with sword, amen,
With fire an' with sword, here come the men of war,
Ah, the world must be comin' tae an end.

Wi' their bayonets an' their bombs, amen, amen,
Their bayonets an' their bombs, amen,
Wi' their bayonets an' their bombs they'll be tearin' down our homes.
Ah, the world must be comin' tae an end.

There's blood upon their hands, amen, amen,
There's blood upon their hands, amen.
There's blood upon their hands in this an' other lands,
Ah, the world must be comin' tae an end.

They massacred the young, amen, amen,
They massacred the young, amen.
They massacred the young tae make them hold their tongue.
Ah, the world must be comin' tae an end.

Oh, will they have their way, amen, amen?
Will they have their way, amen?
Will they have their way, or will the young folk say
That the world will not be comin' tae an end?

2 Music-learning in traditional societies

PETER COOKE

What else can we learn from 'the folk' apart from their tunes and texts? If one looks through the recent BBC pamphlets such as the Singing Together series, one might well say that our school children are getting enough folk music already and have been doing so for many years. But it is one thing to transplant songs, say from the bothies of rural Aberdeenshire into the classroom, and quite another thing for the teacher, let alone the children, to have any understanding of the social situations in which the so-called 'bothy ballad' evolved and was re-created with each perform-ance, or to ask such questions as what the singing does for the singer and for his audience, how he handles his material, and how he learned. Yet such questions should be important to one's thinking about formal music education today.

One does not need to leave Britain and spend time living within another culture, in Africa for example, to understand the way music works in so-called 'folk' societies, though it is a salutary experience to witness the important place music and dance occupy in many non-Western societies and to realise that the enormously rich and varied repertory is created and handed on without the help of notation. A look at music-making in some of our own traditional societies could be equally profitable: most of the remarks that follow stem from the writer's own experience recording and studying traditional music in the western and northern islands of Scotland. The music of ceremonial religion and other ritual will not be discussed here: it is usually well taken care of in all societies and often takes special forms. In contrast, my subject will be the informal music-making which emerges so often when friends get together of an evening. In Gaelic-speaking parts of Scotland such an event is called a *ceilidh*: the term means no more than 'a social gathering' and should not be confused with its urban relation of the same name, which is a more formal entertainment. Yet it is just such occasions that produced our great wealth of British folk song, and must in earlier times have been a very satisfying mode of social communication. I stress social rather than purely musical satisfaction, because it is clear that the music is not looked upon as an end in itself, but used as a very special form of social interaction. As one traditional singer put it, 'it's not so much the song you enjoy but the person'.

This is true of the ceilidh. The emphasis is on a sharing; room is made for the gifted and the less gifted to offer musical or other items for the enjoyment of all. In this situation singing is principally a solo activity but many of the songs and most of the ballads contain end refrains (often middle refrains too) which allow the assembled friends to endorse the sentiments of the song and the efforts and sincerity of the singer. British ballads are tales sung by individuals; most other songs are solo-istic expressions also. At a ceilidh people take it in turns to sing — to share what they have — and the act of sharing is appreciated as much as the song itself is enjoyed. Thus there is room for individual offerings and general participation. All too often in school, group singing is seen as an end in itself, rather than merely an efficient and inexpensive means of teaching a repertory of songs and ballads which evolved as solo music. In the classroom, group effort often seems to be compulsory, certainly unspontaneous — whether the songs are particularly attractive to different individuals or not. Such performances in music lessons are often conducted. This would be an exception in a more natural context, where in any case there is no fixed stereotype to which the singer must adhere. It is seldom realised sufficiently that folk songs which appear in books are often merely skeletal representations of what one singer sang on the occasion when the song was collected. Yet it becomes obvious, when one studies verse variants or recordings made at different times from the same singer, that singers carry a fluid model, to be realised in an infinite number of ways according to their own re-creative ability and their own mood and that of their audience. By this means songs or certain 'ways' of a song become the property of individuals. It is possible that this feeling of owning one's own song is akin to that experienced by the literate composer as he hears his work performed for others to hear (though in folk societies there is rarely, if ever, such a dichotomy of com-poser and performer—interpreter). In the classroom such freedom for expression and creativity can be stifled by tightly controlled group singing which necessitates the adoption of a single stereotype.

There is room too in the ceilidh for those who do not wish to sing or who feel they cannot. Indeed non-participants often enthusiastically encourage music-making — are often the patrons. The truth is, of course, that they are participating, inas-much as they are there, sharing and enjoying the musical offerings (and in any case since the ceilidh frequently includes story-telling, joke-spinning, riddle-asking, they often make an offering of a kind other than music). Should there be less compulsion in class music-making than there often is? Should there not be room for those who just want to come and listen, as well as the chance to opt out temporarily? In some parts of Scotland if a relative dies there is no singing or dancing by his kinfolk for three months or more. There is no room in this chapter to examine the reasons for this: it should suffice to recognise that there can be times when children, as much as adults, do not wish to make music. We should ask if sufficient account is taken of the powerful relationship between music-making and the emotions, when at 9.30 in the morning, regardless of the state of mind of any one of them, thirty individuals are brought together to sing lustily a programme of songs varied in emotional con-tent and chosen by the teacher.

Another aspect of the ceilidh that has bearing not only on the richness of the experience but on the question of learning, is that it is not usually segregated by age or sex, nor even by social class. Young children and pensioners, local doctor and crofting labourer meet, the children learning by watching and listening until the time when they also have something to offer. Anyone who has taught in an institution where there is streaming by age (usual in secondary institutions) and by ability (also frequent, but becoming less so) must have experienced the depressing shortage of gifted musical leaders in the nth stream. The leaders are necessary in any society. Taking out the musically gifted and educating them at a faster pace than their peers has no doubt been hotly debated among music educationists, so the point need not be laboured here, save to stress that such a socially divisive action is foreign to more balanced, homogeneous societies. They too have their gifted musicians, but it appears unnecessary to segregate them from their peers. One sees neat solutions to the problem in many parts of Africa, and even in London among West Indians. The apprentice musician or dancer continues to learn his skill by watching and imitating even during public performances: spectators at the Notting Hill 'Mas' sometimes see, on the lorries carrying the steel bands, a tiny boy seated in the lap of an elder, who is helping him to drum his correct part in the total musical texture.

Watching the crowds dancing around the lorry, or alongside the other steel bands, as they make their way slowly around the jammed streets, one is reminded that in many non-Western societies and to a lesser extent in British folk societies, music is usually associated with dance. In many parts of Africa and Asia, for instance, music and dance are indivisible. Roderyk Lange (*The Nature of Dance* (MacDonald and Evans, 1975)) has commented on its vitally important role in society — yet it is neglected in our schools, at best taught by physical education specialists and usually divorced from other musical activities. In Shetland, by contrast, concerts of all kinds usually end with dancing, and in some islands dance is still central to the wedding rite — putting a seal on the church ritual and bringing the whole village or island community together. Taking a cue from more homogeneous societies such as Shetland, there is clearly a case for blurring the present sharp division between music and dance in our schools and bringing dance into the music room.

Turning now to the question of excellence, we find specially gifted persons in all societies, and qualities such as virtuosity and other manifestations of musicianship are always valued. Nevertheless there is probably no society in the world where the *cult* of excellence is so strong as in our own. It is common for professional critics, competitive festivals, and prognostic tests to single out musical pupils, with a resulting sharp division between performers and listeners. Taken to such an extreme, the cult is inevitably inhibiting. The majority are educated into thinking themselves unmusical; violins are rationed out among the 'talented' only. This offers a strange contrast with the Shetland Islands, for instance, where most men can 'knock out' a tune on their fiddles. True, there too there are the 'house fiddlers' (those who would not take their fiddles with them to a dance or a concert) as well as the dance fiddlers (those who are asked to play at wedding dances, regatta dances, etc.), but the 'house fiddler' gets his turn, and, in his own house, will be asked to play for his friends. As one Shetland crofter, Bobby Peterson, put it (when describing life in the fo'c'sle of a whaler when he was a youth), 'there were some good fiddlers . . . the like of Jacky Laurenson and his late brother, Bob . . . you see . . . they were crack fiddlers, good fiddlers. And they would play, and everybody played a tune, and although they were good fiddlers they were just as keen to hear the like of me playing a tune'.

Equally interesting were the remarks made by Belle Stewart, one of Scotland's best-known 'travellers', when she sat as a judge at one of the annual traditional singing competitions of the Traditional Music and Song Association of Scotland (a strange event this, since in attempting to encourage traditional music, it makes a competitive spectacle of the singers and their songs; fortunately few take the competitive element seriously). Strength and quality of voice mattered little to her; she was looking for the singers who 'had the coinyach', an ill-defined quality but one in which sincerity and conviction are two vital ingredients.

How many young people are sacrificed on the altar of excellence? How many adults are there who say that they cannot even sing? The answer is, unfortunately, far too many: they learned this during their school years because of the emphasis on certain 'high standards' which, while relevant to the concert-hall platform, unfortunately have little to do with the requirements of domestic music-making. In the Outer Hebrides, for example, the good singer is the person who has learned good texts, long texts, who understands them and loves them, who can hold a tune and has a voice which needs only to carry across the room of the croft house.

This brings me to the process of learning in 'folk' societies. Sincerity and conviction come easily when a singer has learned his repertory orally. Once stored in the memory the song becomes his own property, to be reshaped and worked on continually, albeit, in some cases, unconsciously. Good musical memories can be readily developed among the young. Andrew Polson of Whalsay, Shetland, learned to play his fiddle in the dark: 'I went up a dark loft . . . and I'd sit there and try and learn. I knew a lot of tunes, just myself like . . . I could sing them and I knew when I was wrong and when I was goin' on the right.' His repertory consists of, among other dances, more than one hundred rare and lovely Shetland 'springs' (reels); he received no formal instruction but absorbed the island style, as all traditional fiddlers seem to do, by watching the older men around him, and he learned many of the tunes from the singing of his mother before ever he began to attempt to play them on an instrument. Watching and listening appears to be the key, even where instrumental learning is involved. Many Scottish pipers are quite happy to handle rhythmically inadequate notations of their bagpipe repertory, particularly in the case of that classical solo repertory known as 'pibroch'; for many of them use the notations only as useful mnemonics, after having learned 'the way' of the tune from a teacher. Suzuki's teaching lays stress on this important aspect of 'imitative and tactile learning allied to motor co-ordination', considering musical literacy to be something quite separate from the task of acquiring an early repertory (G. Russell Smith, preface to *Suzuki Violin School*, vol. 1 (with accompanying record

SBHED007)). These ideas, along with his others (i.e. that there is an innate ability in all children to learn musical instruments, and that family participation is import-ant), are admirable, but they are not new — not to the folk tradition in Britain at any rate.

It should not be thought that folk musicians deliberately turn their backs on literacy, though there is a long tradition of this in Gaelic-speaking areas; and the writer has been told of the scornful comments of one gifted South Uist bard about another in a nearby township, 'Och! he has nothing but what you find in books!' In other rural parts one comes across collections lovingly and painstakingly com-piled by seamen and farm labourers, who have noted down songs and ballads that took their fancy wherever they heard them; but only on the rarest occasions do they record the melodies. The tune is already committed to memory, to be worked on as one wills: the verses serve as a mnemonic, sometimes one suspects solely as a safety precaution, so that should the memory ever go bad the song is preserved.

No one who has attempted field research in the 1970s can fail to have noticed the great use which folk musicians make of tape recorders and long-playing records, not simply for passive listening purposes but as a means of expanding their reper-tory. Some fine new Gaelic songs have come into the archives of the School of Scottish Studies which were composed by emigrant Scots in distant lands like Nova Scotia, recorded on tape and sent home at Christmas-time as personal musical messages to friends and relatives, sometimes passing quite quickly into the local repertory. Those folk who could afford it have not been slow to take advantage of new inventions, but the primacy of oral learning is still there. Perhaps one should ask, how important is skill in handling musical notation today? If one considers it less important to teach one's young pupils to play standard orchestral works and sing extended choral pieces than to teach them to be able to handle less complex (if no less 'deep') forms such as ballads and lyrical songs or dancing tunes, and to be able to re-create them, or even to compose their own material, then the teaching of notation need no longer be a central feature of music-teaching.

Of course it is one thing to describe these idyllic folk customs and processes, and it is another to decide how far they can or should be incorporated into institutional teaching. A radical approach could lead to the abandonment of the standard class music lesson completely, replacing it with an informal 'folk club' attended option-ally by older and younger pupils simultaneously. One could then make use of the skills of older pupils as well as music teachers (while not neglecting the use of practice rooms for those who prefer to get on by themselves with the task of acquiring instrumental skills). Another approach could be to make increased use of cassette recorders and listening booths for learning new songs and instrumental pieces aurally. Yet another could be to make more use of older pupils (and even parents) to teach the younger pupils new items for their repertories, and so help in teaching the kind of social co-operation that is very necessary in today's highly interdependent society. One might decide only to modify the teacher-directed curriculum, and give more scope for solo singing, more teaching by rote, but, more importantly, placing more emphasis on song-making and adaptation (e.g. a school 'broadsheet' packed with topical comment to known melodies).

Other experiments could be attempted. To discuss them further is outside the scope of this chapter. The least one should ask for is that the music of the 'folk' be treated with respect and understanding for what it is and how it came about — through the creative activity of individuals working with and for the common wealth of their society.

3 *Folk music in junior and middle schools*

MICHAEL POLLARD

For educational purposes, at least, the definition of folk music can be fairly tolerant, and it shades off at the edges into clearly different, but related, material such as children's skipping and counting-out rhymes, early music-hall songs and Sharp's 'vulgar street songs' of the turn of the century, brass-band music, and even Nonconformist hymnody. The variety of ways in which traditional material may be used is perhaps best illustrated by quoting examples of classroom work which I have either organised myself or seen in other people's schools.

Playground games make an interesting starting-point for younger children. It is worth remembering that those immensely complex skipping and ball-bouncing routines that break out in primary-school playgrounds in early summer are possibly the last example we have of genuine oral transmission on the folk pattern. Like folk music, they bridge the generations without benefit of direct teaching or the printed word; and like folk music, some of them take on something from each generation that they pass through, while others preserve their now-forgotten period flavour. An example of the latter kind is one of the standard skipping games, in which two children turn, or swing, a rope while the rest of the group take a verse each in the middle:

> Queenie, Queenie Caroline
> Dipped her hair in the turpentine.
> The turpentine began to shine,
> Queenie, Queenie Caroline.

> N— sat on the shore,
> She had children, three or four,
> The eldest one is twenty-four
> And she's getting married to the boy next door.
> How many children will they have?
> One, two, three, etc.

Subsequent verses deal with what they will live on (salt, mustard, vinegar, pepper) and where they will live (house, flat, pigsty, lavatory) and so on. Survival in this game depends not only on skipping over the rope but on remembering the details of the routine.

Closely related to these singing games are some of the remnants of folk drama which still survive here and there, usually as seasonal excuses for making a collection: mumming songs, souling songs, and so on. These have such a complex history that it is hazardous to attempt a brief summary, but it is sufficient to say that many of them seem to be derived from the calling-on songs of folk players. A typical example is the 'Lancashire Pace-Egging Song', collected in the nineteenth century by the Lancashire historian Harland and still performed regularly in the 1860s (J. Harland and T.T. Wilkinson, *Ballads and Songs of Lancashire* (1865)). (Other versions survived in oral transmission much later.) Pace-egging is a spring ritual, Christianised to become associated with Easter, and its songs fulfilled the same role as carol-singing at Christmas. The Lancashire song was clearly the opening chorus of a mumming play in which St George has been transmuted somewhere along the line to the heroic figure of Nelson. The first two verses run:

> We're three jolly lads and we're all in one mind,
> We are come a-pace-egging and we hope you'll prove kind.
> If you will prove kind with your eggs and strong beer
> We'll come no more singing until the next year.

> The first to come in is Lord Nelson you'll see,
> With a bunch of blue ribbons tied round by his knee,
> And a star on his breast that like silver do shine,
> And he hopes you'll remember it's pace-egging time.

('Lancashire Pace-Egging Song', coll. J. Harland.)

Later verses introduce other characters, some known only locally, and the song ends with a renewed appeal for alms. This particular song, like its counterparts in other parts of the country including the well-known 'Padstow May Song', has survived only through the conscious efforts of antiquarians, though the odd verse turns up occasionally in other songs from the oral tradition. Nevertheless, it and many other songs of ceremony are available in printed collections and on records, and there is no apparent reason why seasonal singing should be confined to Christmas. There is also scope here, as with performances of folk plays, for the introduction of local allusions and new material. In introducing young children to creative work, there is something to be said for working within a known format, and improvisations — musical as well as verbal — on existing material offer a useful introduction to problems of metre and form.

Two further examples illustrate how traditional song spills over into children's experience. The first concerns the story of the Babes in the Wood, not now very common as a children's story but still current in pantomime. The story first appeared as a play in 1601 with the title *A Lamentable Tragedie of a young child Murthered in a wood by two Ruffians, with the consent of his Unkle*, and is popularly thought to have been based on the story of the princes in the Tower. In fact, the play borrowed its story-line from an even earlier ballad entitled 'The Norfolk Gent', based on a local scandal at Wayland Wood near Watton in Norfolk. Neither 'The Norfolk Gent' nor the 1601 play appears to have survived, but a long ballad based on it did, to be collected — all twenty verses of it — by Pepys among others. A truncated version of this was still current in oral tradition at the beginning of this century, when it was collected, with minor variations, in Oxfordshire, Sussex and elsewhere in southern England. Interestingly, the dramatic high point in the song, as collected from country singers, is a verse describing the birds covering the children with leaves — a scene which is, of course, still the big tear-jerking moment in pantomime versions of the story. Somewhere along the way, too, the story had acquired two children instead of the original one, perhaps as a result of the link with the princes.

The second example concerns another long-lived ballad, 'The Cruel Mother', which turns up all over the place — in North America and Newfoundland as well as all over Britain — in a variety of versions. The slightly macabre story-line is of a mother who stabs her own children and, on the way home, sees some other children playing (the numbers vary wildly). If they were hers, she tells them, she would care for them lovingly; at which the children sing (to quote one version):

> O dear mother, when we was thine,
> You neither put on our coarse or fine,

and condemn her to seven long years in hell. Teachers who find this bloodthirsty fare for primary-school children may be comforted by the fact that some versions of the song leave out the more gory elements in the story — it appears in some collections as 'The Lady from Lee', 'There was a Lady lived in York' or 'Down by the Greenwood Side', among other titles. In fact, variants of 'The Cruel Mother' survive in the playground in a skipping rhyme collected widely in Britain, beginning:

> There was an old woman and she lived in a wood,
> Down by the river Sila,
> She had three children and she had no food,
> Down by the river Sila.

That children in today's schools should be chanting a version of a ballad which, according to Ewan MacColl and Peggy Seeger, can be traced back to a broadside printed in 1690 is something altogether remarkable, and a powerful argument for those who, like me, believe that the culture of the playground is a living, vital thing which teachers should not ignore. (Five variants of the song are recorded by MacColl and Seeger on the first record of the *Long Harvest* set, Argo ZDA 66.)

This is all fascinating stuff, teachers may argue, but what do we actually *do* with it in the classroom? I have already suggested incidental opportunities that may arise — the skipping-rhyme season, a local Babes in the Wood pantomime, a St George play at Christmas-time — but there is a case for a more planned and deliberate attempt to surround children with traditional music. In this connection, I am not sorry that I cannot play a musical instrument, a fact which forces me to use the record-player. No teacher needs to be told how easily children learn by ear — consider the number of television jingles in the average primary-school child's repertoire — and this is a facility which comes into its own here. There are a number of times in the classroom day when folk music can be played incidentally, perhaps with other kinds of music: the beginning and end of school assembly, art and craft lessons, other periods when children are doing work which does not demand complete concentration. These are opportunities to experiment with a wide variety of folk music — from Morris tunes through songs in traditional performance to modern revival arrangements — to get some idea of the children's likely response to deeper treatment. In my own experience, strong melodic lines with fairly heavy instrumentation will go best and produce requests to hear particular items again. When this happens, the teacher has of course scored his first success. It's worth noting, incidentally, that the words should be available of any songs which become popular. As teachers know who have ever listened carefully to a primary-school child's recitation of the Lord's Prayer, the young ear can do curious things with the English language!

This 'incidental' use of folk music has the advantage that it accustoms the children, without any commitment on their or the teacher's part, to the kind of music they will come to if the material is used more directly as a teaching resource.

One interesting use for folk music is as a stimulus for creative work — writing, painting or drama. Most teachers are familiar with the use of poetry, passages of prose, paintings and photographs in this way, and in recent years many have turned to classical music as a source. Folk song offers for this purpose a whole range of simple yet fundamental story-lines, from the plain heroics of 'The Heights of Abraham' and many of the whaling songs to delicate stories like 'Hynd Horn' and its many variants. Perhaps it will be useful to explore how the two songs mentioned might be developed in classroom work.

'The Heights of Abraham' (alternatively known as 'Bold Wolfe' or 'Brave Wolfe') is a contemporary account of the death of Wolfe at Quebec in 1759. It is, incidentally, remarkable in that it is one of the few songs of its type to have survived in oral tradition; most songs celebrating national heroes tended, if they were ever taken up, to go out of fashion and die, partly because many of them were officially inspired (and for a period, in the case of naval songs, were actually produced by an officially appointed balladeer). The song contains some vivid imagery, as the following verses indicate:

> There stand the French on the mountain high
> While we poor lads in the valley lie.
> I see them falling like motes in the sun
> > Through smoke and fire,
> > Through smoke and fire
> Arising from the British gun.
>
> . . .

'Here's a hundred guineas in shining gold.
Take it and part it, my blood runs cold.
Take it and part it', General Wolfe did say,
   'Brave lads of honour,
   Brave lads of honour,
For you have fought the French, and have gained the day.'

(This version can be heard on Topic 12T 142, *The Watersons*.)

The complete song conveys an impression of great loyalty among Wolfe's troops and genuine grief at his death. But, for all that it is a folk song, it is to some extent a 'literary' account of the battle. Children might be asked to use the information in the song as a basis for a soldier's version of events, perhaps as in a letter home or in a story told to his friends and relations on his return. Another approach, which I have always found interesting, is to make a 'story-board' — a series of up to a dozen rough drawings, as in a film treatment — based on the verses in the song. Alternatively, there is scope for a short documentary treatment of the battle on tape, with sound effects whose devising will give plenty of scope for experiment. Finally, with older children of middle-school age, the words suggest a number of themes for classroom discussion — loyalty, patriotism, the concept of a 'hero's death', the lot of the common soldier, and so on.

'Hynd Horn' ('our only important ballad based on medieval romance', A.L. Lloyd has written in *Folk Song in England* (Lawrence and Wishart, 1967), p. 158) is a seminal ballad which was revived by broadside-printers in the early nineteenth century and has since appeared literally hundreds of times under such titles as 'The Dark-Eyed Sailor', 'A fair maid walking all in her garden', 'The Broken Token' and many others. However, the basic plot is remarkably consistent: a girl out for a walk meets a sailor, who asks her why she is so sad. She explains that some years before (the number varies) she loved another sailor, and they split a gold ring (or sometimes a coin) between them as a token of their love. She hasn't heard from him since. The sailor then shows the girl his broken token, and the lovers are reunited. (Readers of H.G. Wells's *Kipps* will recognise this as a source of the incident early in the novel when Kipps and his sweetheart Ann split a sixpence between them.)

Children might be asked to transfer this central incident to another setting — perhaps a modern one; they could make a play from the story; they could retell the story as it might be remembered by the girl as an old woman; they could develop the story further; or older children might compare one of the 'Hynd Horn' variants with one of the many versions of 'The Watery Grave' (sometimes known as 'Scarborough Sands' or 'Scarborough Banks'), in which a similarly forlorn girl finds the body of a sailor on the shore and recognises her own former lover.

Some care has to be exercised in choosing versions of ballads for classroom use. It is well worth casting the net wide, bearing in mind tone, feeling, vocabulary and length, before choosing a song which is going to be used as a basis for other work.

The selection of folk music as a resource demands as much care and preparation as the selection of, say, a film-strip or a film.

Another part of the curriculum in which folk music can be valuable is in religious education, especially in the top junior and the middle-school age-ranges where the syllabus tends to turn from mere story-telling and Christian observance to wider issues, such as other religious cultures. The way in which many primitive festivals were Christianised — the solstices and equinoxes, harvesting, and many local red-letter days — provides an excellent introduction to the idea that ceremony and ritual do not depend only on the Christian tradition. The most direct link between Christian and primitive observance is, of course, in the repertoire of carols; even Christian hymn-books contain some carols which echo primitive midwinter customs, 'The Holly and the Ivy' being the outstanding example. 'Wassailing' is an older cus-tom than carol-singing, and the huge number of wassail songs has a longer ancestry. So too with harvest songs. The legend of the corn-king which survives in the folk song 'John Barleycorn' stretches back into prehistory, and even the custom of the harvest ale, a comparatively modern one, is far older than that of the Church harvest festival, with its nineteenth-century hymn-tunes and sentiments. But the recesses of hymnody, especially among Nonconformists, contain some treasures which should not be ignored. The tune to which 'While shepherds watched their flocks by night' is customarily sung by West Country Methodists, for example, is a fine example of what might be called church folk composition; so, too, is the hymn 'Shepherds Arise', collected from the Copper family of Rottingdean, Sussex, which survives only in its folk version and, as A.L. Lloyd has said, 'reminds us what musical riches have dropped out of church use, due to the flannel ears of nineteenth-century hymnbook compilers' (sleeve note to Topic 12TS 212, *Welcome to Our Fair*).

This is an appropriate point at which to mention Morris dancing, another reflec-tion of primitive ritual. We are on tricky ground here, because the Morris, in so far as it has been involved in education, has become overlaid with various false notes — including the antiquarian interest of Victorian clergymen, the 'health-and-beauty' connotations of the revivalists of the 1920s, and the vulgarisations of television comedians. It has also become confused with that educational hybrid 'country dancing', which has always seemed to me (though, in my innocence, early on in my teaching career I helped to foster it) the archetype of that process of bastardisation through education of which 'nature study' is another example. I can see no point in teaching the Morris in primary school as dancing, because apart from anything else it demands adult stature and an adult sense of timing and performance. At the same time, the Morris tunes are so vital that some means should perhaps be found to let children hear them, preferably in the open air. The ideal answer is, of course, to get a local Morris side to perform in the playground or at some school function, because the music itself on record — and there are remarkably few satisfactory recordings of Morris tunes, except for practice purposes — fails to convey the contra-movement, the ebb and flow of form, and the pace which is Morris's essence.

I once persuaded a local Morris side to come into the school one morning at playtime. No previous announcement was made about it; they simply turned up and danced. The effect was interesting; the initial giggling at the sight of a team of grown men dressed in ribbons and bells gave way, as they danced on, to interest in the patterns and movements they were making and, at the end, to a whole host of questions: about how the dances started and what they were all about, about the instruments, and indeed about why on earth the Morris men were engaging in this outlandish activity today. This was merely an isolated occasion; we had had no preparation, nor did we do any 'follow-up' in the traditional college-of-education way, but I like to think that at least a handful of the children in the playground that day may have remembered the occasion long afterwards.

But it is, of course, in the teaching of history – or, if you will, the humanities or social studies – that folk song has most to offer the primary- and middle-school teacher. This is equally true whether a traditional history syllabus is being followed, or whether 'projects', 'patches' or 'topics' are being pursued, or whether the class is studying themes, as in some approaches to the humanities. The wealth of material ranges from reasonably accurate accounts of historical events, through material of local interest and frankly propagandist songs of various kinds, to songs which illustrate the timelessness of certain themes and ideas in popular culture.

An interesting example of the first category – what might be termed 'the folk song as news' – is the ballad on the Great Fire of London, 'London Mourning in Ashes', which is easily available on records (for example, on Argo ZDA 46, *A Merry Progress to London*). This appeared as a broadside soon after the event. Pepys included it in his collection of ballads, though it does not appear to have survived in oral tradition, since in later collections it appears only as a quotation from Pepys.

'London Mourning in Ashes' has every mark of the good journalistic eye-witness account of the spread of the Fire and of the population's reaction to it, and it would be interesting for a class to compare it with a contemporary piece of radio or television reportage. There are many echoes of contemporary journalistic hyperbole:

> The second of September in
> The middle of the night,
> In Pudding Lane it did begin
> To burn and blaze outright.
> When all that gazed were so amazed
> At such a furious flame,
> They knew not how or what to do
> That might expel the same.
>
> It swallowed Fish-street Hill and straight
> It licked down Lombard Street
> Down Cannon Street in blazing state
> It flew with flaming feet.
> Down to the Thames, whose shrinking streams
> Began to ebb away,
> As thinking that the power of fate
> Had brought the latter day.

The second verse quoted above might almost have come straight from a television reporter's script! But the account of the Fire in this ballad (an extremely long one, by the way) tallies with most historical accounts — though a sceptical historian might put this down to the fact that it is one of relatively few contemporary records. There are also some interesting references towards the end to the popular search for a scapegoat, the simple explanation of a runaway fire at the baker's shop at the corner of Pudding Lane and Lower Thames Street being too tame for most people's taste:

> Many of French and Dutch were stopped
> And also are confined.
> 'Tis said that they their fireballs dropped
> And this plot was designed
> By them and those that are our foes,
> Yet some think nothing so,
> But that our God with's flaming rod
> For sin sends all this woe.

Suspicion of foreigners, one of the less endearing but most enduring English traits, was not just the balladmonger's fancy, incidentally. It was not until 1830 that the inscription at the base of the monument to the disaster was altered to remove a reference to 'Popish frenzy which wrought such horrors'. But in any case the ballad ended with good Protestant sentiments:

> If this do not reform our lives
> A worse thing shall succeed.
> Our kindred, children and our wives
> Will die for want of bread.
> When famine comes, 'tis not our drums,
> Our ships, our horse or foot
> That can defend, but if we mend
> We never shall come to't.

The possibilities of 'London Mourning in Ashes' range from plotting the spread of the Great Fire with the help of a large City of London street map (or, of course, for schools within reach of London, on foot) to exploring, with an older age-group, some of the themes implicit in the ballad — religious fervour, propaganda, chauvinism, reactions to civil disaster.

'London Mourning in Ashes' is perhaps the archetypal local folk song as far as teachers of history are concerned, but there are many others, dealing with less apocalyptic subjects, which lend themselves to equally interesting treatment in the classroom. In particular, there is a collection of songs which celebrate vanished features of our cities. Many major cities, including London, Birmingham, Dublin, Glasgow and Newcastle, can lay claim to a variant of the widespread Jack-of-all-trades theme, in which the trades practised in different streets are enumerated.

Songs of similar local interest include 'I Can't Find Brummagem' and 'The Streets of Brummagem Town' (Birmingham), 'Blaydon Races' (Newcastle upon Tyne), 'The Manchester Ship Canal' (a spirited send-up of the sailor's hornpipe) and innumerable songs about London, particularly the now-disappearing dockland area east of Tower Bridge. Many of these, incidentally, date from the heyday of music hall, when bills were kept going largely on local talent, with only the top names coming in by train. Songs with local allusions — the tradition still persists in pantomime — could always be assured of a laugh. It is at this point that purists of folk music are inclined to raise their eyebrows, but whatever the academic rights and wrongs of including 'vulgar street songs' among folk song proper, they are useful sources for the teacher looking for a different angle on local history.

A far larger group of songs deals with subjects with particular local relevance but which are also of national interest. These include the songs of coal-mining (especially of the Northumberland and Durham fields), of spinning and weaving (especially of Lancashire and Glasgow), of sailors and of deep-sea fishing. They are an important historical source, and more acceptable for primary- and middle-school children than the cold facts as recorded, for example, in the proceedings of the various official commissions on mills and the factory system. Some examples of songs of this type are included in Roy Palmer's *Poverty Knock* (Cambridge University Press, 1974).

Similarly, the true shanties and forebitters, as recorded notably by Ewan MacColl and A.L. Lloyd (for example on *A Sailor's Garland*, Transatlantic Xtra 5013), reflect many aspects of nineteenth-century life in the merchant fleet, from the cut-throat competitiveness of North Atlantic trade to the way in which sailors ashore were fleeced by publicans, lodging-house keepers, sailing-masters and girlfriends alike. Given a good reference library, a selection of these songs can lead to many 'finding-out' activities and will suggest many themes for group or individual research.

Apart from using these songs as historical resources alongside other material, there are many other ways in which they can enrich the curriculum. Many of them are worth studying in English as examples of economical story-telling. Others raise questions for class discussion. Others might inspire the children to write new words, especially if one of the better-known tunes is chosen, perhaps based on current national or local events. Humanities themes like the role of women, attitudes to work, war or family relationships can usefully draw upon folk song as a resource which is valuable in presenting a 'popular' rather than a political view on such issues. But these are all, in a sense, mere excuses to justify what teachers in primary and middle schools should be doing anyway — reminding children of their cultural heritage. And folk music has as important a place in British culture as our poems, novels and plays.

4 *Folk music in the music lesson*

PAT PALMER, JACK DOBBS, GEOFFREY BRACE, AILIE MUNRO

This chapter consists of four contributions from practising music teachers. **Pat Palmer** explores the role of musical activities in child development and the part folk music can play in musical education, and then describes some work in a junior school in Birmingham. **Jack Dobbs** makes some practical suggestions about the use of folk music with older primary and younger secondary pupils. **Geoffrey Brace** continues from the viewpoint of the secondary school and **Ailie Munro** describes some of her work with less able and disadvantaged children in inner-city secondary schools in Scotland.

I PAT PALMER

Primary-school teachers are less concerned than secondary-school teachers are with the content and disciplines of specific subjects. The most important considerations in the education of young children are fundamental principles of learning and child development. However, it could be suggested that the aim of all education is to provide opportunities for physical, emotional, intellectual, aesthetic and social development. The teacher's main function is to provide the means by which this experience may be acquired and assimilated. Music is a rich source of all these forms of experience and an ideal vehicle for expressing them.

Folk music has long been a part of the school music curriculum. What has radically changed is the choice of material and the style of performance. A brief glance at current BBC school music pamphlets will illustrate this. The choice of music is wider and more cosmopolitan. Generally it is more suited to the experience and interests of the age-group for which it is intended. Traditional games and humorous songs are frequently used; folk songs of other countries and continents are also a feature; the drawing-room type of piano accompaniment is often replaced by the guitar and extra spice is provided by percussion instruments. Much of the accompaniment can be played by amateur musicians and the general presentation of singing programmes is more relaxed and informal. Involvement is the keyword in music, as in other subjects.

There is also the workshop approach. Its growth is largely due to the work of the great composer—teachers Kodály and Orff and their disciples. Their influence has greatly stimulated the use of traditional music for training in musical literacy. Both suggested that the child's natural forms should be the starting-point for musical education. Chants, singing games and dances are still invented and transmitted from children to children. Some are old and long established, such as 'The big ship sails' and 'There came three gypsies'. More recent characters, George Best and Cliff Richard, are immortalised in rhymes. New ones also appear. Was 'Sock-a-ball'[1] played before the invention of nylon socks, which seem ideally suited for this game? These games and songs are acquired soon after the child starts school and fade naturally in the last year of the junior school, girls using them much longer than boys. There are dips, claps, skipping and ball games and elastic-jumping, all accompanied by songs and chants. There are also song-dances such as 'Going to the countryside' and 'A sailor went to sea, sea, sea, to see what he could see, see, see', and songs with semi-dramatic or stylised movement such as 'When Susie was a baby . . . infant . . . junior . . . teenager . . . pregnant . . . mother . . . grannie . . . skeleton . . . ghost'. Choosing games with songs include

> Monday night down the lane,
> Tuesday night back again,
> Wednesday night a visitor,
> Out goes . . .

and

> These two sailors . . .

The tradition remains because it appears to be necessary at a particular stage in a child's social development. An interesting deviation in modern times is that these games are now used much more by girls than by boys. Four main needs appear to be satisfied: physical/kinaesthetic, social, technical (i.e. handling concepts such as number and colour), and aesthetic.

When children perform their own songs they never stand still and the movements they use demand considerable co-ordination and skill. This physical response to a

---

1. In this game the player stands with back to a wall and legs astride. The ball inside a long flexible sock is hit backwards above the shoulders on alternate sides and between the legs on the word 'sir' in the rhyme.

> Want a cup o' tea, sir?
> Yes, sir.
> Why, sir?
> 'Cos I've got a cold, sir.
> Where'd you get your cold, sir?
> From the North Pole, sir.
> What're you doing there, sir?
> Catching polar bear, sir.
> How many did you catch, sir?
> One, sir, two, sir,
> The third caught me, sir.

song or rhyme develops skills and balance that may otherwise not be acquired. Mental retardation is often associated with lack of rhythmic co-ordination and special educational programmes including perceptual training recommend the use of music and rhythmic exercises in clapping and moving to music. Similarly, language-teaching programmes, including those for immigrants, suggest that the rhythm of language is reflected in the rhythm of traditional music.

Together with rhythm and physical response, social skills are also a significant ingredient of children's traditional songs and games. Such techniques as counting and naming colours, days of the week and months of the year are practised. Also social modes of conduct are observed and described. Primary social roles, including those of sex and family, appear in 'When Susie was a baby', 'The farmer's in his den'. Choosing or capturing a mate occurs in many singing games. Developing interest in language as the most important medium of social communication shows itself in the play with language, encouraging fluency and articulation. (See Peter and Iona Opie, *Children's Games in Street and Playground*, Oxford University Press, 1969.) There are many 'dips' − a characteristic choosing strategy − with this feature − for example, 'Eenie, meenie, macha, racha', and 'Dippy, dippy, dation, my operation . . . ' Intrepid observation of social conduct recognises the tart-like figure in 'Going to the countryside, going to the fair'. Primitive law and order appears in 'Who stole the apple from the old man's tree?' Similar social skills and observations appear in the adult tradition in counting and cumulative songs and love and courtship songs.

Though kinaesthetic and social features seem to be the most important ingredients of children's games, aesthetic appreciation is revealed in the obvious enjoyment of form and musical phrasing. Question-and-answer structures give the satisfaction of balance and symmetry. However, segmentation of phrases for special effect also occurs, as in

> Who stole the apple from the old man's tree?
> Number one stole the apple from the old man's tree.
> Who, me?
> Yes, you!
> Couldn't have been.
> Then who
> Stole the apple from the old man's tree?
> Number two . . . etc.

The phrase overlap 'then who' produces a syncopation which is even more highlighted by the clapping accompaniment which is an integral part of this splendid chant. The contrast provided by a solo voice in dialogue with the group is also an important aesthetic feature, and the relentless beat is a deliberate artistic device in this rhyme.

It is advisable for all teachers of music in primary schools to have a knowledge of the children's tradition in the context of individual schools and areas as well as of national trends. The features of the songs and dances and the needs they appear to satisfy are highly relevant to early musical education. For example, the loss of vitality in children's singing in the classroom may in part be due to the frustration of their natural physical response to music. A weekly music and movement programme from one of the BBC's lists does not satisfy the need for the formal, controlled and socialised movement that characterises their own traditions. When left to their own devices girls will often accompany songs they have learned in the music lesson with patterns made from clapping and slapping with two pairs of hands and knees. Perhaps the most unlikely example of this kind of treatment I have observed was 'Jubilate', a sixteenth-century canon which can be found in James Wild (ed.), *Roundabout* (*Sing for Pleasure*, book 2) (Oxford University Press, 1968), p. 15. The climax of the final Amen was beautifully expressed by four hands together on the first syllable and two pairs of knees for the second, expressing the physical sensation of the falling fifth as well as the slower note values! This natural form of accompaniment should be encouraged where appropriate. The refrain of, for instance, 'Johnny Lad', the Glasgow street game in Ian Campbell's school collection, works well with it. In my school we've even tried it with everyone in assembly turning to a neighbour and clapping in this way for the last chorus of 'The Family of Man'. It's a bit riotous but helps reinforce the spirit of Karl Dallas's song! In the children's tradition handclaps often reinforce tongue-twisting chants, hands thus helping tongues. Might this be a tip for helping children to learn difficult word patterns in songs or rhymes? Both Kodály and Orff suggest that the natural physical response to music should be exploited and developed in early musical education. Jacques Dalcroze went further, believing that many musical concepts and principles could be experienced and reinforced by movement.

A more advanced and disciplined use of hands and feet can occur in reading early rhythmic patterns and in the recognition of differences in time. For example, one left-hand tap followed by two right-hands may represent the sensation of triple time. Similar treatment may be used for $\frac{5}{4}$, which occurs in Eastern European music. Such asymmetrical movement demands considerable control and concentration from children. Triple time appears to be the first real obstacle. Duple suggests the natural pendulum of right—left, up—down, in—out, bad—good. To hold a dotted minim for three full beats or to maintain a minim—crotchet rhythm is much more unnatural and therefore difficult. A quick glance at nursery rhymes will reveal few in triple time ($\frac{3}{4}$), though triple division of the pulse ($\frac{6}{8}$) is very common in English sayings ('Look before you leap', 'Too many cooks spoil the broth'), as well as in traditional songs.

The relevance of the appearance of the highly socialised forms of children's traditional singing games may be appreciated if reference is made to Piaget's interpretation of development and behaviour. As the child becomes less egocentric and achieves conservation, in Piaget's terms, he is less dependent on immediate experience and adopts a form of communication that reflects the deeper and extended view of social reality.

The counting and cumulative songs, which are great favourites with young children, besides expressing and practising social skills also exercise the memory. Storing experience for reference is a relatively new skill which is recognised, albeit subconsciously, as needed for further intellectual and social development.

As an understanding develops of consequence and logic, with such concepts as are implied by the words 'if', 'but', 'because' and 'although', children begin to enjoy such nonsense songs as 'There was a man and he went mad. He jumped into a paper bag.' Observation of social ritual leads to appreciation of incongruity or inappropriate behaviour, as in 'When shall we get married, John?'

The concept of time and history is attained relatively late in a child's development. Folk songs are useful in this context. At a very basic level the early experience of time passing and the recognition of a rhythm of life, work and leisure may be reinforced by the celebration of the seasons. Harvest, Christmas, spring, May and summer are marked by special forms of celebration or activity. Children are very involved in and affected by these celebrations. Musical experience is often far more memorable in these contexts than any other. Probably more children will remember the carols they sang last Christmas than the card they made for mother. Traditional material is often the most potent because it has the permanence and strength that specially composed material does not.

Orientation in a geographical and mathematical sense may be experienced by children in easy folk dances. Right-hand/left-hand recognition is a common problem. In 'Old Brass Wagon', an American singing dance where a circle of girls faces a concentrically moving circle of boys, 'Circle to the left' means going in opposite directions. Children love this paradox as much as they enjoy the casting figure in country dances. Similarly in dance making lines from circles and circles from lines fascinates them.

The use of a variety of folk songs and dances will run parallel to the children's own tradition and many social and physical needs will be satisfied. For the non-specialist teacher this may represent the limits of his ability in the use of folk music. However, the aesthetic and intellectual aspects may be developed much further by the music specialist using traditional material.

Early aural training begins in the infant school and includes rhythm and pitch work as well as musical appreciation. Children at this age will readily respond to differences in speed and recognise this as a factor in expressing a mood or atmosphere. For example, a lullaby might be unrecognisable if sung too quickly. Later, characteristic rhythms will produce appropriate movement responses. A march will suggest strong walking steps and 'Girls and boys, come out to play' will evoke skipping. The 'jig jogs' from the Opies' *Puffin Book of Nursery Rhymes* (Penguin, 1963) provide excellent examples. The trotting rhythm of 'Trit trot to Boston' contrasting with the gallop of 'To market, to market' may be reinforced with the use of un-pitched percussion such as sleigh bells, claves, coconut shells and wood blocks. Nursery-rhyme collections will provide further examples of trotting and galloping or skipping, as will folk-song collections. Some teachers may like to use written note symbols to represent those basic rhythms of walking, running and skipping.

A later step in rhythmic training is in the recognition of characteristic patterns. These should be taken from songs already learned, as aural recognition should precede written symbol or sign. For example the counting song 'Navi-o' has a recurring pattern on the words 'Hit him on the radgie-padgie' which is easily recognised and memorised. The ability to reproduce this by tapping or clapping or using an instrument every time it occurs is an elementary aural exercise which is also enjoyed. The song appears under the title 'As I got up one morning' in G. and M. Polwarth, *Folk Songs from the North* (Frank Graham, 1970), p. 39.

Later on some of these familiar patterns may be used on flashcards or on wall sheets. They may also be used as rhythmic ostinati for other songs and pieces. A common body of experience which may be acquired from nursery rhymes and traditional songs is essential for continued reference. Music students often refer back to such sources for familiar rhythmic and melodic patterns.

Experience of rhythm in a bigger dimension, that of musical form, originates in the features of balance and repetition found in singing games and other traditional material. Dancing to traditional tunes is one of the easiest and most immediate ways of recognising and responding to musical phrases. Children should never be taught to count steps when they are learning dances but should be encouraged to match the figures of the dance to musical phrases. Given experience in basic movements and figures found in early folk dances, children will readily make up dances to fit tunes they know as well as inventing new ones.

This kind of work begins with singing games, not the ones that children use themselves in the playground, but some that have passed out of oral tradition and some from other countries. The game element or 'story' diverts attention from possible clumsiness or self-conscious movement. Free dance and movement may also be done to traditional music. Different instrumental colour and texture may be illustrated from the numerous recordings of folk instrumental music now available. Children at my school were intrigued by the 'diddling' tracks in a Scottish recording. The delicacy and neatness of foot movement suggested by the sound of a single man's voice vocalising for the dance was spontaneous and far more impressive than anything a dancing teacher could have taught.

'Hello, how are you?' movement sometimes begins our lessons. Children move freely to music and extend an arm of greeting as they dance. A brief turn or figure may be done with a classmate before moving on again. The next step may be to invite the pupils to make up a short dance. A tune with a clear rhythmic and phrase structure is used and is heard several times before any movement is done. The children are then expected to match dance figures to phrases. Different versions may then be compared and assessed.

Soon after this type of exercise children begin to make up dances to tunes and songs they already know. Good examples may be performed at morning assembly. Performance is a very important part of musical training. It is also the musical equivalent of 'putting it up on the wall', which most children of this age enjoy. It is a refreshing change to have something to see as well as to hear for a musical voluntary before the service. Harvest, Christmas, and May festivities provide further opportunities for such performances. A class band or the school orchestra will enjoy providing a live accompaniment. This type of work contrasts with music and movement programmes broadcast for school use. In these the focus is on the mood of the music rather than its structure, and very often the music is the backcloth for the story. Children benefit from both kinds of experience and approach.

Pitch-training may proceed in a similar way, that is, from the aural experience of traditional music. With infant-school children pitch-training may be sometimes hindered by language deficiency. For example, although the physical sensation of high and low may be felt by young children the matching of this experience linguistically to the musical concept is often inaccurate. Children up to the age of seven or eight confuse 'high' with 'loud' and 'low' with 'soft'. 'Low' seems to suggest restfulness — a low voice means gentle and soft to a young child. 'High' is shrill, painful, loud. As this appears to be a linguistic problem rather than a musical one the point need not be laboured. However, frequent use should be made of the terms 'high' and 'low' in their musical context.

The basic melodic interval of falling minor third — 'soh'–'me' — occurs in calls and chants heard in streets and playgrounds as well as in street cries and souling songs:

A soul, a soul, a soul cake, Please, good mis-sus, a soul cake, An ap-ple, a pear, a plum or a cher-ry,

A-ny good thing to make us mer-ry. One for Pe-ter, one for Paul, One for him who made us all.

The melodic pattern 'soh–me–lah–soh–me' is common. It occurs in many children's songs, including 'I'm Shirley Temple' as well as this newly created one from my school:

We are little Irish girls

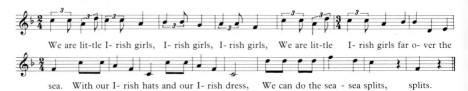

We are lit-tle I- rish girls, I- rish girls, I- rish girls, We are lit-tle I- rish girls far o- ver the

sea. With our I- rish hats and our I- rish dress, We can do the sea - sea splits, splits.

(Tune and words: Shirley Boron, Maxine Pugh)

Most teachers start with the pentatonic scale nowadays because of the prevalence of those intervals in primitive tunes. After two or three years, however, the intervals and tonal relationships of the major scale may be taught. John Curwen, who greatly influenced Kodály and others, began his programmes with 'doh' and 'soh', or the tonic and dominant relationship. The other tonic sound 'me' was then introduced. The dominant-to-tonic and tonic-to-dominant opening in English traditional music is probably more common than true pentatonism. Examples of it are 'Baa, baa, black sheep', 'The big ship sails', 'There came three gypsies', and 'I sowed the seeds of love'.

The frequency of the Ionian mode and an often basically major tonality makes the introduction of the mediant easy; for example, 'Here we go round the mulberry bush', 'Girls and boys come out to play', and 'Ally, bally, bally, bally bee'. After the tonic sounds, the non-tonic beginning with the leading note 'te' and then 'fah' and 'ray' encourage recognition and use of tonic and dominant harmony. Of all the musical concepts that of harmony is believed to be attained latest. It is also fashionable to despise the Western European preoccupation with harmony. This is a further argument used to support prolonged use of pentatonic scales which produce picturesque pseudo-polyphony.

Whether we like it or not, harmony has been exploited as a musically expressive device as well as a powerful agent in the shaping of highly sophisticated musical forms. Teachers cannot ignore the whole musical history of Western Europe, which has also influenced and shaped our traditional forms, in favour of more exotic fields. Harmony still is a powerful factor in much of the music children hear. Teachers themselves may have had a surfeit of the three-chord guitar accompaniment but, like so many experiences common to adults, it is new and exciting to children.

Earliest experience of making harmony often comes in the singing of rounds, many of which come from the seventeenth century. Most of them, with the basic pillars of tonic and dominant, have a greater affinity with harmony than polyphony. Many songs in the Ionian and major modes may be found in traditional music which provide examples of characteristic melodic intervals and patterns, as well as tonal relationships. Folk-dance tunes also contain basic tonic and dominant harmony. American play-party games are useful as examples. The autoharp is the easiest instrument to provide complete harmonic accompaniment in the early stages. Barred percussion instruments (glockenspiel, xylophone and the like) played chordally by one person provide similar experience. Later, simple guitar strumming fulfils the same purpose.

Other modes than major should of course, be experienced and recognised. When the minor scale is introduced many songs in the Aeolian and Dorian modes may already be in the children's repertoire. One example – 'I will give my love an apple' – besides being an Aeolian tune, has the added advantage of metaphorical language which appeals to the older junior-school child's interest in linguistic device. (Note the love of puns and riddles at this age.) 'The Drunken Sailor', in the Dorian mode, is a great favourite and sounds best with harmonies on the tonic and flattened lead-ing note. 'Land of the Silver Birch', a song from Canada, is pentatonic with strong tonic and dominant and a beautiful repeated minor third at the end of the tune.

Folk songs of other lands and other cultures will also be in the repertoire. How-ever, they should not submerge native material in the early stages, as a reliable home base is essential for identity as well as security. Musical appreciation of regional and national styles may be cultivated. A way to begin this is to use folk recordings as introductory and concluding music at morning assembly. Folk records need not replace the more usual classical material: the two kinds of musical expression should be alternated, complementing and contrasting and thus cultivating the faculties of musical discrimination and appreciation. Examples of Scottish, Irish, Australian, Spanish or Hungarian traditional music may be grouped and illustrated in the same way that a 'composer of the week' might be used. Folk and regional music can often be related to topics and projects. Other views of folk music may be obtained by hearing various individual and traditional styles of performance. Differ-ent vocal and instrumental groups may be heard and evaluated. Sometimes with young children such records may be used for simple aural discrimination; for example, identifying the instruments to be heard on a particular record.

Characteristic forms such as shanties, work songs and industrial ballads may be illustrated. These can also be grouped for performance. For example, a set of shanties can be compiled and be built up with simple costume and a few props into a sequence or story. Christmas carols and harvest songs can be used in a similar way. Dramatisation of songs will increase appreciation. Traditional lullabies can be used alongside examples by composers like Mozart, Kabalevsky, Tchaikovsky, Schumann and Brahms.

At the school where I work we held a May festival which included processional May songs and dances, with further diversions from flower-sellers (who made their own baskets), self-styled jugglers, clowns and acrobats. The preparations stimulated two girls into producing a May song, which was printed and sold by the composers and friends. The modality was quite natural and unsophisticated.

Spring is coming

(Tune: Elva Griffin. Accompaniment: Catherine Harbert)

A dance was devised by a group of third-year girls to Morley's madrigal 'Now is the month of maying'. One of the recorder groups was learning a three-part setting and the tune was so admired that a dance setting was worked out during playtimes, presented for my approval and performed at the festival. Costumes for the various entertainers were found in the dressing-up cupboard and the whole occasion was colourful and gay in the gorgeous summer sunshine. Happy memories of the day produced written work, pictures and a further song from one of the 'clowns' who cribbed the tune from one of the group of folk-dance tunes which had been arranged for the school orchestra.

Clowns' Song

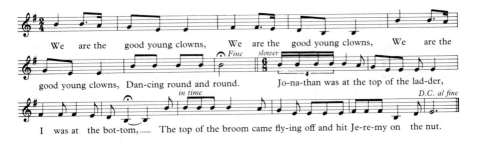

(Words and tune: Jeremy Crombleholm)

The same children continued to make up songs, sometimes using poems, sometimes making up words for their own tunes. 'Pebbles', by Elva, who composed the May song, has a Lydian flavour.

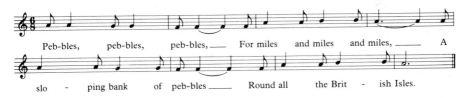

She also composed a setting of 'June', which she found in a poetry book.

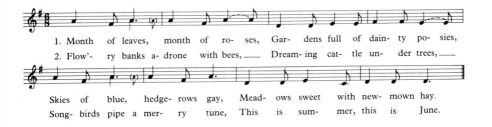

Her class teacher noticed a growing interest in poetry as a result of her success in composition. Elva taught this song to a group of first-year children; a friend played a simple rhythmic accompaniment on percussion instruments, and it was performed at a lower-school morning assembly. The composer, a shy girl, left school about a month later, subsequently joined the choir at her secondary school and returned one evening about Christmas-time to tell me of her continuing interest and bringing a new song she had composed.

The boy with a stammer who came out of his shell to be a clown also continued to compose, mainly comic songs, often writing his own words as well as music. He also made great strides with his violin lessons and now proudly leads the school orchestra.

A festival of traditional singing games based on a collection of playground material from five schools in different areas of Birmingham produced a crop of new song-dances of traditional types. 'Irish girls' (p. 5) was made up by girls of Irish parents. The words, tune and dance were made up together. This pair of composer—dancers was joined by two West Indians from the same class. The quartet have produced a crop of song-dances. 'There's a little girl in the corner' has a simple social message, particularly relevant in our multi-racial school.

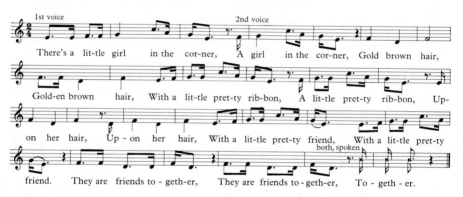

(Words, tune and dance: Shirley, Maxine, Mavelin and Ann)

The children's creative work has not been limited to traditional style, however. They have also made up descants and obbligato lines to tunes already known. Two of their hymn descants, 'Far around the world' and 'Silent Night', have been performed at morning assembly. The strong harmonic feeling of one of the West Indian girls was also expressed in our guitar club where she supplemented the simple guitar and autoharp harmony for hymns and songs on barred percussion. This girl can also provide a simple descant line which she plays by ear. Her delight in simple harmony has led her to make a piano piece based on tonic and dominant harmony, though she has no instrument at home. She also frequently harmonises songs we learn in class lessons at the piano. She is now learning to play the cello. Another West

Indian girl, musically literate via the recorder and violin, also followed up her harmonic experience at guitar club with a piano piece. She is now taking piano lessons and is a most promising all-round musician.

The four dancers initiated a lunch-time traditional dance club. The culmination of a term's informal work was their invention of a group of dances using traditional figures, to accompany the school orchestra's Christmas dance suite which had been arranged for a mixed group of recorders, strings, piano (played by a beginner) and percussion. These were performed as the opening item of a Christmas concert in the local church. One of the group also composed a delightful tune to a poem she was given to copy for handwriting practice from the blackboard! She sang it consistently in tune despite the high tessitura. This was the final item of the concert. The sound of her silver-clear voice in the tall church will be a treasured memory.

A Christmas Song

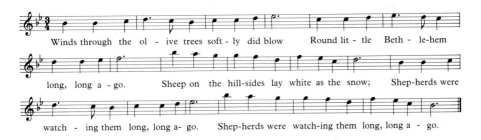

(Tune: Shirley Boron)

These examples of creative work are only a small part of the musical activity of the school as a whole. Many and varied forms of musical expression and different styles are encouraged. I have only been in the school for four complete terms — there are also two peripatetic teachers of violin and cello — and I do not pretend that my interest and abilities ensure a comprehensive or even progressive view of musical education. However, I have attempted to observe children's needs and modes of musical expression as manifest in their own tradition. In addition, my own musical training, which has continued uninterrupted in some form for over twenty years, has compelled me to recognise basic skills in children which I have believed worth trying to extend in order to enrich their musical performance.

Creativity, particularly in the arts subjects, is nowadays regarded as paramount in education. Music is often linked in this regard with arts and crafts. Although the craft aspect of music is not ignored the affinity with language is often forgotten. Music can be as much a means of communication as of self-expression. Most musicians, both amateur and professional, mainly practise interpretative and re-creative skills, performing music that others have created but which lies dormant unless it is re-awakened by performance. Also most musicians perform with and for others. Pouring out one's own idea for oneself in one's own creative work is rare. Dabbling with musical effects, though a necessary preliminary to musical expression and discovery, cannot be prolonged or replace the acquisition of definite skills. Even quite young children recognise skill. Watching an older child or teacher play an instrument, they believe at first they can produce the same effect merely by handling the same materials. Some sense of shock and frustration is experienced when they realise that patience and hard work are required. However, they may be helped to build a repertoire of music which provides the basis from which further skills and knowledge may be acquired. The style that is nearest to their own traditional expression is the one that provides the confidence and interest needed to do this.

II JACK DOBBS

As a result of the growth of folk clubs in colleges and universities as well as in pubs and other places where people gather socially, many primary-school teachers now know the pleasure of singing folk songs together. Having enjoyed the songs themselves they have also recognised the valuable contribution these can make to the education of young children, giving them an insight into local and national events, commenting on occupations past and present, and bringing into the classroom the customs and traditions of other countries. Poetry and literature, religious education, environmental studies and any number of other activities come into the ambit of folk music. Indeed, folk music and particularly folk songs often seem to be used for the teaching of almost every subject except music itself. How can this situation be remedied?

Clearly, one of the main responsibilities of any music teacher is to provide for his pupils a repertoire of beautiful music, to introduce them to music of lasting value. Here folk songs come into their own. Many of their tunes are the equal of the most beautiful tunes in the world, and yet are within the capabilities of young performers and accessible to them. Most of these songs were not composed especially for children. They are expressions of common human feelings and descriptions of events of universal interest. But children can nevertheless appreciate them at different levels and identify with them in their own individual ways. They can grow into them as they could never grow into songs that have been written down to what was considered their level.

These songs that have proved themselves over the years belong to an oral tradition and so make an excellent basis for sound aural training. The value of regular training in concentrated listening cannot be overemphasised. Such training is not possible if all our songs are read from printed notation; but if the songs are learnt in the traditional manner from someone else's singing, the ear has to remain wide awake throughout to catch the musical and verbal nuances. And the musical memory is also being trained.

A reliable musical memory is essential for any musician. Music moves through time, and unless the listener can relate its various elements as they pass before him the gestalt cannot be perceived. Notation can become a crutch and if for some reason it is removed the music limps rather badly. The child who has memorised his songs carries his repertoire around with him and is able to produce items from it on any occasion he wishes, for his own and others' pleasure.

This process of oral transmission keeps folk songs alive by re-creating them every time they are performed. We are not dealing with museum pieces, but with living entities developing organically and always adapting themselves to contemporary needs. Once the folk song becomes static it begins to petrify. There is much less likelihood of such petrification if the songs are passed on orally from teacher to pupil and from child to child. Indeed, children are themselves custodians of many intriguing tunes associated with their games and street songs, often from the immediate locality. Within the school there are many opportunities for encouraging local adaptations and for creating new compositions, weaving into their fabric contributions from individual pupils who benefit from each other's offerings as well as from the shared responsibility for the final product.

If the teacher is to pass on the songs in this way the pupils must be seated in the classroom in a position which allows them to follow his or her facial expressions and any bodily gestures he may happen to use. For his part, he must sing the melody clearly, and enunciate the words with precision. The intonation must be as accurate as possible, and the rhythms vital even when the song is slow and melancholy in nature. Such patterning does not require a professional singing voice: warmth of personality and an ability to communicate are the essentials.

The first sing-through should give an impression of the song as a whole, conveying its character and meaning to the pupils. This can only be done really effectively when the teacher has made the song a part of himself — when instead of being read from the pages of a book it flows freely from the singer. One hopes that like the pupils he will have had the opportunity to learn it from another singer, in person if possible, but failing that, from an authentic performance on tape, record or radio.

This need for communication is underlined by the fact that the purpose of many folk songs is to tell a story. The melody is the vehicle for the words, and it is the words that were usually uppermost in the traditional singers' minds. In fact, many English singers were unable to sing the tune without its words. This element of story-telling in the songs is very important to young children, who usually respond more immediately to the dramatic and eventful than to the lyrical and pastoral.

If songs are transmitted orally the melody is also more likely to take wing, for the artificial barriers erected visually by the bar-lines are removed, and the phrases can be learnt as wholes instead of as accumulations of bars. Visually difficult intervals often prove easy to grasp aurally, and apparently complicated rhythmic groups like those in 'Sweet water rolling' no longer hold up the learning. They are more quickly learnt by imitation from someone else's singing, and the learner's own singing takes on much greater flexibility and fluidity as a result.

Sweet wa-ter roll-ing, Sweet wa-ter roll,   Roll-ing from the foun-tain,   Sweet wa - ter roll.

(Ruth Seeger, *American Folksongs for Children* (Doubleday, New York, 1948), p. 65)

In the early stages of such learning of songs it is prudent not to spend too much time on unimportant details in case the whole is lost in the parts, and the element of pleasure is killed. Nor should we try to put in or extract too much 'expression'. A simple, unselfconscious patterning at the song's natural speed is more effective. This allows the child to identify with the song as he wishes, and to let it grow within himself in a way which is impossible if the song is moulded too completely to an individual interpretation in the early stages of its life.

We need not be unduly worried if not all the children are eager to join in the singing at first. Some may prefer to sit and clap their hands or tap their feet, even to move about the room, and it is only later that their parents discover how much of the song they have taken in. Ruth Seeger, who has had a great deal of experience with young children, reminds us in *American Folksongs for Children* (p. 39) that children who are shy about singing will sometimes join in on an important single note or interval when they would not think of attempting a whole phrase. Such a song might be 'Frog went a-courtin'':

Frog went a-cour-tin' and he did ride, *m-hm,*   Frog went a-cour-tin' and he did ride, *m-hm,* etc.

(Ruth Seeger, op. cit., p. 116)

Songs requiring an answer to a question sometimes encourage such children to participate:

Who built   the ark?   *No-ah, No-ah,*   Who built   the ark?   *Bro-ther No-ah built the ark.*

(*Oxford School Music Books*, beginners' series, no. 3 (Oxford University Press, 1954))

So do nonsense refrains like that in 'The Herring Song' and the parts in shanties where the sailors make a united effort for some physical action like hauling the sails.

There was an old man who came from Kin-sale, *Sing: ab-er-um-vane,*   *sing: ab-er-o-ling,* And

he had a her-ring, a her-ring for sale,   *Sing: ab-er-um-vane,*   *sing: ab-er-o-ling.*

(Peter Kennedy (ed.), *Folksongs of Britain and Ireland* (Cassell, 1975), no. 296)

Repeated phrases within a song also give the pupils something to hold on to while they gradually grow acquainted with the remainder of the song.

Some teachers may object that this oral teaching will prevent children from ever learning to sing at sight, and that folk songs have for many years been used as a rich source of material for this very purpose. That is true, and what is now being suggested is not the neglect of notation but a reconsideration of its place in a child's musical education. The printed book does not become valueless because a child first learns to speak without it, and when Suzuki teaches his young violinists to play their tunes by imitation he doesn't thereby repudiate notation. Rather, he encourages them to 'speak' first and only then to recognise in written form the sounds they have already produced. In due course, as the aural and visual become more closely associated, the notation acts as more than a reminder of what has already been performed: it presents its own message to be interpreted on the voice or instrument. The same principle can apply equally to the use of folk songs to aid musical literacy. They are first learnt aurally, and then appropriate sol-fa syllables and staff notation will show the pupils what they have already sung. They will discover that the interval with which the song began or which was prominent else-where in it was 'soh,'–'doh' or 'doh'–'me' or 'doh'–'doh''. From then on that par-ticular interval will be familiar to them and they will not only recognise it aurally and know its name, but also be able to read it visually. And the same thing can happen with the rhythmic groups. Our pupils will experience the difference between ♩ ♫ and ♫ ♩ or ♫♫, and will find that the last is not more difficult to sing or comprehend than the first two, although it is called compound time and they are described as simple. In this way the pupils' musical vocabulary will be continuously and systematically enlarged, and the regular practice in associating sound with symbol will enable them to read accurately from staff notation.

Heaven forbid that we should sing our folk songs only for this purpose and in a graded order calculated for the development of literacy. But the standard of musical literacy in schools is not so advanced that we can afford to treat it in a cavalier manner — and other countries have been helped by folk music in this context. The nature of English folk music makes it, perhaps, less easy to use as an exclusive foundation for our musical education than was the case with indigenous folk music in Hungary. Kodály had available a vast collection of songs, the result of his own and Bartók's labours, which could be classified and graded from the two-note calls based on the minor third (increasingly familiar at our own football matches) to the most complex melodies. We have very few tunes with as limited a range as three notes, and no unifying scale like the pentatonic — unless it be the major. So if we wish to use folk music as the basis of our scheme for musical literacy we must include music from other countries and welcome the richness this brings into our schools.

When teaching folk songs using the voice it is assumed that the accompanying instrument will not be the piano. The teacher who has become thoroughly familiar with the song and really wants to share it with the children gathered around won't feel the need to cling to the piano, still less to hide behind it. His eyes and attention must be on the children, not on the keyboard. The playing of the melody as the children sing makes their ears lazy, and in any case it is far more difficult to pattern a legato, cantabile tune on the keyboard than it is using the voice or a melody instrument. Moreover, away from the piano and printed notation the teacher is more likely to sing the song at a pitch suitable for children's voices, which often have a lower tessitura than is recognised by song-book editors.

Kodály has made unaccompanied singing the basis of his choral method, pointing out that the use of equal-tempered tuning on the keyboard, with every note slightly out of tune, is hardly the best way to train children to sing accurately in tune. Much better to let them sing unaccompanied and as early as possible in parts, making this the check on the correctness of the intervals. There is, then, educational value in singing the songs unaccompanied, quite apart from its stylistic appropriateness. That being so, we should be very cautious about adding any accompaniment that may rob the melody of its flexibility, subtlety and directness, for the melody and its words are always more important than any accompaniment, however tasteful.

Nevertheless, it is also a fact that not all folk songs were sung unaccompanied. The fiddle, flute, pipes, concertina and melodeon have all been used by traditional singers, and more recently singers have added the double bass, guitar, banjo, mandolin, harmonica, dulcimer, drums, cymbals, bones and autoharp. This last-named instrument, which produces chords by a simple mechanical device, has proved of great value to inexperienced teachers. This is a practical consideration, for some teachers take a little time to lose their self-consciousness in front of their children, and feel more at ease when they are strumming or plucking an instrument. For them the autoharp, dulcimer or guitar may be useful aids.

The guitar is certainly one of the most versatile instruments, able to provide accompaniments from the simplest three-chord *um-cha-cha* to the most demanding requirements of the Spanish flamenco. It can also offer an acceptable imitation of other harp- and zither-type instruments as far removed from our own culture as the Chinese *ch'in* and Japanese *koto*. And it can be carried around easily, so that it is not long before a young soloist singing quietly to her instrument acts as a magnet for a lively group, swopping songs and extending their repertoire at a rate that might surprise many teachers.

The purpose of an accompaniment is not just to provide a harmonic background or to give the singer rhythmic support. It can also bring hidden potential out of the tune. Material from the melody may suggest interwoven improvisations within the mode of the song, melodic motifs may shadow the tune until the ends of lines or during rests, and an entirely new countermelody, developed from the song itself or completely independent of it, may provide exciting new rhythmic interest. At all times simplicity and economy must be our guides so that the accompaniment does not distract from the singer.

We may not have all the instruments just mentioned in our schools, but there may be others equally suitable. Recorders or clarinets can create a lyrical and pastoral atmosphere and can be used effectively instead of the pipes that accompany songs in some Eastern European countries. The violin has always been associated with both folk songs and dances: the lower strings of this and of the cello provide a good bagpipe drone when that is required.

The Holy Child

Born on earth is the ho-ly child, Praise him with o-boes and bag-pipes play-ing; Born on earth is the ho-ly child, Sing to wel-come the sa-viour mild.

(Translation: Sally Wright) (Jack Dobbs, *Ears and Eyes*, teacher's manual (Oxford University Press, 1978), p. 62)

We can also use a vocal drone which may lead through ostinati and rhythmic figures derived from it to independent part-singing. The glockenspiels, xylophones and percussion of the Orff instrumentarium can add colour and provide dramatic effect when these are needed and prepare the way for an understanding of the *gamelan* music of Indonesia as well as of many contemporary compositions. The instruments should not be limited only to the accompaniments. Children should also play instrumental folk tunes themselves and accompany folk dances, not just for functional purposes but because of the sheer beauty and vitality of the tunes.

We must make sure that we explore fully the varied collection of songs available, and that they meet the needs of the children to whom they are given. Young children enjoy ball-bouncing songs, skipping games and traditional singing games.

Simple spontaneous chants, recognisable all over the world, grow naturally out of the children's games and can be heard in almost any playground. They make good starting-points for songs. Cumulative songs are enjoyed; so are songs containing a humour acceptable to children. At Christmas when we sing carols we sometimes forget their close association with the old ring games, the word 'carol' itself being derived from 'carole' — 'a ring dance'. The wassailing songs, too, lend themselves to movement. We should also remember that carols do not only belong to Christmas. Some of the loveliest, especially for the older children, deal with the events of Passiontide — for example, 'Mary's Wandering' (*Oxford Book of Carols* (Oxford University Press, 1964) no. 93). Others relate to Easter (*OBC*, no. 94). There are mumming plays, pace-egging songs and songs relating to the changing seasons. Let us use particularly any songs that are common in the children's own locality — rural or industrial.

The singing of folk songs with their dramatic possibilities allows us to think in terms of individuals and small groups rather than to treat the class as a single unit, all singing in unison throughout. Individuals can take the parts of the main characters and the rest of the class can be involved in the narrative or the crowd's comments. In the shanties there are ready-made opportunities for solo and chorus work. The acceptance of responsibility for such individual parts prepares for the independence required in part-singing. The shanty gives a good chance, too, to try out different styles of singing in the shantyman's part — bold or intimate, in strict time or rubato, straight or with decorations. Improvisation played an important part with some shantymen: verses moved about from one shanty to another and new ones were created on the spur of the moment to suit particular situations or send up well-known characters.

In the shanties as well as in many other songs there is an opportunity for improvisation, making the words relevant to the world known by the children, while still retaining the traditional words for use at other times. Some teachers feel that children should be able to understand all they sing. But apparently meaningless words (like those in foreign languages) may still be enjoyed by children for their fascinating sounds, and may at the same time unconsciously extend their horizons. The 1905 *Handbook for Teachers* spoke wisely when it said, 'It is not necessary that infants should understand all the words they sing, as the chief appeal is not to the intellect, the training of which is the purpose of almost every subject in the curriculum, but through the spirit of the song to the unconscious mind of the child.'

This section has been about folk song in the primary and middle schools, but one of the fascinating things about folk songs and dances is the way they elicit a response from people of all ages. As children grow up their appreciation of folk music can deepen and increase: in introducing them to it early we are giving them a treasure which will continue to increase in value throughout their lives.

III GEOFFREY BRACE

Music teachers in secondary schools are in a particularly difficult position these days. Music is the focus of young people's lives and of their developing emotions and personalities. It is their own principal form of entertainment. It is associated with good times, romantic encounters, high spirits and all kinds of intense personal experience, real and imaginary. A lesson in school, in a classroom, under the heading 'Music', cannot possibly be the same thing — even with the same music. The setting is wrong. The whole ambience is wrong. Setting up the frenetic disco in the lunch hour achieves something in the way of emotional outlets, release of physical energy, public relations. But (much to the disappointment of the young teacher *and* his expectant class) playing pop records in the classroom seems too often to be a cover-up for doing nothing (or the barely-noticed background for doing something else). Another big problem is that young people can become violently partisan about pop music. This usually has very little to do with music — it is a loyalty to *something* that they feel they want to have. Similarly, positions in the top twenty are nothing much to do with music either; they are results — classifications — by means of which people can get expectant and excited, with something to talk about until the next results and classifications come along.

Trying to talk about music without having to include all these other appendages is often a problem, but there are redeeming factors in the young person's attitudes to music that make things easier than they might be. Young people are, in fact, far more open-minded about music than is usually appreciated. The top twenty is hardly ever unmitigated pop 'personality' music. It produces the most surprising items — from medieval carols to slightly souped-up classics and old standards of the thirties. It is nothing like as predictable as people think. Ask men in the business. They are continually in despair at the flops they have backed and the crazy, completely un-pop things that take people's fancy. Obviously there are youngsters who go through stages when only one group or star can do anything right but, generally speaking, there is real receptivity to all kinds of music. In common with most people, young people like the familiar, but the familiar actually includes a wide variety of types of music. For instance they are likely to hear on television, if only in advertisements or opening titles, all kinds of snippets which may arouse a curiosity to hear more, even if this curiosity is at first latent. It is not the idiom which people reject so much as the supposed intellectual demands made by the music or the teacher. These must not be too heavy, too subtle or too long-winded. Within these limitations, most youngsters will try anything.

The other redeeming factor is the eagerness of people — young and old — to participate actively in some kind of music-making, provided, again, it is not too demanding in the initial stages and a sense of some achievement can be felt reasonably quickly. In this context the actual music is far less important. The experience of being involved in producing a recognisable tune — even if it is only 'Country

Gardens' or 'Scotland the Brave', can far outweigh the fact that it isn't a currently popular hit. In this context, folk music, in its many guises, is one very *practical* proposition available.

The music of rock groups, symphony orchestras and bands, however much others may like to try their hand at it, is professionally orientated. Out-and-out pop requires costly equipment. Orchestral and band playing demands a high standard of technique. With both there is always the knowledge that we are falling short of the standards we know exist — it doesn't sound the way we know it ought to sound. Though there *are* professional folk performers, the same sense of inadequacy doesn't obtain in folk music. One is not dependent on expensive gear, technical virtuosity or vocal training. The chances of a keen amateur providing a satisfying performance (satisfying to *him* especially) are much greater than in any other genre. And we all know what a crucial part a sense of success plays in all aspects of education.

Under my definition of folk music comes an enormous range of material. The English and American repertoire of ballads and broadsides, of course. But also American country music, Afro-American blues and gospel and their near-pop off-shoots; the 'new' folk songs of the singer—writers in the American and English revivals; the traditional music of every country in the world, not forgetting the *dance* music too. There is material here for several years of active and fascinating music-making and study — adaptable to every level of intellectual and technical ability.

To be a little more specific now about the musical knowledge that can be acquired through the use of folk music: to begin with, some traditional tunes are simple, limited in range and (with some notable exceptions) rhythmically straight-forward. They are therefore excellent material for the beginners on any instrument and for the non-player/non-reader to try to work out on melodic percussion. The harmonic basis of much Western folk music has a fundamental tonic—dominant and occasionally subdominant harmonic scheme and so is well-suited to elementary guitar and other chordal work (autoharp, accordion, bass, chime-bars and so on). The modal, minor and pentatonic tunes of Western Europe and countries further east are again not difficult to play or read but lend themselves more to drones, canons and ostinati in accompaniment — vocal or instrumental. Part-singing of the Northern European and American material comes easily and can be learned by rote, the simplest third-above or third-below harmonies being the most effective and usually the most authentic.

It is extremely important to use the right instrumental colour in accompaniment if at all possible — or at least something close to it. If one is going into the subject really intensively, one needs not only a guitar and bass but also, if possible, a fiddle and that even more ubiquitous folk instrument — the accordion. Rhythmic accompaniments must be chosen carefully, with a view to creating the right sound and not just to giving someone something to hit. Latin-American and Caribbean songs suggest certain obvious sounds. Greek, Latin, Spanish and Irish tunes all have their own characteristic settings which need to be explored, observed and reproduced.

This is an exciting and rewarding exercise in itself. Budding pop drummers and guitarists can easily be incorporated — as the excellent English and Irish dance-tune arrangements of the Fairport Convention, Steeleye Span and the Albion Country Band have shown — and this collaboration could easily be extended to the dance music of other nationalities.

Pupils are rarely reluctant to play. They are often reluctant to sing. Again, the folk-music repertoire probably has something for the most unforthcoming voices — raucous drinking songs, for instance, may bring involvement from older boys while the newer romantic folk-style songs like 'Last Thing on My Mind' and 'Suzanne' appeal to many girls.

Here also, the manner of performance is all-important. Many music teachers suffer by having trained or partly trained voices which, when applied to folk song, can sound most inappropriate. This does not mean that one does not take care to breathe well, to enunciate and to use all possible devices to put the song and its story across. But it does mean that one has to forget about cathedrals, opera houses and concert halls and think of a small company of people listening to one of their number in the intimate setting of a bar-room or front parlour. Excessive production of the voice and choir-style enunciation are quite out of place. The voice must sound natural, unforced and effortless, with clear but not affected diction, good breath control and a strong sense of the drama or humour of the song. As a model of how it can be done I would quote such artists as Tom Paxton, Richard Digance and Judy Collins. They do use microphones — but only in order to reproduce that unforced, easy style in large halls and arenas. In the classroom or saloon bar the same style will not need any amplification. There are other styles of singing that may be called for too — the hearty, rather rough style of drinking songs, the nasal whine of American country music, the aggressive, sonorous drive of African songs, the cheerful, extrovert singing of Mediterranean and Latin-American traditions. Obviously, if one can manage the original language that helps too — even if one is only imitating sounds without having any idea of their specific meaning.

All this is in the realm of practical musical activity — which is, to me at any rate, the essence of musical education. You do not in fact teach folk music, you just do it — pass on the tunes, work out the arrangements together in a co-operative work-shop atmosphere. You can teach guitar chords and notation for simple melody instruments and, as we have seen, folk material is ideal for this purpose. If, how-ever, the conscientious academic has a niggling feeling that some of his more promising musicians are not being extended by this sort of fare, there are higher levels at which to work on the subject. For example:

— the analysis of melodic formulae on the lines of Walter Wiora's *European Folk-song* (Anthology of Music series, no. 4 (Arno Volk, Cologne, 1966)).
— the various traditional scales — pentatonic, hexatonic, modal, Magyar — and those of the East — India, Indonesia, Japan.

— the elements that go to make up American folk music — German, Irish, Dutch, Negro, Spanish.
— the part that folk music has played in the work of composers like Bartók, Janáček, Copland, Holst.
— the strong German and Austrian folk influence to be found in Mozart, Schubert and Beethoven.

Then there is the whole realm of primitive music in Africa, Australia etc. — music and its associations with ritual and magic — the very raison d'être of music and its continued connection with the mystical and religious throughout history.

Basic composition can come through this line of study too: persuading students to conjure rhythms and short melodic figures out of the tops of their heads very quickly — to look at some words of verse and just sing them straight off instead of reading them — to trust their ability to do this and not have to rely on written notes to create ideas — to build something from small repetitive units as folk musicians do.

Out of all this activity at its many levels could come some more ambitious projects. A concert devoted to traditional music from all corners of the globe could include much more than a succession of guitarist—singers. It could include some of the folk-inspired music of Bartók, Holst etc. from the school orchestra, band or other instrumental groups, as well as dance-tune arrangements for more traditional-sounding groups — perhaps even the dances themselves — and songs in a variety of settings, aimed towards the near-authenticity advocated above. Costume and scenery might also play a part. If an all-out folk concert is not required, it is easy to see how items of the kind we have described could provide contrast and variety within the more usual concert programme, and at other not specifically musical functions like fetes and open days.

A project that is particularly near to my heart is the folk musical — the natural successor to the ballad-opera genre which has had very little development since the eighteenth century. The basic idea of taking well-known tunes and giving them new words to fit into the plot of a play would seem admirably suited to school music-drama requirements. The ballads and broadsides of the English tradition with their traditional instrumental settings (concertina, fiddle etc.) could be used most suitably in a musical—dramatic version of some classic novel like *The Vicar of Wakefield* or something from Eliot, Dickens or Hardy. We once based a very effective music drama on Hardy's *Under the Greenwood Tree* — an absolute natural for such treatment: there are many other possibilities.

The two great advantages of this kind of production are that the melodies and musical arrangements are fairly easily and quickly produced and that the performance of them does not make elaborate demands on individual voices or on the technique of instrumentalists. What is more, a young performer will find it much easier to sing to a small folk band than to the terrifying array of visiting orchestral players that suddenly starts belting forth at the dress rehearsal of the standard school operetta. I would be most interested to hear of anyone taking up this ballad-opera idea — particularly where the original procedure of adapting well-known tunes to new lyrics is used.

I have been fascinated by folk song and dance all my adult life, while being equally fascinated by most aspects of art music, from Dufay to Berio. There is nothing inferior or even less substantial about folk music. It has its own disciplines, its own background of knowledge, and its own academicism if you want it. Above all, it is accessible to the multitude emotionally, technically, and financially in a way that no other branch of music is. That alone must recommend it to every poverty-stricken school in the country.

IV AILIE MUNRO

In Scotland, for the last ten years and more, there have been schools of all kinds which consciously foster folk music, during or after school hours. But the teachers concerned are still rarely music teachers — whose own training, at academy, university or college of education, has left them almost totally ignorant of traditional music and indeed has often actively conditioned them against it. The teacher who tries to reach *all* the pupils, not just those already predisposed by their backgrounds towards an interest in music, will come up against a gulf which is arguably greater than for any other school subject. What follows are a few notes on one teacher's attempts to bridge that gulf, in state secondary schools around Glasgow during the mid sixties.

These attempts began, appropriately, at a modified secondary school for girls in Govan, one of the tougher parts of Glasgow — appropriately, because, to quote A.L. Lloyd in a recent interview (*Folk Review*, September 1974), 'folk songs are very closely bound up with the history of underdogs', and the word 'underdog' describes most of the inhabitants of Govan; also because a modified secondary school in Scotland is for those children not 'intelligent' enough to go to a secondary modern. (In Scotland at that time, senior secondary school corresponded to grammar school, and junior secondary to secondary modern.) Many of these girls had to do the family shopping after school, clean the house, mind the baby and cook the evening meal. Their home conditions were often difficult, psychologically as well as materially. But they were not stupid: I used sometimes to feel we should change places and I should sit and learn from them.

They liked to sing when a tune — and the words — of a song appealed. A record of Peggy Seeger with her banjo, in particular that sad little song 'I never will marry' (Topic 10T 9, now deleted), was a favourite. This song had an accompaniment which sounded quite good on the piano. I found the girls could let themselves go in singing, and were less self-conscious than many academically 'brighter' children. This was an important discovery, and at Christmas we put on, for the rest of the school, a kind of Nativity show, with as much dressing up as possible. A selection of carols was included.

The success of this venture increased the girls' confidence. Then I discovered that they had a great liking and a talent for blues songs. There are some fine examples in the four books of reprints from *Sing Out*, published in New York, so a group of four girls entered a local festival, singing 'Trouble in Mind'. They found the appeal of this music so powerful that we went on to do another show in costume with the school as audience. This was a short history of slavery and of black people in the United States, using gospel songs, spirituals, a chain-gang song, blues and 'Summertime' from Gershwin's *Porgy and Bess*. One of the girls read a simple script and introduced the songs as they fitted in. The most onerous task for the teacher in putting on this show was making up thirty-five girls with Max Factor Negro Pancake No. 2. The girl who sang 'Summertime' (and sang it beautifully) looked so attractive this colour and wearing gilt hoop earrings that she didn't want the make-up removed afterwards and went home still black.

Then there was a shorter spell in an even tougher boys' school, not modified this time, but junior secondary. A sizeable number of these boys had been in trouble with the police and some were on probation. Some first-year boys composed and played a drum part for a performance of the 'Carol of the Drums' at a school concert. They practised nearly every lunch-hour for weeks and achieved some quite complex rhythms, building up and increasing the tension towards the climax and then dying away again. Most of the boys in this school liked the faster-moving songs of action – 'Jesse James', 'Casey Jones', 'The Tarriers' Song' ('Drill, ye tarriers, drill', from a splendid set of arrangements by Alan Bush), 'The Calton Weaver' (published in G. Brace, *Something to Sing 1* (Cambridge University Press, 1963)), and so on. None of them would sing solo, though the girls in the previous school quite often would.

But the favourite with second- and third-year boys – and this applied in all the other types of school – was 'Stewball'. It never failed, as a song both for listening to and for singing. It was from a disc by Peter, Paul and Mary (Warner Brothers WB 121). Some years later, I heard Martin Carthy and Steeleye Span sing 'Skewball': a much more authentic-sounding version, but it would not have gone down so well with these boys, I'm convinced. For one thing, Martin Carthy's words are not nearly so clear, and the accompaniment is more complicated. The story is very important: the racehorse who 'never drank water, he always drank wine', and the poignancy of the loser who backed the wrong horse. And verse 6 ('I'm a poor boy in trouble, I'm a long way from home') had an obvious impact. (Billy Connolly has since used this tune for his comic song 'MacGinty was a greyhound' – another proof of its popularity.)

Oh, Stew-ball was a race-horse, _____ And I wish he were mine, _____

He nev-er drank wa-ter, _____ He al-ways drank wine. _____

Variants:

(v. 4)   My no-ble Stew-ball.___   (end of v. 7) wine._____
(v. 5) I'd be a free man to-day. ___

Oh, Stewball was a race-horse,
And I wish he were mine;
He never drank water,
He always drank wine.

His bridle was silver,
His mane it was gold,
And the worth of his saddle
Has never been told.

Oh the fair-grounds were crowded
And Stewball was there,
But the betting was heavy
On the bay and the mare.

And away out yonder
Ahead of them all
Came a-prancin' and a-dancin'
My noble Stewball.

I bet on the grey mare,
I bet on the bay;
If I'd-a bet on old Stewball
I'd be a free man today.

Oh, the hoot-owl she hollered
And the turtle-dove moaned;
I'm a poor boy in trouble,
I'm a long way from home.

(As verse 1)

On the recording by Peter, Paul and Mary, this song is sung with simple vocal harmonisation and guitar accompaniment, and introduced by the tune played through once. It's an uncontrived, straightforward, *simple* version — the kind of thing that was being sung in folk clubs all over the country — and again has an accompaniment which sounds tolerably good on the piano.

I think this illustrates the point that *appeal*, the kind of attractiveness which accords with their own conditioning, is more important for young teenagers than authenticity: we can hardly expect them to be ethnomusicologists.

All this work involved active participation, still perhaps on the fringes of folk song. Then came music appreciation classes — boys again, but in two senior second-ary schools with third- and fourth-year boys (fourteen- and fifteen-year-olds). The very words 'music appreciation' are a joke in some circles, yet one can't always approach listening through doing, and some help may be necessary to achieve criti-cal and enjoyable listening.

I did not have to stick to any syllabus, so I experimented: we discussed the characteristics of folk songs — oral transmission, variants, modes, different styles — and the impact of various performers and groups we heard on record. (I used far more genuinely traditional music, including Scottish, than in the two previous schools: I was learning along with my pupils.) We also discussed the collecting of traditional music and its influence on certain composers of art music, such as Bartók. This all took place in the classroom. The boys were interested and responded well in discussion, but only two of the fourth year volunteered to sing and brought their guitars. For most of them it was their first introduction to live folk singing, although a few were already listening enthusiasts and lent their records for these lessons.

At the end of the first term, a third-year boy having asked to hear 'some Bartók', I played them part of *Music for Strings, Percussion and Celesta*; this went down well — the third movement, they said, was like 'space music'. So folk music had provided a link with art music, some further examples of which I introduced later in the course. Finally I asked the fourteen-year-olds to write down what they thought of it all: these essays were unprepared and were written in school, and a few extracts may be illuminating. (It must be stressed that such reactions are important: few adults can remember how they felt at fourteen.)

Woody Guthrie, a folk singer . . . was very good — although his voice was terrible the noise he made was good, and it was the rotten voice which held your interest in the music. Some singers with excellent voices very well trained were outshone by Woody's voice.

This point was echoed by several others and opens wide the whole question 'What do we mean by good singing?' (This question is also becoming relevant in art music today.) Kodály wrote in 1953 that he had 'heard the finest singing in the world by the world's worst voice — Toscanini's, when at rehearsal he demonstrated a phrase in his blunt, hoarse voice' (*Selected Writings of Zoltán Kodály*, ed. F. Bónis, trans. L. Halápy and F. Macnicol (Boosey and Hawkes with Corvina Press, Budapest, 1974), p. 193).

I hate to hear these operatic singers with their very deep or very high pitched voices. It makes me very annoyed to hear these people singing because half the time you cannot hear a word.

Truly an 'Emperor's clothes' remark; nevertheless it articulates a difficulty which many composers have themselves been aware of.

I myself like some of the music . . . by . . . e.g. Bach, Beethoven, Mozart. But I think that because these composers lived in the 17th and 18th [*sic*] centuries, teenagers regard them as ancient . . . this I think is the reason teenagers do not buy any of the classical records unless they are publicised on television or radio, and there is someone like a disc-jockey telling everyone how good it is or it is a great new sound. But teenagers like to buy something that is up to date and in the fashion.

As Professor John Blacking has said (in *How Musical Is Man* (University of Washington Press, 1973), pp. 32–3), 'What turns one man off may turn another man on, not because of any absolute quality in the music itself but because of what the music has come to mean to him as a member of a particular culture or social group.' I think this pupil was also expressing the need to hear what the *living* artist has to say. André Previn and Anthony Hopkins in their book *Music Face to Face* (Hamish Hamilton, 1971; p. 128) united in a plea for composers now to 'write for young people and not be too remote'.

In commenting on classical, pop and folk music the essays showed clearly that pop was by far the favourite. And these were senior secondary pupils, so one may assume that this verdict would be even more decisive among the academically less able. It is not possible to discuss here the complex phenomenon of pop music but it is of paramount importance to all those concerned with secondary-school music, for it is from the commercial exploitation of this age-group that its chief profits are drawn.

What then are the general effects of folk music, and more particularly folk song, on the young teenager? First, there aren't the age barriers; the content of some pop builds up to a positive hatred of parents and older people, whereas this hardly occurs with folk song: middle-aged and old people at festivals and clubs are given as big a welcome and command as much of a response as the young. This mutual acceptance between different age-groups could help discipline in school work, where music has notoriously involved greater discipline problems than any other subject.

Moreover, the music can command a fairly ready emotional response from the children: it's not too arty, not too cerebral or too complicated, and it's not anti-life (for there's such a thing as artistic pollution as well as material pollution). All pupils can become involved in a practical way.

The verbal content provides what A.L. Lloyd has described as 'a whole education in pride and courage and love, conveyed through characters and situations that have been found typical by generations of common people through the changing scenes of time' (*Folk Song in England* (Panther, 1969), p. 121). Of these situations love, and sex education in its broadest sense, is one of the most important — and, closely linked to this, the changing role of women.

But above all, shining through folk song is the theme of the dignity of the human being irrespective of rank, wealth or class. In a recent 'Man Alive' TV programme entitled *Education Today*, an important point arose from discussion, the idea that *it's not the job which defines the person*. This was one of the attitudes which education should inculcate in all types of children.

Pop music is the most pervasive musical influence on the majority of young teen-agers, and pop has some doubtful effects; art music is distant and unfamiliar and requires a bridging of the gulf; folk music not only can help to provide that bridge, but is not too difficult to involve the children in, for its own sake, and with good results for their development towards adult life.

Three practical suggestions:

First, Education Authorities should appoint good folk singers, with a wide repertoire, to visit schools, sing to the pupils and get them singing, and perhaps start clubs. Archie Fisher had such a post in Fife, and Jean Redpath, the Scottish singer, for a longer period in the United States (she also taught folklore and folk song in Wesleyan University, Middletown, Connecticut). Tom Anderson, the fine Shetland fiddler, is teaching traditional fiddle playing in schools throughout Shetland. He has nearly a hundred pupils and in 1975 he took two of them to the centenary con-ference of ESTA (European String Teachers' Association), with which Yehudi Menuhin is closely associated. (I have said nothing about instrumental folk music but it could be most valuable. The teaching of guitar in some schools has proved extremely popular, but there are many other suitable instruments too, such as the penny-whistle. And listening to different kinds of instrumental music from other parts of the world would lead to the broadening of horizons and to the discovery that sophisticated virtuosity is not exclusive to the Western concert platform.)

Second, we should get more recorded folk music not only into school libraries but also into public libraries.

Third, school music teachers could encourage the pupils to do some collecting themselves, of songs they've heard at home or in their locality.

I should like to make my final point as a Scot — originally a 50 per cent Scot who has become a 90 per cent Scot in recent years. A great renaissance — artistic, spiritual and political — has been taking place in Scotland as in other small countries. Zoltán Kodály once said that the collection and publication — and by implication, the singing — of folk songs 'is one of the first signs of national con-sciousness . . . Because of this, we know we are a branch of an ancient tree, our roots are deep, and since we differ from so many peoples, we do have something new to say to others' (*Selected Writings*, p. 38).

Helping the young to find their own identity is, I think, an essential part of education.

5 *Folk song and the English lesson*

GEOFFREY SUMMERFIELD

*They are little traits from life and other things which were somehow not
forgotten; nowadays there's a lot worth throwing away. But that older
impulse was there too, to listen to stories, good and inconsequential alike
... which, if they come to their end, have to end by touching us. It's a
reading of traces everywhere, in all directions, in bits and pieces variously
divided. For in the long run, everything that meets us, everything we
notice particularly, is one and the same.*
(Ernst Bloch, *Spuren*, trans. Fredric Jameson).

Cultural divisions abound, and often find expression in categorical distinctions: high
(or elitist) culture and low culture; literature and vox pop; respectable and vulgar.
Ever since the Reformation, the 'culture' of the 'vulgar' has been condemned from
above: along with the more bizarre superstitions, folklore of all kinds was associated
with Popery and under the grim regime of the Puritans received an onslaught of
moral and religious disapproval that both predicted and enlarged that cultural sub-
ordination that we are all familiar with. Sanctioned by some obscure, unknowable,
and distant authority = good; local, indigenous, familiar = inferior. With the spread
of schooling in the nineteenth century, promoted by do-gooders either indifferent
or hostile to local culture, and the emergence of a powerful addiction to limiting
forms of 'useful knowledge', the demoralisation of autochthonous culture that was
a feature of both seventeenth and eighteenth centuries gained momentum and was
reinforced by the demographic chaos of the Industrial Revolution and by the
ruinous waves of agricultural depressions.

That is one, microscopic-thumbnail, way of putting it — grossly simplified and
politically tendentious. But a scrupulously detailed account of particular moments
in the last two hundred years would provide the requisite corroborations: Boswell
browsing through chapbook tales and acknowledging his sense of their remoteness;
Maria Edgeworth advocating a total separation of genteel children from vulgar servants; Archdeacon Wrangham setting up village libraries in East Yorkshire, full of
improving evangelical theology, and not a story-book to be seen; Mrs Trimmer and
a thousand other worthies driving myth and folk tale from the early nineteenth-
century nursery; Keightley, and Hugh Miller also, noting in 1828, that the spread of
printing and of good coach-roads, not to mention the looming railway, was pushing

the oral tradition further and further into remote, 'uneducated', corners. So, relentlessly, 'culture' became the intellectual commodity offered by schools and universities: those who received no 'schooling' had no culture — were defined in terms, not of having something older, deeper, wider, but of not having, of being without.

Folk song, like the tales of oral tradition and of the chapbooks, was something to be discarded and disowned by the child entering the school: the meritocrats turned, and turn, their backs on their parents. Not a bad thing, when it is a matter of transcending the darker ignorance and xenophobia of parochialism; but one recognises a loss too, especially when the exchange is a bartering of forms of life for juiceless chaff.

The reclamation of folk song, its retrieval and rehabilitation, can be seen in larger cultural terms as a desperate attempt to rediscover a true voice of feeling, the singing voice of peculiar passion, of distinctive power, in a world that has grown old, is weary of sophistication, of electronic noise, of overcultivation. Future historians will perhaps see these things more clearly than we can, but there is no doubt that, at times of various crisis, societies return to the primal springs, the deeper roots — the metaphors are unavoidable. 'The Primitives are the salt of the earth. Through their existence alone does contemporary art . . . preserve in its depth sources of freshness and life', said Jean Cassou of the Musée National d'Art Moderne in Paris, on the occasion of Grandma Moses's hundredth birthday. 'All great literature is rooted in folk-literature', said Isaac Bashevis Singer, in 1975 downtown Manhattan, the concrete jungle. 'There is the literature of knowledge, and the literature of power', said de Quincey in 1848, preferring that which moves to that which merely informs.

Historically, the academic pursuit of literature has largely robbed it of its power: Landor and Scott wept over stories that moved them: we breathe a cooler air, an air of rational, analytic detachment. We have learned techniques for robbing the most powerful literature of its dynamite: generation upon generation of English teachers learned, as students, that *Beowulf* is philological debris, an archaeological tip, strewn with the bric-à-brac of a dead language spoken by a dead civilisation. Who can ever be moved to pity or terror by such dry bones? Curiosity, inquisitiveness, the pure and lucid emotions of the grammarian, maybe, but these are relatively specialised and rarefied motions of the mind.

Elizabeth Eastlake, in some historic essays on children's literature in 1844 (*Quarterly Review*, vol. 71), saw the cloud rather larger than Goliath's hand on the horizon, and she called it didacticism, the itch to instruct, to mediate. Mediation is a fine thing, in its place, as she acknowledged, but it is essential that something shall have happened, something shall be felt to have happened, before the explanations and explications start. In Miroslav Holub's poem, the 'functionary' is so busy telling his pupils to listen that they hear nothing, and two hundred years ago, Maurice Morgan, recoiling from the 'rules' of the scholar—critics, insisted that while the commentators were busily explaining Shakespeare's aberrations and disunities, women and children could 'feel' the coherence of his plays. The moral that he derived from such an ironic contrast was simple: we must not try to possess Shakespeare; we must let him possess us — Wordsworth's 'wise passiveness'; Keats's 'negative capability'; William James's tranquillity.

What then do we 'do' with folk song in the English lesson? Microanalysis of English-teacher behaviour reveals that a great deal of time is devoted to questions and answers: less time is given to the 'experience' that yields the raw material for such interrogations. If I say that the first thing we must learn to do with a work of art is to learn to 'let it be', what does that mean? First we have to have it, in as auspicious a form as possible: folk song by definition has, then, to be sung. But I can't sing, not even in the bathroom. So what do I do? I 'buy in' a singer, or I use a record-player or tape recorder. The former is obviously preferable: there is nothing more stirring, more disconcerting, more shocking, than a person singing with passion and manifest energy in a confined space, close up — it is a remarkable event. More than an event, because all manner of intense happenings can occur inside us on such an occasion. As a result, we all have something, inside ourselves, to reflect on. There is nothing quite as vivid, compelling, moving; after such a feast, we teachers must be careful not to spoil it all by turning an epiphany into a lesson: we must let it be. It is rich soil, but we must not spoil it by trying to wrench a crop from it immediately. Years of schooling often make pupils nervous, anxious to be seen to be instructed. For many, it is not enough that something should have happened, that they should have apprehended vivid forms of life: they need to know what it is that they have learned. What we do in such circumstances will depend on our guile, cunning, candour, freedom from fear, temper; but we must wean our pupils from their pathetic infatuation with 'useful knowledge'.

But many songs depend on a sense of context. How often, we note, do singers introduce their songs with a few lines of explanation: historical, geographical, economic, social, cultural, linguistic? In this sense, many songs are like anecdotes: they presuppose a community which recognises all the references — the original audience all knew about those particular fragments of the local scene. To explain a joke is to kill it; to give context to anecdote or song is to place and locate it. The rule seems to be a matter of proportion — the song shall not be overshadowed by its preface: avoid offering a paraphrase that does the work of the song before it is sung.

But contexts are relative: some are limited, specific, spots in time, merely footnotes; others are extensive — the context created by half a term's work on a topic or theme, for example. Do we then reduce songs to the status of evidences, of demonstrations, of particular manifestations of realities that are to be found primarily *outside* the songs? If so, are we then demeaning the songs, reducing them to something less than what they in themselves actually are? If we 'place' a song, are we also inescapably holding it at arm's length, preventing it from doing its proper moving work? Is 'The Unquiet Grave' merely to be offered as evidence of long-dead superstitions?

The answers to such questions must surely be quite specific and carefully judged: we each have to work out our own taxonomy of integrity; we need a variety of strategies, a range of uses. Above all, songs do not offer information, as such, but help us to recognise, if ever, 'how it felt'. In so doing, they animate what might otherwise remain dead historical information. It is one thing to be told of the peculiar intensity of the Eskimos' dependence on successful fishing or seal-hunting: it is quite another to hear and feel the compelling, relentless, and manic rhythms, the sheer concentration of will and energy, in their hunting-songs and dances.

But before we try to enter into remote and exotic states of being, it is better, first, to recognise again what we already know: my own rule is to explore first forms of the familiar, the near-at-hand, before venturing into remoter, stranger corners. Let us, then, recognise the sheer localness of our worlds. Intellectual history suggests that major *intellectual* enterprises have generally been conducted by those with very tenuous local roots: metaphysics or philosophy ranges widely and at a high level of abstraction; but, equally, artistic achievements grow from rootedness, from particular people in particular places: for the artist, the songmaker, 'the particular object is a very remarkable phenomenon', as it was for Wittgenstein. Let us then learn to stop apologising for local, parochial, provincial vividness: let us take a leaf from the book of Hardy, Wordsworth, Dickens, Clare, or Crabbe, and celebrate the peculiar idiosyncratic vividness of the local fact. In practice this means that the English departments of London schools will be as familiar with the cockney repertoire of John Foreman as they are with their Advanced-level set texts; that schools in Yorkshire will resound to the Watersons' *A Yorkshire Garland*; that each and every school will say '*Here* we are; not there, but here; what local vividness what peculiar near-at-home spring can we tap?' And all this, not in the spirit of folksy antiquarianism or phoney quasi-resuscitation, but in the pleasure of recognition: I still recall the shock of 'discovering' 'The Wednesbury Cocking' in Samuel Butler's *Alps and Sanctuaries* under the dust of a chaotic second-hand bookshop in Wolverhampton when I was seventeen. Six years in the grammar school had effectively denied the existence of the surrounding Black Country: separation of curriculum and environment was virtually *total* – two worlds that had nothing to say to, or of, each other. And, suddenly, the voice of my grandfather leapt out of Butler's pages. (Butler had met the ballad when he was a pupil at Shrewsbury School: an eccentric classics master had the boys translate it into Greek hexameters!) The 'Cocking' gave me a strong, almost nauseating, whiff of the life of the Black Country a hundred or more years ago: miraculously, Wednesbury had an almost tangible past, and a past that was expressed vividly in my own non-standard dialect which I had been anxiously suppressing and chiselling away.

The dissociation of languages is hard to live with: 'refined' at school, but snared by shibboleths; relaxed and natural, comfortable as old shoes, at home. When, later, I did teaching practice at Willenhall Comprehensive School, it struck me that most of the carefully hand-picked and able staff were 'foreigners' and found the local dialect virtually incomprehensible. Similarly, when I taught at Churchfields School, West Bromwich, few of the staff could understand a joke in the local language of most of the pupils. It was clear from the start that the language on the pupils' lips

WEDNESBURY COCKING.

AT WEDNESBURY there was a Cocking,
A match between NEWTON and SKROGGING,
The Colliers and Nailors left work,
And all to SPITTLE'S went jogging;
To fee this noble fport,
Many noted men reforted,
And though they'd but little money,
Yet that they freely fported.

There was JEFFERY and COBBUR from HAMPTON,
And DUFFY from BILSTONE was there;
FRUMMETTY he came from DARLASTONE,
He was as rude as a bear;
And there was OLD WILL from WALSALL,
And SMACKER from WEST BROMWICH come,
BLIND DOBBIN he came from ROWLEY,
And ftaggering he went home.

RUFF MOEY came limping along,
As though he'd fome cripple been mocking,
For to join the blackguard throng,
Who met at WEDNESBURY Cocking;
He borrow'd a trifle of DOLL,
To back old TAVERNER's grey,
He laid four-pence halfpenny to four-pence,
Loft and went broken away.

But foon he return'd to the Pit,
For he'd borow'd a trifle more money,
So he venturerd another bet,
Along with blubber mouth CONEY;
When CONEY demanded the money,
As was usual upon fuch occafions,
He cry'd B— you, if you don't hold your prate,
I'll pay thee as Paul paid the Ephefians.

SKROGGING'S breeches was made of nankeen;
And wore very thin in the groin,
In ftooping to manage his cock,
His a— was all open behind;
Befides his fhirt tail was befhit
Which occafion'd a very great laughter,
SKROGGING turn'd himfelf round in a pet,
And cried," B— you! what's the matter."

The morning fport now being over,
Old Spittle a dinner proclaim'd
That each man fhould dine for a groat,
If he grumbl'd he might be afham'd;
For there was plenty of beef,
But SPITTLE he swore by is troth.
The d—l a man fhould dine,
Till he'd eaten his noggin of broth.

The beef it was old and tough,
Of a bull that was baited to death;
BUNNEY HIDE got a lump in his throat,
It had like to have ftopp'd his breath,

So the company fell in confufion,
At feeing poor BUNNEY HIDE choak'd,
They took him into the kitchen,
And held his head over the fmoke.

They held him fo clofe to the fire
He frizzled juft like a beef fteak,
And then threw him down on the floor,
So had like to have broken his neck;
One gave him a kick on the ftomach,
Another a thump on the brow,
His wife cried—"throw him into the ftable,
And he will be better juft now."

Then foon they return'd to the Pit,
And the fighting it went on again,
Six battles were won on each fide,
And the next was to decide the main,
For thefe were two famous cocks,
As ever the country bred;
SKROGGING's a duck wing black,
And NEWTON's a fhift wing red.

The conflict was hard on each fide,
Untill braffy wing blackly was choak'd
The Colliers was nationly vex'd;
And the NAILORS were all provok'd;
PETER STEPHENS he fwore a great oath,
As SKROGGING hadn't play'd his cock fair,
So he gave him a kick on the a—,
And fwore he had no bufinefs there.

Then the company arofe in diforder,
A bloody fight quickly enfu'd,
Kick, b-ll-ck and bite was the word,
Untill the WALLSALL men fubdu'd.
Ruff MOEY bit off a man's nofe,
It's a wonder that no man was flain,
They trampl'd both cocks to death,
And fo they made a drawn main.

The cockpit was near the church,
An ornament neat to the town,
On one fide an old coal pit,
And the other was well gors'd round:
PETER HADLEY peep'd thro' the gorfe,
In order to fee them fight,
SPITTLE jobb'd his eye out with a fork,
And cry'd, b—ft thee it ferv'd thee right.

Some people may think this is ftrange,
Who WEDNESBURY never knew;
But thofe who have never been there,
Won't have the leaft doubt but its true;
For they are all favage by nature,
And guilty of deeds the moft fhocking;
JACK BAKER he wack'd his own father,
And fo ended WEDNESBURY Cocking.

T. R. WOOD, PRINTER, NEW MEETING-STREET BIRMINGHAM.

Plate 1

rarely, if ever, got onto paper. So I encouraged them to write stories, sketches, vignettes, chapters of autobiography in their own often 'grossly' non-standard dialect. The only rule was to pack their writings so densely with the syntax and vocabulary of West Bromwich that most of the teachers (from the effete South, North, East and West) would find them totally incomprehensible. The results were often as rich as plum pudding or black pudding: they had the same quality of 'bludginess' that excited Juliana Horatio Ewing in the Mummers' Pace Egg Play and that Bernard Miles discovered in his memorable radio programme of Bible stories rewritten and spoken by children from the provinces.

Inevitably, the enterprise was extremely problematical. Imagine a continuum, the left-hand end of which is the standard dialect, the right-hand the extreme of local dialect. Where would *you* place 'We haven't got none', 'We don't have any', 'We ai' got any' and 'We ai' got none'? Questions of grammar and orthography arise, willy-nilly, on all sides — not as rules, but as discoveries and as speculations. Was 'Please give me one, mate', nearer to the standard and therefore less 'opaque' than 'Eh, give us 'n, our kid'? If then, the latter was to be preferred in this context, what of the orthographic problems? How *can* one write down an unwritten language — a language that never had been written down, and that had come down to us through generations of illiterate talkers, who had to *hold in their head* all that they knew, or else not know it? Why was 'Give us' (= me) preferred to 'Give me'? Did it lie more comfortably on the lips? Is 'our kid' more friendly than 'mate' — does it enforce a bond more effectively? Is it claiming a quasi-familial relationship? Such questions are deeply *educative*, yet all the richly educational, intellectually taxing, aspects of native speech-use are generally neglected, indeed frowned upon, by a profession that is, like Beckett's Maddie Rooney, de-animated by the subtle disease of gentility: 'If we close our eyes, perhaps it (all that vulgar, local, coarse, life) will go away.'

The kids' stories were tested by the whole class and, if too 'open' were reworked. 'Do you have one?' yielded to ''Ast got e'er a one?' (Hast (thou) got ever a one?) or ''An yo' got one?' just as 'you are, aren't you?' was displaced by 'Thee bist, bistn't?', and 'You aren't, are you?' by 'Yo' bay, bin ya?' But the snag about what I've just written down is that a hint of 'you' is phonically present in 'yo'', whilst the vowel is nevertheless emphatically closer to $\bar{o}$ than to $\bar{u}$; and 'bay' looked oddly wrong; it is a contraction of 'ben't', but the vowel is closer to $\bar{a}$ than to $\bar{e}$, and the 'n't' is dropped in the cause of economy of effort and a quick elision.

There is a rich and powerful discipline in all this, and it is for real; it involves both a teasing and complex *mimesis*, sheer registration, and also the kind of generalisation-generating activities of the grammarians. As a linguistic activity, it seems to me entirely appropriate to the secondary-school English lesson; as an exercise of the mind, it has inexhaustible intellectual possibilities. You take it as far as the kids can go; and the language that they are attending to is not something 'out there' but rather the behaviour of the self, studied reflexively and with peculiar authority. Kids from the back streets of X, Y or Z, wherever it may be, are the *authorities* in the matter of *their* language: this should be both recognised, celebrated and exploited; and such recognition can move into ways of breaking down the curious cultural isolation of the school vis-à-vis the local community. In my experience, grandparents are often sitting around twiddling their thumbs and waiting to offer such gifts as 'Oh we used to . . . ' or 'No, we didn't say that; we said . . . ' and 'Do you know what they called . . . ?'

Such work, well done with pupils in their first and second years, bears many rewards. The third year is too late: by that time the awkward adolescent is into the complexities of alienation, privacy, gauche transformations, and an increasing sense of self-consciousness. And such work can move in a variety of directions: language of the family leads into family history, wedding-days, continuity and change, births and deaths: some of the best work that I have ever seen from fifteen-year-old girls was in autobiographical form: 'my story' — but not solipsistic; delighting, rather, in mothers' revelations of what they had been like at fifteen. As Isaac Bashevis Singer has insisted, each of us has a story to tell that no one else in the world can tell — a dazzling thought. And grandparents' reminiscences lead naturally into many aspects of folk song: what was it like? how did it feel? And, in this matter, to be 'purist' is to cut off a great deal of fascinating material: fathers and grandfathers remember wars, and wars throw up a vast repertoire of song — not 'ethnically' impeccable, perhaps; but sorrows and joys, the heights and the depths, are not the place for pedantry. For my purposes, I choose to include under the category of folk song any song that has worked its way into oral tradition: so 'Tipperary' qualifies as folk song. The purist shudders, alas; I have no wish to inflict gratuitous injury on him: he will simply have to go away and hug his virtue to his chest, while I browse through Denis Johnston's *Nine Rivers from Jordan* (surely ripe for reprinting?).

Work in dialect — and no one lacks a dialect — can also move into the exploration of texts. Write a sleeve-note transcript of Lou Killen singing 'Sair Fyeld Hinny' and, for comparison, Britten's setting of William Soutar's 'The Ald Aik's Dead'; or just listen, without the itch of pencil and paper, to one or the other and see how many of the words you can recall. Is there a rhyme-scheme? Does it help memory? Does it clinch the point? Is there anything quite as dead as the words of a folk song when printed? Where is the centre, the source, of the life of the song? Consider a song such as Fairport Convention's version of 'Tam Lin': until the collectors, the early folklorists and antiquarians went to work, it only existed when it was being sung. Except when being performed, it did not exist. With the spread of printing, it became words on the page, out there, tangible, visible, an object. And so arises an illusion: the 'object' is 'real' — so 'objective' is a complimentary term; conversely, 'subjective' means less satisfactory than 'objective' — private, illusory, prejudiced! Hence, again, the importance of the performance — the song is 'something that happens' within and between the singer and his audience. The song is *not* words-on-the-page; not even a melodic line; it moves and changes, subtly and even dramatically, on the lips of the singer; and the eye-movements and swaying motions of the listeners subscribe, contribute, to the song-as-sung. Folk song can thus serve as initiation into, or reminder of, the primacy of speech/vocalisation/lip-and-tongue, in the sound that a poem, or any passionate utterance, makes. If only we learned this lesson from folk song we would perhaps help our pupils to escape from the odd, unwitting prejudice that a poem is only words-on-the-page and to retrieve some adequate sense of poetry as words spoken.

Many university students are unaware of what is happening to them as they experience a poem — the poem as internal event and as social event — unaware of the poem as an experience through which to pass, during which one is shocked, disconcerted, amused, puzzled, delighted, disappointed, teased, amazed, and so on, as in a lively and animated conversation: the poem as 'forms of life' — what it feels like to be in suspense, to be kept waiting, to be relieved, and so on. Such recognitions come more directly through folk song, especially when experienced live.

The peculiar virtue of the folk song is, I have suggested, its local vividness. Conversely it also offers a democratic and universal world: democratic, because it is rarely obscure, complex, or esoteric; universal, because it touches our lives at those places that we share in common with everyone else — birth, love, hatred, misunderstanding, accident, separation, despair, joy, zest, weariness, sorrow, and death. This is nowhere more vividly apparent than in the great ballads of the industrial areas, and in particular of mining communities. It is worth noting that the most conspicuous failure of nerve in Victorian poetry was in its inability to deal with industrialism; indeed it is arguable that only Lawrence, Auden and Edwin Morgan, of all postindustrial British poets, have in any decisive way managed to incorporate the legacy of the Industrial Revolution in their poetry, and even Auden's interest in the industrial landscape is primarily a geological and political matter — a view of mineralogical curiosities and of social set-pieces — rather than a matter of any vivid inwardness. Again, one must recognise that by the time of the agricultural depressions following the Napoleonic wars and the implementation of avaricious enclosure acts, a strain of radical protest had entered the English ballad: the broadsheet ballad was edging closer and closer to the disaffected political pamphlet; indeed at times they were indistinguishably irreverent and scurrilous. In matters of social awareness English folk song came of age as a result of unprecedented misery, squalor, and exploitation: in the ballads of transportation, in sharp political squibs, and in the songs of strikes, blacklegging, and periodic disaster that came out of the mining communities. Traditionally, the decorum of English teaching has always, at least officially, steered clear of political issues: they ruffled the even tenor of our judiciously neutral ways. It is a bit that we should be prepared to take emphatically between our teeth: popular literature — the songs and ballads of the industrial working class — has never received an adequate recognition for its vigour, its sharp ironies, its lively and unkillable antinomianism, and it is something that should now belatedly be given its proper place. The work of such a songmaker as Thomas Armstrong is something that requires no apology, for the same reasons that the popular hymns of Methodism require no apology, for the reasons that Wordsworth made clear in his historic letter to John Wilson in June 1802 (quoted in Graham McMaster, *William Wordsworth* (Penguin, 1972)), when he asked, 'Pleasing to whom?' It is a demotic literature that is not inferior to Matthew Arnold's dandified 'Scholar Gypsy', but simply different, going about rather different business — and, some would claim, more important, more urgent business. Certainly it is pleasing to rather more people, as Wordsworth had already anticipated when he himself strenuously remade himself into the form of a populist and demotic balladeer. The great industrial ballads can be left to speak for themselves, just as they manage to let horror and squalor speak for themselves: a minimum of contextual explanation is requisite, and again the vivid material is local. Jo Manton's biography of Sister Dorothy Pattison, Sister Dora of legendary virtue in the Black Country, provides an interesting example: not a stuffy civic-pride-inspired official history of Walsall, but an enthusiastic account of one woman's superhuman pioneering work to ameliorate the vileness of the common lot in a filthy industrial slum: a remarkable book that provides the perfect context for such local Black Country ballads as have survived from the 1860s and 70s (*Sister Dora* (Methuen, 1971)). For such purposes, then, the official histories of standard English Literature are worse than useless: we need, rather, to go to the local history rooms of our public libraries — the real stuff is there if we are prepared to dust it off: and, of course, in many places we can look to the local history societies for guidance and collaboration. It is, emphatically, always worth the trouble to go to the primary sources — the broadsheets and other ephemera — for most editors have been deplorably cavalier in their handling of the texts: it seems that the words of the anonymous working-class poet deserve less scrupulous editorial care than those of their more respectable counterparts, and too many editors seem blandly ignorant of the distinctive nuances of the non-standard dialects involved: Matthew Hodgart's mishandling of 'The Wednesbury Cocking' (in the *Faber Book of Ballads* (1965)) is a classic case of such aberration. Contextually, every area has its topographical literature, and this again is worth digging out: for contrastive purposes, anyone teaching in a large city or conurbation will find it worth his while to nose back into the eighteenth century: de Quincey's father, for example, published a tour of the North Midlands and the Black Country that saw the innovations of the industrial scene with euphoric eyes, before the slums had congregated. As a general guide, W.G. Hoskins's classic *The Making of the English Landscape* (Penguin, 1970) is an essential and brilliant adjunct to any work on popular song and literature in the eighteenth and nineteenth centuries: a topographical mirror-image of social and economic change and vicissitude.

In my own experience, urban pupils take much more readily — especially in adolescence — to the folk songs of the industrial and commercial nineteenth century and to such vivid adjuncts as Mayhew's records of child-workers and scavengers than they do to the more emphatically rural tradition. Similarly the ballads of the trans-portation system, and of such magnificent outlaws as Ned Kelly, stir them power-fully; ballads of the hiring-fair, of Van Diemen's Land, and the eye-witness accounts of such books as W.H. Hudson's classic *A Shepherd's Life* constitute a rich and heady brew that much so-called 'good' literature finds it impossible to match. It is of course an open secret that we have as yet done very little serious work on 'literature for adolescents' — adolescence is a phase of life with its own distinctive intensities, passions, concerns, and anxieties: exploratory, prickly, sensitive, and compassionate to a degree. It's clear that if ever we have energy and wit enough to consolidate and refine such a repertoire of *appropriate* (as distinct from 'relevant') literature, it will include a great deal that lies outside the official, time-honoured, high-culture-orientated province of familiar classics: certainly, a central place must be found for the industrial ballads of the factories and coalfields, alongside the appropriate chapters from Mrs Gaskell and Dickens.

For the teacher of English, the larger forms — e.g. the novel — constitute a severe problem, a test of ingenuity, stamina, ordonnance, cohesion, timing, relationship. All the essential elements of the matter of the novel, of what it deals with, are present also in folk song; and the same is true for drama. Hence, through the folk song, pupils can come to recognise, within relatively narrow bounds, in an economic fashion, the essential dynamics of what we call a work of art — the presentation and resolution of tensions: the relatively brief journey through time, in which the protagonist is tested, and found adequate or wanting: in which not everyone 'can win', in which a price has to be paid. So the great tragic songs, the great ballads, form an ideal and powerfully affecting entry into the world of tragic literature: not less than 'literature', but distinctively themselves, equivalent in power and range to the best literature. I can think of no better preparation for the experience of Shakespeare's tragedies than the great ballads of family and state calamity, wherein the range of action, crisis, and emotion is miraculously contained within such an unwasteful form. And for the introduction of older pupils to the critical study of texts, what better than to compare Matthew Hodgart's bungled text of 'The Wednesbury Cocking' with the version offered by Robert Graves in his *English and Scottish Ballads* (Heinemann, 1967)? Again comparatively, place a text of folk song alongside an unascribed poem by Edward Thomas, John Clare, William Soutar, William Barnes, Thomas Hardy, Wordsworth, Thomas Moore, Brecht or Housman, and ask pupils to decide which of the two is the real folk song: initially, their answers will be necessarily speculative, but they will come to recognise the peculiar economy of folk-song idioms: how is it that they so consistently avoid all trace of literariness? Similarly, as a comparative experience, play alongside each other Bridie and Jacqueline's performance of 'Scarborough Fair' and the (to me, lamentably affected) Simon and Garfunkel version of the same song. What has happened to the razor-edged poignancy of the original song in the tarted-up, arty, version? Are S. and G. simply playing with patterns of sound? Are they taking away in the act of adding to the *ur-*song; is more, in this case, less? And, in the original song, is less more? And have S. and G. lost not only the breathtaking, audacious, simplicity of the original version, but also submerged the diabolical riddling tests of the lover under a sickly-sweet embroidery? Such questions can, I suggest, be posed as open questions: they need not be pre-empted, whatever one's own views. The peculiar virtue of such a song as 'Scarborough Fair' is its inexhaustible variousness: twelve-year-olds enjoy it as a riddle — a rich vein in folk song that touches directly on one of the great passions of one's early years — whilst fifteen- and sixteen-year-olds relish it as a love song.

The riddle is one of those forms that one can use quite opportunistically: to plug a gap when one's 'lesson' has finished ten minutes before the bell, or as light relief on a wet Friday afternoon. The topic leads in all sorts of directions — secret societies, initiation rites, tests of courage and valour. Christmas crackers, puns — all the serious and frivolous play with language that is so important especially in one's pre-adolescent years and that most English syllabuses woefully underplay. As for songs of love, one can do worse than start with chapter 1 of Willa Muir's *Living with Ballads* (Hogarth Press, 1965) on courtship games in childhood — a subject that, in my own experience, is of great interest to adolescent girls but one that tends to leave most boys tongue-tied or hostile. My own prejudice is not to point one's work *directly* at the pupils' *present* lives, especially in adolescence, and particularly in matters involving sexual relationships. For this reason, I prefer to have them look at *other* people's lives, allowing the attention to be *implicitly* reflexive, i.e., they are free to recognise themselves, if and when they do so, but there is no explicit insistence on such recognition: it seems to me an important freedom, the freedom to dissociate oneself from 'difficult' or problematical questions. So one offers the possibility of 'detachment': 'This is how it was for X and Y, 10 or 100 or 200 or 300 years ago': Romeo and Juliet, or Bogie's 'Bonnie Belle'. Consider, for example, Davy Stewart's magnificent performance of this last song (Topic 12T 157): it is inelegant, unsweet, melodically unpredictable, broken-footed; conversely: intensely impassioned, elegiac, heartbroken, tragic. It is a performance that would presumably have excited Verdi; the accordion provides an extraordinary 'orchestral' resonance, with the tense suspense of a high operatic prelude, and the singing is of a startling declamatory power and intensity. The story is allowed to speak for itself and there is no explicit moralising. But it is not a song, or performance, likely to appeal to the fans of Queen or the Rolling Stones: advocacy in such matters is a dubious business. I don't see it as my business to 'prove' that Davy Stewart is 'better' than the Stones — such exercises in odious comparison seem to me counter-productive; and there is room in most lives for both. But is the world of folk song an irredeemably 'old' and past world, a world we have lost never to know again, a world in which we, let alone our pupils, are no longer at home? This is a question to which each of us, individually, will find an answer: but I think that as a general rule it is unavailing to offer the world of traditional folk song as a 'better' world than the one that we all live in, the very world which is the world of all of us. There is much unproductive Jeremiah-like commination in the view of the world as it is, held by those who continue to yearn for the 'organic' past: far better to explore with one's pupils a wide range of folk song, all the *Folk Songs of Britain* records from Topic, for example, and to locate those idioms and styles that one's pupils find most captivating; and to build on that.

Some of my happiest experiences with ballads have occurred when a particular story has fired the imagination of a class of twelve-year-olds and they have asked to use it as the basis for improvisation: they are still un-demythologised and find the archetypal patterns of such tales deeply stirring; the action is limned with vivid primary colours, especially red, black, and white (cf. the preface to John Arden's *Serjeant Musgrave's Dance* (Methuen, 1960)), and the relative absence of psychological complexity suits their perceptions very well. With adolescent pupils, the ballads of revenge compel attention and lead into a consideration of the values of honour, loyalty, and self-sacrifice. What price honour when it involves massive carnage and the deaths of the innocent unwittingly swept up into the patterns of anger and retribution? The sweep of *hubris* and *nemesis* belongs of course to heroic times when the issues were less teasingly grey than those that we have to deal with: but does all heroic ballad-poetry depend on a radical simplification of the issues? If *Beowulf*'s poet had tried to see Grendel's point of view, where would the heroism of Beowulf be, where the distinctive terrors of the epic? These are not questions for twelve-year-olds to bother their heads with — most of them live in a morally simplified world — but they are good issues for sixteen-year-olds. It seems to me a pity that Ordinary-level and Advanced-level examiners seem to have heard of neither epic nor ballad poetry, perhaps because the current literary critical orthodoxies find themselves virtually unequipped to deal with these forms, if only because we seem to be stuck at the moment with a pervasive and uncritical set of assumptions resting on a rather naive notion of psychological 'realism': 'verismo' and 'social realism' are fashions singularly uncongenial to the art of the great ballads. In this respect, it is instructive to look at popular prose versions of the ballads; take up the question posed by Coleridge in *Biographia Literaria* (chapter 18): do stories depend for their survival on the use of metre, rhyme, and all the distinctive economies and resources of verse? Is prose inherently a feebler medium than verse? Less memorable in all senses? Coleridge's answer is that the sinewy prose of the great chapbook stories can more than hold its own, and cites the astonishing image of the rookery flying out of the giant's beard in a version of the story of 'Tom Hickathrift'; but the fact that no version of the story with such an episode has turned up disproves, or at least throws doubt on, Coleridge's case! Give your pupils Joseph Jacobs's *English Fairy Tales* and Barbara Leonie Picard's *Hero Tales from the British Isles* (both in Puffin editions) and their ballad originals, and let them decide for themselves. Ask them, for example, to try to memorise both verse and prose versions, and see which is, in the event, more memorable.

The province of folk song embraces not only heroic feats of strength, stories of dire retribution and tragic love stories, but also the world of spirits: in the light of the recent recrudescence of interest in the more idiotic fringes of the occult, it seems to me at least desirable to take note of the dark world of magic, of hauntings and of strange sprites. One can do worse than to go back to the beginnings of the folklore movement; look at the writings of Grose and Brand in the late eighteenth century: the Introduction to Brand's *Popular Antiquities* (3 vols., 1849—53) is particularly useful in this respect, as a preface or entry to Walter Scott's essay on fairy beliefs in his *Minstrelsy of the Scottish Borders* (vols. 1 and 2, Kelso, 1802; vol. 3, Edinburgh, 1803), and to Thomas Keightley's *Fairy Mythology* (2 vols., 1828). For anyone venturing into this territory for the first time, Richard M. Dorson's *Peasant Customs and Savage Myths* (Routledge and Kegan Paul, 1968) is an invaluable guide to the tangled undergrowth of the nineteenth-century folklorists, and if one wishes to take one's pupils back to the fairy lore that Shakespeare drew on in *Macbeth* and *A Midsummer Night's Dream*, Keith Thomas's *Religion and The Decline of Magic* (Penguin, 1973) and Katharine Brigg's various books (such as *A Dictionary of British Folk-Tales* (4 vols., Routledge and Kegan Paul, 1970–1)) provide inexhaustibly rich primary source material. There are many strands to tease out in the field of fairy-mythology, both malign and benign: the prettification and domestication – the neutering – of the world of faerie in the nineteenth century was one of the greatest misfortunes of our culture, yet some writers have succeeded, by tact and independence of genius, to sustain a potent paganism: Edward Thomas in his best poetry on the theme of *genius loci*, for example, and Mrs Ewing in her magnificent tale *Lob-Lie-by-the-Fire* (reprinted by Dent Dutton in 1964), in which the spirit of Robin Goodfellow walks abroad again with undiminished energy: one of the great stories for children, and not for them only.

But folk song celebrates not only the heroic and the magical, the extraordinary and the sublime: it also comprehends the familiar world of our own streets. The Opies have performed a useful service in their collecting – *The Lore and Language of Schoolchildren* (Paladin, 1977) is a marvellous collection, however miserably, mealy-mouthedly, bowdlerised. Here are riches indeed: a pity they didn't print any tunes. This is a great harvest to explore with adolescents: let us see if we can remember how we resolved quarrels when we were six or seven; how many magic spells we used to ward off the malign emanations of the ambulance or the funeral cortege; how many songs we sang to celebrate the end of term, bonfire night, the approach of Christmas, not to mention the songs of the football stadium. How do they compare with our parents' repertoire, our grandparents' legacy? There is material in plenty here for compilation, collation, comparison, performance, charting the decline and fall of film-stars as they enter and then disappear from the early songs of the street. Does Charlie Chaplin go on for ever? Whatever happened to Betty Grable? (Who?) And Davy Crockett? What skipping-songs did *your* grandmother sing fifty years ago? As in the matter of dialect, one of the virtues of such work is that, again, each individual has a peculiar authority: he knows what he is talking about. Consider the traditional 'grammar-school curriculum': on the one hand a teacher who has been reading, say, history for thirty years; on the other hand, a group of twelve-year-olds with an imperfect and confused sense even of two or three generations of the family's past, let alone the street, the town, they live in. Such asymmetry is manifestly nonsensical as a feature of any *learning*, if such is to be allowed to take place. As a corrective, it seems to me important to explore and tease out bits of the world in which the pupils have some degree of expertise (see, for example, Robert Roberts's excellent book *A Ragged School* (Manchester University Press, 1976)): conversely, again, I see little gain in forcing an examination of current experience: the distancing, be it of only six or seven years, seems a necessary feature of such enterprises. Reductive analysis, again, seems to me to be no proper or necessary element of such activity: '*Why* did you sing such songs?' is as useless and defeating a question as that old conversation- or lesson-stopper 'Why did you enjoy that?' Short of invoking the next millennium's work in neurology, biochemistry, and depth-psychology, such a question is absolutely futile. If one *has* to catechise one's pupils, perhaps one can learn to ask such clarifying, consciousness-raising, questions as 'Were you surprised by anything in that song? Yes? When? Was it a pleasant surprise?' (Such questions, and some of the interesting answers, are emerging currently from the work of Stanley Fish in what is off-puttingly termed 'affective stylistics'.)

Finally, what is the *tone* of your classroom? Is it lively, energetic, but relatively free of anxiety and painful tension? Is it friendly and informal? Can *you* do things on the spur of the moment? Do you enjoy having free-flowing conversation with your pupils? Do you find their jokes amusing? Such an ethos seems to me the most conducive to the distinctive gifts and rewards of folk song: if you have five minutes to spare, can you go over to the record-player or the tape recorder and 'give' your pupils Sandy Denny singing 'Crazy Man Michael' or something similar — a cheerful, genial, good-humoured song that is simultaneously animating and pacifying, something to delight in and to soothe the nerves, not least your own? Not the least of the virtues of folk song is that it can bring a breath of sweetness and light into parts of the world too long regulated by too many people who look as though they never want to break into song, not even in the bathroom.

6 *Folk song and the teaching of history*

ROY PALMER

At the outset I should confess that I am a renegade modern linguist who, over a period of many years, has become progressively more interested in the teaching of history. With French classes I used to make extensive use of folk songs since, apart from being enjoyable, they communicate the feel and flavour both of the language and the national character. In the field of French history I was particularly impressed by the *Histoire de France par les chansons*, by Pierre Barbier and France Vernillat (8 vols., Gallimard, Paris, 1956). The title is self-explanatory, though it is worth saying that the work draws not only on folk song, but on allied material from the street singer, the vaudeville artist, and the hedge poet. From this point, it was only a short step to the idea of exploring a similar field in Britain, and of propounding the straightforward thesis that such material constitutes an invaluable resource for the historian. To many, this might seem a truism. Yet when I wrote a few years ago to offer some ballads to a historian who had just published a book on the Luddites, he replied that he was not interested. I found it difficult to understand that any historian could fail to be interested in a possible source; no doubt the gentleman in question was tacitly doubting the validity of ballads as source material.

On the face of it, to take another example, it does seem a little unlikely that a Warwickshire villager interviewed in 1950 would have very much to contribute by way of commentary on certain events in the Caribbean some 250 years earlier. This is what Sam Bennett had to offer:

Admiral Benbow

Come all ye sea-men bold and draw near, and draw near, — Come —
all ye sea-men bold — and draw near. 'Tis of an ad-m'ral's fame, — brave Benbow was his
name, — How he fought all on the main you shall hear, you shall hear.

87

Come all ye seamen bold and draw near, and draw near,
Come all ye seamen bold and draw near.
'Tis of an admiral's fame, brave Benbow was his name,
How he fought all on the main you shall hear, you shall hear.

Then Benbow he set sail for to fight, for to fight,
Brave Benbow he set sail for to fight;
Benbow he set sail on a fine and pleasant gale,
And his enemies they turned tail in a fright, in a fright.

Said Burke unto Wade, 'We will run, we will run',
Said Burke unto Wade, 'We will run;
For I value no disgrace, not the losing of my place,
But the enemies I won't face till I die, till I die.'

Then Ruby and Benbow fought the French, fought the French,
Then Ruby and Benbow fought the French;
They fought them up and down till the blood came trickling down,
Till the blood came trickling down where they lay, where they lay.

And Benbow lost his legs by chain shot, by chain shot,
Brave Benbow lost his legs by chain shot;
Brave Benbow lost his legs, down on his stumps he begs,
'Fight on, my English lads, 'tis your lot, 'tis your lot.'

When the doctor dressed his wounds, Benbow cried, Benbow cried,
When the doctor dressed his wounds, Benbow cried,
'Let a cradle now in haste on the quarter-deck be placed,
That the enemies I may face, till I die, till I die.'

When in death he closed his eyes, they all cried, they all cried,
When in death he closed his eyes, they all cried,
'What a shocking sight to see our brave hero of our day',
And they carried him to Kingston Church: there he lay, there he lay.

(Collected by Peter Kennedy, to whom I am indebted for permission to reproduce it. This version appears in print here for the first time. It is available on a tape-cassette, *Down by the Greenwood Side-i-o* (FSA-60-098, Folktracks Cassettes, Harberton, Totnes, Devon).)

Essentially, the song says that Benbow, because of the reluctance of his captains to fight, came off the worse in a battle with the French, died of his wounds, and was buried at Kingston. This is correct. John Benbow was a Shrewsbury man who owned and captained a ship (John Campbell, *The Lives of the Admirals* (4 vols., 1742–4); the quotations which follow are from vol. 4, pp. 257–86). In 1685 he was boarded off Cadiz by Moorish pirates, who were rapidly repulsed. On Benbow's orders, the thirteen Moorish dead were decapitated, and the heads 'thrown into a Tub of Pork-Pickle'. He took them ashore in a sack, telling the 'officers of the Revenue' at Cadiz that it contained 'Salt Provisions for his own Use'. Not surprisingly, they were suspicious, so Benbow produced the severed heads. The officers were duly impressed, Charles II of Spain admiringly summoned Benbow to Madrid, and when James II of England heard the story he gave him a command in the Royal

Navy. Perhaps I have laboured this point, but the fact that Benbow was known to
be tough, and was a tarpaulin captain — one who had obtained command through
his own efforts, outside the usual network of patronage — endeared him to his men.
John Campbell noted that 'the Seamen generally considered Rear-Admiral *Benbow*,
as their greatest Patron; one, who not only used them well, while under his Command, but was always ready to interpose in their Favour, as far as his Interest went,
when they were ill-treated by others'. Perhaps this reputation was not liked by his
officers, which might explain their reluctance to fight under him.

Nevertheless, Benbow was 'a very able Commander', and after successes in
Europe, King William sent him to the West Indies in 1701 as Admiral of the Blue,
with a flotilla of ten ships. The following year, Benbow sailed from Jamaica to seek
out the French fleet. In August they sighted the French off Santa Marta (now in
Colombia) and chased them across the Caribbean for five days. Benbow was enraged
and deeply disappointed when his captains refused to engage the enemy, or to help
him when the flagship engaged. On the fifth day, Benbow had to abandon any hope
of bringing the French into a decisive battle, but not before his 'Right Leg was
shattered to Pieces by a Chain-shot, and he was carried down; but he presently
ordered his Cradle on the Quarter-Deck, and continued the Fight till Day'.

Although he was 'ill of a Fever' on returning to Kingston, Benbow ordered that
seven of his captains should be court-martialled on charges including the cardinal
offence of cowardice in the face of the hereditary enemy, the French. One died a
few days before the trial, one was vindicated, two were suspended from duty
(though the sentence was not to take effect until Her Majesty's pleasure — Queen
Anne had come to the throne — was known). The two worst offenders, Kirby and
Wade, were found guilty of 'Cowardice, Breach of Orders, and Neglect of Duty',
with Wade in addition convicted of drunkenness, and were sentenced to be shot.
Benbow died — of his wounds, of fever, and perhaps of chagrin — in November
1702, and was buried at Kingston. Kirby and Wade were shot on board the ship
which had carried them home when it docked at Plymouth in April 1703.

Although Sam Bennett's ballad does not contain all these facts, it is true to them
with the single exception of an error over a name (Burke for Kirby in verse 3). It
did not survive for 250 years without the assistance of print, for versions appeared
on ballad sheets in both the eighteenth and nineteenth centuries. It is interesting to
note, however, that the verse about Kingston Church did not appear on the printed
sheets (cf., for example, the version printed by Davenport of London (in J.
Holloway and J. Black, *Later English Broadside Ballads* (Routledge and Kegan Paul,
1975), p. 15).

The ballad emphasises the virtues of patriotism and personal courage; it is full of
bottom, to use an eighteenth-century term, meaning dependability and the refusal
to let go. The vocabulary is sturdy, monosyllabic, almost organic. The tune wove in
and out of many different sets of words for several centuries, beginning with a
Diggers' song from the time of the Civil War. The ballad is illuminated by a study of

the circumstances which gave rise to it, but in turn it provides an insight into those circumstances with immediacy and vigour. It is memorable, revealing, satisfying, and full of reverberation. Is this not a worthwhile piece of history?

Since the oral version of 'Admiral Benbow' squares with the reported facts, the historian may be willing to accept it as admissible evidence. However, confirmation from alternative sources is not always possible. In which case, would he be prepared to take a similar item on trust? Here is a song which was circulating orally until recent years, apparently without any assistance from print. Roy Harris, now a professional folk singer, but then a soldier, learned it while serving in the Royal Artillery in 1951.

McCafferty

When I was just sixteen years of age,
To the British Army I did engage;
I left my home with a good intent
To join the Forty-second Regiment.

To Fulwood Barracks I did go,
To serve my time in that depot.
From troubles then I was never free:
My captain took a great dislike to me.

When posted on duty at the barrack gate,
Some soldiers' children came along to play;
From the officers' mess my captain came
And ordered me to take their parents' name.

I took one name instead of three;
'Neglect of duty' they did charge me:
Ten days' C.B. and the loss of pay,
That's what it cost me for those children's play.

With a loaded rifle I did swear
I'd shoot my captain on the barrack square;
I aimed my rifle and fired to kill,
And hit my colonel against my will.

At the Liverpool Assizes my trial I stood;
The jury they all banged on wood.
The judge he said, 'McCafferty,
Prepare yourself for the gallows tree.'

Well, I've no mother to break her heart;
I've no father to take my part.
I have only one friend, and a girl is she;
She'd lay her life down for McCafferty.

Come all you young officers of the present day,
Just treat your men with civility,
For if you don't, there's sure to be
Another hard case like McCafferty.

(Sung by Roy Harris on his solo record *The Bitter and the Sweet* (Topic 12TS 217, issued in 1972). I am indebted to him for permission to reproduce it here.)

All very far-fetched, or so it would seem. The unfortunate soldier tries, for an inexplicably trivial reason, to kill an officer, and manages to kill two with a single shot. The information that the assassin is an orphan seems a transparent attempt to gain our sympathy. The 42nd Regiment — the Black Watch — was never stationed at Fulwood Barracks in Preston. Even an observer predisposed to be favourable — Roy Harris himself — can only suggest that the ballad is a fantasy 'conceived by a disaffected soldier, perhaps Irish, some time in the latter half of the nineteenth century'.

Yet even if we accept all this, is the song worthless to a historian? One would have thought that the last verse, for example, pointed significantly towards a particular relationship between the rank and file and officers in the British Army, and was therefore of some value. Versions of the song were widely known, though it was regarded with awe, and even fear. A Shropshire singer called May Bradley (quoted in Fred Hamer, *Green Groves* (EFDSS Publications, 1973), p. 47) tells how she once started to sing it and 'a man jumped up and said "Mrs Bradley we mustn't allow that song in this house." And I said "What's that got to do along o' you?" and he said "If you was found singing that song you'd get ten years in gaol." ' To sing it in the army was rumoured to be a chargeable offence. One wonders whether some luckless swaddy did find himself charged for singing it, under the compendious clause of Queen's Regulations (now, I believe, amended) which covered 'conduct prejudicial to good order and military discipline'.

I hope that my readers are at this point reflecting on the shakiness of my defence of the song, for I shall now reveal that it basically tells a true story. Patrick M'Caffrey, a young Irishman, whose mother was dead and whose father had vanished in America, enlisted in the 32nd Regiment (not the 42nd) at Preston. Rightly or wrongly he felt himself to be persecuted by the adjutant, Captain Hanham. When M'Caffrey was on picket duty outside the officers' mess he was told to take the names of some children who were making a nuisance of themselves by larking about near-by. He complied with the order in a half-hearted way, and was placed on a charge by the adjutant, which resulted in his being awarded C.B. by the commanding officer. Confined to barracks, by the way, was far more than merely having to stay in camp: it included parading in best kit, pack drill (remember the saying 'No names, no pack drill'?) and fatigues (extra work). Incensed by what he felt to be an injustice, M'Caffrey took his rifle and shot at Captain Hanham when he was walking across the barrack square with Colonel Crofton, the commanding officer. Both men were killed, though M'Caffrey afterwards said that he had only intended to kill Hanham. He was handed over to the civil police, tried at Liverpool Assizes, and executed in front of Kirkdale Gaol before a crowd of 30,000 people, in January 1862. The only romantic invention which the anonymous songwriter had permitted himself is M'Caffrey's sweetheart, who does not appear in any of the contemporary reports.

Thus a wildly improbable song is proved to be a valid document, save for a few details. (The song appears, with an extensive commentary and newspaper accounts of the trial of Patrick M'Caffrey, in my *Rambling Soldier* (Penguin, 1977).) It circulated for almost a century in a semi-clandestine fashion, with no assistance from print. It was widely known, as the variety of versions attests, because of its striking story and its deeper implications. In fact, it was nationally known.

The Luddite songs of Yorkshire survived in a very similar way, though they were confined to a relatively small area. The song of M'Caffrey made a fairly general point, whereas the Luddite songs tended to be very specific. They have survived thanks mainly to Frank Peel's assiduous questioning of old people, the results of which he included in *The Risings of the Luddites* (first published in 1888; the second edition of 1895, from which I quote, was printed by Cass in 1968 with an introduction by E.P. Thompson). Incidentally, this is an early example of the techniques of the oral historian, which have recently begun to be more widely used. 'There are evidences', wrote Peel, 'that the Luddite rebellion was not destitute of poets who celebrated in rough but vigorous rhyme the progress of the triumphant croppers in their crusades against the machines that robbed their children of their food; or appealed solemnly to the God of Heaven to smite with swift vengeance the oppressors who despised the cries of the poor and needy and ground them down to the dust' (op. cit., p. 119). One of the 'evidences' which he quotes is a song sung by John Walker, of Longroyd Bridge, near Huddersfield. Walker was hanged at York in 1813 for taking part the previous year in the attack on Cartwright's Mill at Liversedge, but he was remembered for a long time at the Shears Inn in the same town for his singing: 'long before Walker had come to the end of his song the rollicking chorus was eagerly caught up by his delighted audience, and when the end was reached the refrain was twice repeated with extraordinary vigour, many of the men beating time on the long table with their sticks and pewter mugs (op. cit., p. 48). The song itself is clearly a home-made product, closely based on a poaching ballad which told of a conflict between keepers and poachers. It is printed here for the first time with a tune similar to that which Walker must have used.

The Croppers' Song

Come cropper lads of high renown,
Who love to drink good ale that's brown
And strike each haughty tyrant down
With hatchet, pike and gun.

(Chorus) Oh, the cropper lads for me,
          The gallant lads for me,
          Who with lusty stroke the shear frames broke,
          The cropper lads for me.

Who though the specials still advance
And soldiers nightly round us prance,
The cropper lads still lead the dance
With hatchet, pike and gun.
(Chorus) Oh, the cropper lads for me, etc.

And night by night when all is still
And the moon is hid behind the hill,
We forward march to do our will
With hatchet, pike and gun.
(Chorus) Oh, the cropper lads for me, etc.

Great Enoch still shall lead the van,
Stop him who dare, stop him who can.
Press forward every gallant man
With hatchet, pike and gun.
(Chorus) Oh, the cropper lads for me, etc.

(Text: Peel, op. cit., p. 47. Tune: 'The Gallant Poachers', sung by George Dunn (1887–1975) of Quarry Bank, Staffs.; collected by Roy Palmer, 2 July 1971 (*Folk Music Journal*, 1973, 276).)

The frames mentioned made the work of shearing the nap on cloth into a semi-mechanised process. The croppers, who worked the massive hand-shears, opposed a development which quickly put half of them out of work. 'Enochs' were sledge-hammers made by the firm of Enoch and James Taylor of Marsden, which also made the shear frames. Hence the Luddite saying 'Enoch has made them and Enoch shall smash them'. Shears, Enochs, and a model shear frame can be seen at the Tolson Memorial Museum, Huddersfield.

We know of the doings of the Luddites from a number of records, including contemporary accounts. Most of these were composed by men hostile to the Luddites, who spoke themselves, if at all, only when on trial for their lives. There are a few anonymous letters, and that is all — except for songs. These give a real feeling of the men's strength and pride, which is hard to find elsewhere. Of course, the Luddite view was not in accord with the consensus either among their contemporaries or among most historians. Yet it was deeply and passionately held and, expressed in song, it sends a *frisson* of communication through more than a century and a half.

Not all songs are hostile towards industrialisation, though one must admit that those favourably disposed are harder to find. The excitement of steam power combines in this song, which I take to be late eighteenth-century in origin, with a whimsical look from a Nonconformist point of view at high-church Anglicanism:

The Wensleydale Lad

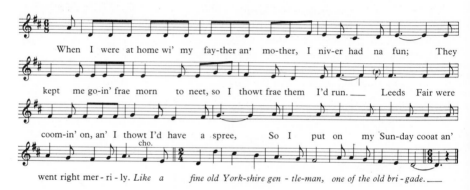

When I were at home wi' my fay-ther an' mo-ther, I niv-er had na fun; They kept me go-in' frae morn to neet, so I thowt frae them I'd run. ___ Leeds Fair were coom-in' on, an' I thowt I'd have a spree, So I put on my Sun-day cooat an' went right mer-ri-ly. *Like a fine old York-shire gen-tle-man, one of the old bri-gade.* ___

When I were at home wi' my fayther an' mother, I niver had na fun;
They kept me goin' frae morn to neet, so I thowt frae them I'd run.
Leeds Fair were coomin' on, an' I thowt I'd have a spree,
So I put on my Sunday cooat an' went right merrily.

(Chorus) Like a fine old Yorkshire gentleman, one of the old brigade.

First thing I saw were t' factory, I niver seed one afore;
There were threads an' tapes, an' tapes an' silks, to sell by monny a score.
Owd Ned turn'd iv'ry wheel, an' iv'ry wheel a strap;
'Begor!' said I to t' maister-man, 'Owd Ned's a rare strong chap.'
(Chorus) Like a fine old Yorkshire gentleman, etc.

Next I went to Leeds Owd Church — I were niver i' one i' my days,
An' I were maistly ashamed o' misel, for I didn't knaw their ways;
There were thirty or forty folk, i' tubs an' boxes sat,
Then up cooms a saucy owd fellow. Says he, 'Noo, lad, tak off thy hat.'
(Chorus) Like a fine old Yorkshire gentleman, etc.

Then in there cooms a great Lord Mayor, an' over his shooders a club,
An' he gat into a white sack-poke, an' gat into t' topmost tub.
An' then there cooms anither chap, I thinks they call'd him Ned,
An' he gat into t' bottommost tub, an' moack'd all t'other chap said.
(Chorus) Like a fine old Yorkshire gentleman, etc.

So they began to preach an' pray, they prayed for George, oor King;
When up jumps t' chap i' t' bottommost tub. Says he, 'Good folks, let's sing.'
I thowt some sang varra weel, while others did grunt an' groan;
Ivery man sang what he wad, so I sang 'Darby an' Joan'.
(Chorus) Like a fine old Yorkshire gentleman, etc.

When preachin' an' prayin' were over, an' folks were gangin' away,
I went to t' chap i' t' topmost tub. Says I, 'Lad, what's to pay?'
'Why, nowt', says he, 'my lad.' Begor! I were right fain,
So I clock'd hod o' my gret club stick an' went whistlin' oot again.
(Chorus) Like a fine old Yorkshire gentleman, etc.

The song, whose text appears in F.W. Moorman, *Yorkshire Dialect Poems, 1673–1915* (1916), pp. 12–13, continued in oral tradition to the present day, often with more ribald words. The tune commonly used is a variant of 'The Fine Old English Gentleman', and the chorus has been added with the tune. It circulates in a relatively restricted area straddling the Pennines between Oldham and Huddersfield, which, as it happens, is almost the same territory as that of 'The Croppers' Song'. Precise local dialect in the one case and relevance in the other have restricted the songs' appeal. 'McCafferty' and 'Benbow', however, although based on specific incidents, had a wider appeal which enabled them to have a national, and even international, circulation. All these songs give a strong feeling of communication from the past, especially when one knows that they have been passed on and treasured by many generations of ordinary people.

In the case of 'Benbow' and 'The Wensleydale Lad' there was assistance from print, in the shape of ballad sheets. From the earliest days of printing, these were popular. In 1631 an author who has remained anonymous wrote of a balladmonger that 'his ballads, cashiered the city, must now ride poast for the country; where they are no less admired then a gyant in a pageant: till at last they grow so common there too, as every poore milk-maid can chant and chirpe it under her cow, which she useth as an harmless charme to make her let down her milk' (quoted in J. Brand, *Popular Antiquities* (3 vols., 1849–53), vol. 3, p. 313). In the 1860s Charles Dickens was still complaining about the 'brazen performers on brazen instruments, beaters of drums, grinders of organs, bangers of banjoes, clashers of cymbals, worriers of fiddles, and bellowers of ballads' who disturbed the London streets (quoted in M. Bass, *Street Music in the Metropolis* (1864), p. 41). 'The ballad-singer', wrote the *National Review* in 1861, 'with his rough broad-sheet, travelled ... over the whole surface of a man's life, political and social.' The past tense is perhaps significant, though there is evidence that songs on topical issues continued to appear until late in the century, and indeed afterwards.

Plate 2 Engraving from 'Pretty Girl Buying a Ballad' by Henry Walton (c. 1790).

Samuel Webber, who was born in Poplar in 1874, well remembered street singers:

Every Friday and Saturday nights there used to be a couple. The man'd have a high-topped hat on — have these music sheets round his hat, and his wife'd be with him, too. They used to have 'em round the tops of their hats — no music, only words. Song sheets, they were called. They cost a penny. A lot of songs on 'em. They both sang them together, in unison. There was always a crowd round the sing-song — they used to make a fair collection.

And I'll tell you a song they sung on the occasion when there was a fire at Forest Gate School, when about twenty-four children — boys — lost their lives.

The Forest Gate Fire

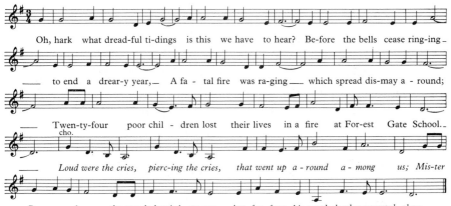

Oh, hark what dread-ful ti-dings is this we have to hear? Be-fore the bells cease ring-ing __ to end a drear-y year,__ A fa - tal fire was ra-ging __ which spread dis-may a - round; Twen-ty-four poor chil - dren lost their lives in a fire at For-est Gate School.__

cho. *Loud were the cries, pierc-ing the cries, that went up a - round a - mong us; Mis-ter Dun-can so brave the poor lads tried to save, but far from his reach death con-veyed them.*

(Reminiscences and song from Samuel Webber (1874–1973), collected by Roy Palmer, July–October 1971, and published in part in *Folk Review*, February 1976, 18–19.)

The fire took place at Forest Gate Industrial School, Poplar, in 1890, when twenty-six boys died. I have not so far traced the printed ballad sheet.

At least one London printer, W.C. Such, of Union Street, Borough, SE1, continued in production until 1929. Plate 3 is a reproduction of one of his sheets. The original is in the Bodleian Library, Oxford, in the John Johnson Collection of Street Ballads (box 8). For a possible tune, see my *Touch on the Times* (Penguin, 1974), pp. 214ff. (I am indebted to Mike Yates for helping me to date this sheet.)

Street ballads were a commodity, sold for profit. The publishers set out to appeal to what they took to be popular tastes and sentiments, though this by no means implied uniformity of approach. On the contrary, these 'narrow strips of history', as they have been called (Douglas Jerrold, *Heads of the People*, 1840), were produced over a long period of time, employed many different styles, and covered an immense field: war, work, crime, living conditions, sensational events, politics, adventure, sex – one could claim, like the *News of the World*, that 'all human life is here'. The historian of popular culture will be interested in the complete spectrum, though the historian *tout court* may prefer the social and political material, which parallels, confirms, supplements, and sometimes corrects information from other sources.

For example, Dorothy George, dealing with the clothing industry in the South-west in the eighteenth century, quotes Dean Tucker, who wrote this in 1757:

in Gloucestershire, Wiltshire, and Somersetshire . . . one person with a great stock and large credit, buys the wool, pays for the spinning, weaving, milling, dyeing,

An Appeal
BY
UNEMPLOYED
Ex-Service Men.

Please purchase a Copy and thus Help.

Some thousands in England are starving,
  And all through no fault of their own,
The troubles of poverty sharing,
  And only to them it is known.
It's hard when the cupboard is empty,
  And through the streets the poor men
    must roam,
And all the week through with nothing to do,
  Yet with poor hungry children at home.

Then pity the Ex-Service workmen,
  Who starve all the week through,
They don't want to shirk any kind of hard
    work,
  But, alas, they can't get it to do!

A man who is fond of his children,
  To keep them alive does his best,
So o him it must be bewildering,
  Yet brings sorrow to both parents' breast,
To see his dear little ones starving,
  In the midst of deep poverty hurled,
For no one can tell what they must feel
  So friendless and alone in the world.

The workman must live by his labour,
  And that he needs have day by day,
And altho' he may have feeling neighbours
  They have nothing they can give away.
For no one knows where the shoe pinches,
  But those who the pain have to bear,
With no work to do, all the week through,
  And just nothing but sorrow and care.

There are many in towns and in cities,
  Who are walking the streets all foot sore,
They surely deserve all your pity,
  As dejected they pass by your door.
At factories and workshops they're calling
  But they're told the same words every day,
There's no orders in hand, all over the land,
  So no wages the masters can pay.

It used to be called happy England,
  But where is its happiness now ?
When people are slaving in thousands,
  At the factory, the loom and the plough.
In this country there's millions of money,
  But those who have got it take care,
Their sovereigns they nurse and they keep a
    full purse,
  So the poor man can't get a share.

Then do what you can to assist them,
  For they're all flesh and blood like your-
    selves.
Their poverty sadly oppresses them
  With no food at all on the shelves.
The help that your fellow-man's needing,
  Should be given the country all through,
So help the poor man, the best way you can,
  Who *would* work if he had it to do.

W. C. SUCH, Printer and Publisher,
183 & 185, Union Street, Borough, London, S.E. 1.

Plate 3

shearing, dressing, &c. That is, he is the master of the whole manufacture from first
to last and perhaps employs a thousand persons under him. This is the clothier
whom all the rest are to look upon as their paymaster. But will they not also sometimes look upon him as their tyrant? . . . The master . . . however well disposed
himself is continually tempted by his situation to be proud and overbearing, to consider his people as the scum of the earth, whom he has a right to squeeze whenever
he can; because they ought to be kept low and not to rise up in competition with
their superiors. The journeymen on the contrary are equally tempted by their situation to envy the high station and superior fortunes of their masters; and to envy
them the more in proportion as they find themselves deprived of the hopes of
advancing themselves to the same degree by any stretch of industry or superior skill.
(Dorothy George, *England in Transition* (Penguin, 1953), pp. 48–9)

Dorothy George, a historian who had an eye for ballads, goes on to quote part of
one which not only amplifies Tucker's remarks but gives the viewpoint of the
journeyman. It was written by Thomas Lanfiere of Wachet, Somerset (a balladeer
who wrote a number of pieces on the clothing trade) and published in London in
about 1679. It now appears for the first time with one of the stipulated tunes,
'Packington's Pound'.

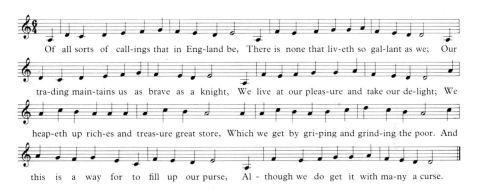

Of all sorts of call-ings that in Eng-land be, There is none that liv-eth so gal-lant as we; Our
tra-ding main-tains us as brave as a knight, We live at our pleas-ure and take our de-light; We
heap-eth up rich-es and treas-ure great store, Which we get by gri-ping and grind-ing the poor. And
this is a way for to fill up our purse, Al - though we do get it with ma-ny a curse.

(Text: J.W. Ebsworth and W. Chappell (eds.), *The Roxburghe Ballads* (9 vols.,
Hertford, 1871–99), vol. VII, pp. 7–9. Tune: W. Chappell, *Popular Music of the
Olden Time* (1859), p. 124. The original is in vol. IV, p. 35, of the Roxburghe
Ballads, in the British Library.)

It seems reasonable to argue that ballads such as this are valuable and illuminating. The example could be multiplied a thousand-fold, ranging from a wide-ranging
ballad cycle produced over several centuries by Anglo-Scottish border friction (see
M. Brander, *Scottish and Border Battles and Ballads* (Seeley Service, 1975)), to a
single sheet on a local crime or disaster. Alternatively, one could take a particular
period and examine the contribution which ballads made to the understanding of
its history. John Aubrey (1626–97) says that 'W. Malmesburiensis pickt up his
history from ye times of Ven. Bede to his time out of old Songs', and adds, 'So my

The Clothiers Delight:

OR, The Rich Mens Joy, and the Poor Mens Sorrow.

Wherein is exprest the craftiness and subtility of many Clothiers in England, by beating down their Work-mens wages.

Combers, Weavers, and Spinners, for little gains,
Doth Earn their money by taking of hard pains.

To the Tune of, *Jenny come tye me, &c. Packingtons Pound, Or, Monk hath confounded, &c.*

With Allowance, Ro. L'Estrange.

By T. Lanfiere.

OF all sorts of callings that in England be,
There is none that liveth so gallant as we;
Our Trading maintains us as brave as a Knight,
We live at our pleasure, and taketh delight:
We heapeth up riches and treasure great store,
Which we get by griping and grinding the poor,
And this is a way for to fill up our purse,
Although we do get it with many a Curse.

Throughout the whole Kingdom in Country and Town,
There is no danger of our Trade going down,
So long as the Comber can work with his Comb,
And also the Weaver weave in his Lomb;
The Turker and Spinner that spins all the year,
We will make them to earn their wages full dear;
And this is the way, &c.

In former ages we us'd to give,
So that our Work-folks like Farmers did live;
But the times are alter'd, we will make them know,
All we can for; to bring them all under our Bow:
We will make them to work hard for a day,
Though a shilling a day before they had pay;
And this is the way, &c.

And first to, the Combers we will bring them down,
From Eight-groats a score unto half a Crown:
If at all they murmur, and say 'tis too small,
We bid them chose whether they will work at all.
We'll make them believe that Trading is bad,
We care not a pity, though they are ne'r so sad,
And this is the way, &c.

We'll make the poor Weavers work at a low rate,
We'll find fault where's no fault, and so we will bate:
If Trading grows dead we will presently show it,
But if it grows good they shall never know it:
We care not whether we keep cloathing or no:
And this is the way, &c.

Then next for the Spinners we shall enter,
We'll make them spin three pound instead of two;
When they bring home their work unto us, they complain,
And say that their wages will not them maintain:
But if that an Ounce of weight they do lack,
Then for, to bate they never we will not slack:
And this is the way, &c.

But if it falls out right, then their wages they crave,
We have got no money, and what's that you'd have?
We have Bread and Bacon, and Butter that's good,
With Oat-meal and Salt that is wholesome for food;
We have Soap and Candles whereby to give light,
That you may work by them so long as you have sight:
And this is the way, &c.

We will make the Market and Workman understand,
That they with their wages shall never buy Land:
Though heretofore a clasp have been lofty and high,
Yet now we will make them submit humbly;
We will lighten their wages as low as may be,
We will keep them under in every degree:
And this is the way, &c.

When we go to Market our work-men are glad,
But when we come home then we do look sad,
We sit in the corner as if our hearts did ake,
We tell them 'tis not a penny we can take:
We plead poverty before we have need,
And thus we do cosen them most basely indeed:
And this is the way, &c.

But if to an Ale-house they Customers be,
Then presently with the Ale-wife we agree,
When we come to a reckoning, then we do crave
Two-pence on a shilling, and that we will have;
By such cunning wayes we our treasure do get,
For it is all fish that bottoms to our Net:
And this is the way, &c.

And thus we do gain all our Wealth and Estate,
By many poor men that work early and late;
If it were not for those that do labour full hard,
We might go and hang our selves without regard:
The Combers, and Weavers, and Workers also,
With the Spinners that works for Wages full low:
By these peoples labours we fill up our purse, &c.

Then let's to the Cloathing-trade, it goes on brave,
We toil for to spoil and moil, no yet to slave;
Our Workmen to work hard, but we live at ease,
We go when we will, and come when we please:
We hoard up our bags of silver and Gold,
But conscience and equity with us is cold:
By poor peoples labour we fill up our purse,
Although we do get it with many a curse.

FINIS.

Printed for F. Coles, T. Vere, I. Wright, and I. Clarke

Plate 4

nurse has the history from the conquest downe to Carl. I in ballad' (*Remaines of Gentilisme and Judaisme* (first published from MS. in 1881), p. 68). Printed sources for those periods are fairly sparse; but even at a time when the contrary is true the ballads have a contribution – possibly a unique contribution – to make. If one takes as an example the decade starting in 1830, then ballads show the impact on ordinary people of the railways, industrialisation, urban change, cholera, reform, agrarian unrest, Chartism. It is outside the scope of this work to give more than a very few examples.

I do not know the identity of Edward Lamborn, the writer of 'The New Poor Law' (Plate 5). Perhaps a local historian could help. The workhouse theme recurs in 'Past, Present and Future' (Plate 6), together with other rural grievances, including enclosure. There is a certain optimism, or perhaps wishful thinking, in the last verse, which is not found in *A Dialouge* (Plate 7). Lord Ashley's bill was introduced in May 1833, then shelved for a time while a committee – proposed by Wilson Patten, a millowner M.P. – sat on the question, and withdrawn in August. It would appear that this sheet can therefore be dated fairly precisely between May and August 1833.

John Frost, Zephaniah Williams, and William Jones were the leaders of a Chartist march on Newport, Monmouthshire (now Gwent) in 1839. Although some of the participants were armed with home-made weapons, the basic intention was to make a peaceful protest. The five thousand marchers arrived at 8.30 a.m. on 4 November outside the Westgate Hotel, where some Chartists were temporarily imprisoned. A scuffle occurred when a special constable tried to take a gun from one of the demonstrators, a shot was fired, and then soldiers who were concealed in the hotel opened fire on the crowd, killing between ten and twenty-two people. The leaders were arrested and put on trial at Monmouth, some on charges of high treason. Frost, Williams, and Jones were sentenced to be hanged, drawn, and quartered, though this was commuted to transportation for life. After serving fourteen years they were pardoned. Williams and Jones elected to remain in Australia, but Frost came home to a hero's welcome at Newport. His spirit was unbroken, and shortly after his return he published a vigorous pamphlet, *The Horrors of Convict Life* (Preston, 1856). The building in which Frost and his colleagues were tried still stands at Monmouth, and there are numerous relics of them in the museums at Newport and Monmouth, including another broadside on display in the Newport Museum and Art Gallery, entitled 'The Trial, Lamentation and Farewell of the Unfortunate John Frost' (the printer was W. Bear of Swansea).

Broadside ballads have a documentary value, as I hope these examples demonstrate, in their printed form. It should be remembered, though, that they were mostly intended for singing: their words seldom take wing unless they are sung. When a tune is indicated there is usually no problem: the air and chorus of 'Home, Sweet Home' adds to the bite of the poor law song. With the other three there is no such help. These are the possibilities: to find the tune indicated by the title of the ballad, if it is well known enough (these are not); to find a tune indicated by what

The New Poor Law and the Farmer's Glory.

WRITTEN BY EDWD. LAMBORN, of UFFINGTON.

I was forced as a stranger to wander from home,
And all through the poor laws to Faringdon to
    come ;
There to have my head shaved, which filled me
    with woe,
And many a poor creature they have served also.
            Home, home, sweet home,
            There is no place like home.

At six in the morning the bell it doth ring,
When every man's allowance of ocum doth bring ;
And if we do not pick it just as the keeper please,
He will be sure to stint you of your small bread
    and cheese.
            Home, sweet home. &c.

When the corn they do bring, to grinding we
    must go,
Both pease and both beans, and barley also ;
And if we do but grumble, or even seen to gloom,
Full well we know the consequence—the blind-
    house is our doom.
            Home, home, sweet home, &c.

At seven in the evening the bell it doth ring,
When every man up stairs is obl iged to swing ;
Upon the iron bedsteads there he's forced to lie,
Some a grieving, some a groaning until the break
    of day.
            Home, home, &c.

And many more things which I know to be true,
Such as parting man and wife and children also ;
O ! what heathens and what brutes are in our civil
    land,
For breaking the good laws which were made by
    God and man.
            Home, home, &c.

Beware you blow'd-out farmers, you noblemen be-
    side,
Though you may laugh and sneer, and at the
    poor deride,
How will you bear your sentence all on the day
    of doom,
When you will call for water to cool your parch-
    ing tongue.
            Home, home, &c.

Perhaps you wont believe me, or care not what I
    say,
I will be bound that you will all on some future
    day ;
For I know that some judgment will soon you
    overtake,
Either in this world, or in the burning lake.
            Home, home, &c.

For those who made the poor laws they are the
    spawn of hell,
And of those that do uphold them the truth to
    you I'll tell ;
For the devil is their master, who put it in their
    heads,
And this they will prove all on their dying beds.
            Home, home, &c.

So now I will conclude, and finish my sad tale,
I've given you all warning before you are in hell ;
And if you wont believe me you will find it is true,
For God has declar'd it to oppressors as this is
    their due.
            Home, home, &c.

T. Hallard, Printer, Oxford.

Plate 5

Past, present and future.

or the Poor Mans' Consolation,

Printed by HILL, 14, Waterloo Road.

Good people give attention, who now around do stand;
While I unfold the treatment of the poor upon the land;
For now-a-days the gentlemen have brought the laborers low,
And daily are contriving plans, to prove their overthrow.

So now, my bold companions, the world seems upside down,
They scorn the poor man as a thief, in country and in town.

In former days the labourers were all called happy men,
And well they might, a labourer could keep a grunter then,
But in these times a grunter, to a poor man, is but lent,
'Tis hard that he must kill and sell the pig to pay his rent.

In older times the poor could on a common turn a cow,
The commons all are taken in, the rich have claimed them
now,
If a poor man turns a goose thereon, the rogues will it surround
The rich will have the kindness just to pop it in the pound.

Now, if a man is out of work, his parish pay is small,
Enough to starve himself, his wife, and little children all,
They'll make him work for a crown a week, to keep his family
And the devil he will shake the rich for all their cruelty.

They build up large workhouses, now, to part the man & wife
That they may no more children get, 'tis true, upon my life,
They take the children from their arms, and send them dif-
ferent ways,
And fifteen pence allow to keep a man for seven days.

There was a time the farmer would work all day at plough,
His wife would to the meadows go, with her pail to milk her
cow,
But work, and him have now fell out, he makes
poor men to jump,
And his wife looks like a scarecrow, with a bustle
on her r—.

So now to end my ditty, may England flourish still,
Let men be for their labor paid, and then with free
good will
We'll all rejoice, with heart and voice, to banish all
our woes,
But long 'ere that, old England must pay the debt
she owes,
And then, my bold companions, the times will
surely mend,
All discontent 'twixt man and man, would then be
at an end.

Plate 6

A DIALOUGE,

BETWEEN OWD CARDER JOAN OTH MUMPS,

An Tum o lung Harrys i Owdham.

JOAN. New Tum ew ar tew getin on new, has te yeard owt obew tis ten Hewrs Bill ut tey mak sich o bother obewt.

TUM. Wha Joan, aw yeard ut th Measters hai gin it sich o slap ith Hews o Commons ut it il never get th better ont this yer.

J. Wha Tum will tha lets year hew theyn orderd to do that, aw thowt ut th evidence upo Sadler's Committee hed settlt o disputes there.

T. Wha Joan, theyn getten a chap ut tey cawn Patten Wilson, to tell um sth hews ut th moast oth evidence ut Sadler's Committee geet, is nowt but o pack o Lies ; un ut iv theyd give um o chonce, ut tey cud proove ut its howsumer ith Factorys tin it is ewt oth Dur.

J. Wha Tum, un dus tew think ut teyn give um chonce o proovein it, because iv ta dun th Measters can proove other that or owt else tey liken, whether its true or not ; but wil to lets year hew theyre orderin new.

T. Wha Joan, theyn getten o set o fellys to come dewn ut tey cawn Commissioners, un theyn look oth fine Factories, un th Measters un do us Hugh Birley, i Maechester did when Owd Nosey coom dewn.

J. Wha Tum, ew wur that.

T. Wha Joan, thew sis tey made oth bons cum i ther Sunday Clons. an o those ut wur Skellurd, an Side Crookd, un Sickly Lookin ; they made um stop ut whom, an for owd Ned they made im goa soa sle, ut owd Nosey thowt ut workin ith factory wur rare sport.

J. Wha but Tum, wene mak um goa into th Shoddy Factorys iv ut tey cum to Owdum, un si thi awl set owd Ned o goin double speed when ut teyre i ewr Factory, un thel o be smothert us sure us tewrt wick, un then weest be bothert wi um noa more.

T. Wha Joan, awl tel thi ew we mun do wi um, when ut tey cum dewn we mun muster o those uts skellowd, un side crookt, an sickly lookin, an lome, an iv wene ony bewt yead wene bring um too ; an wene mak un goa into th shoddy factorys, un into th Hot Rooms ith fine factorys, un then theyne feel whether its fit for foake to work i sich places or not, un then aw think ut teyle tell um o gradely tale obewt it when they getten to Lunnon.

J. Wha Tum, an iv they dun tell um a gradely tale abewt it, Paten Wilson il tell um ith hause, ot ow those uts skellowd an side-crookd en getten it wi wrostlin, an teres a chap ewt e Darbyshaw ut tey cawn Grizzlebone, ur sum sich o nome, seys ut teyne getten a Machiene to purify th air ith Factorys, un th Measters il get sumbody to swear it an tey'll find sum Doctors ut'll sey "tat tey conno tell whether stondin twenty three hews ewt oth twenty four, ul do o yung chilt ony hurt," us tey diden ofore, an ten it il be up wi Lord Eshley's ten hewr Bill.

T. Wha Joan, an ew mun we do then thinks ta, con ta tell ov ony plan o gettin ewr short time bill.

J. Wha Tum I con tell thee tat in a minuit, we mun mak o Paliament ov ewr own, an then we mun pas o Bill to mak oth Dukes, an'th Lords, an'th Nights, an'th Squires, an'th Bishops, an'th Parsons, into Carders, an Stripers, an Grinders, an o ther Wifes into Cotton Batters, an o ther wenches into Card raum hands, an teyne soon want o five hewr Bill ith stead ov ewr ten, I'll warrent ta.

T. Wha but Joan wot mun we do wi owd "Silly Billy" thinks ta, con we mak nowt ov him, wudent he do for a curlooker.

J. Wha Tum, iv thew wur to seek aw world oer, an after that thew cud get dewn into sooty regions an see owd Nick issel, thew cudent get o set o chaps ut ud do as well for owlookers, as o passel ov Cotton Lords, for ther's nobody bigger Tyraits ; an as for owd Billy, he's sich o henpect silly owd woman, ot he's fit for nowt but to stop ut whoam an caunt scales. An as for owd Grey-Goose I'd send im owr to Oireland wi his infernal Burkkin Bill an let th Oirish reken wi him, an theyd pay him off for aw at once I'll warrent ta.

T. Aw say Joan they sen ut th wages il cum dewn iv this ten hewrs bill wur to pass, wot thinks thew.

J. Wha Tum as for that iv ut wede a fifteen hewrs bill ith stead ov o ten hewrs bill, wages il faw under th present sistem for theyne gin notice for another drop both ut Stayley Bridge, un Stopport, soa thew sis ut tats aw fudge obewt wages dropin, but thewst year o bit ov o sung iv thewl stop two or three miults.

Hark ! The Factory Bell is ringing ;
    Yes I hear the dismal sound:
Thousands at its call its bringing,
    Long before daylight comes round.

Listen to the Victims Wailing,
    As they pass your Dwellings by,
When 'tis freezing snowing raining,
    Or Thunder rolling through the sky.

No excuse for non-attendance,
    At the Lordly Tyrants call,
Though they do live at a distance,
    Nay should the very Heavens fall.

Come they must, or pay the forfeit,
    Feel the Strap or turned away ;
If by it they should get a surfeit,
    That attends them to their dying day.

Then for thirteen hours together,
    At their frames they're forced to stay,
With not a moment time of Leisure,
    But just to eat and then away.

Call ye this a Land of Freedom,
    Where such Slavery does abound ;
No ! cursed be the very Kingdom,
    Where such things are to be found.

Tell me not of Negro Slavery,
    Where Afric's sons are bought and sold ;
Nor ever boast of British bravery,
    Whilst Childrens Blood is spilt for GOLD !

Where Factory Lords do strut in splendour,
    Wrung from the labours of the Poor,
Protected in the unholy plunder,
    By the Tyrants now in Power.

Printed by J. Hobson, Swan Yard, Huddersfild.

Plate 7

The Last Farewell to England

Of FROST, WILLIAMS, and JONES.

AS I walked though the town of Ports-
    mouth,
  I heard thee wretched men to say,
Farewell our dearest wives and children,
  We can with you no longer stay,
In agony and broken hearted,
  We are compelled behind to leave
Our native land, our friends and kindred,
  For our awful fate to grieve.

CHORUS.

Across the seas Frost, Jones & Williams,
  Through tempests and dreadful gales,
We leave our native land behind us,
  To end our days in New South Wales.

At Monmouth we were tried for treason,
  Where we was condemned to die,
Great and small throughout the nation,
  For to save our lives did try,
England, Ireland, Wales and Scotland,
  Manfully for us did strive,
And through a deal of perseverance,
  Government did spare our lives.

Sad was the day we drew together,
  Thousands of men from far and near,
Which caused grief and consternation,
  In every part of Monmouthshire.
That fatal day we'll long remember,
  Which caused distress on every mind,
It was the third of last November,
  Eighteen hundred and thirty nine.

Tens of thousands has petitioned,
  Overcome with grief and woe,
Every rank in all conditions,
  A free pardon us to gain,
We anxiously each hour expected,
  That some messenger to see,

To our dismal cells approaching,
  With the sound of liberty.

But oh, alas we was mistaken,
  All our hopes has proved in vain.
We for ever now are banished,
  Never to return again,
A long farewell our wives and children,
  Adieu our friends and neighbours dear,
While in slavery we are pining,
  Oft we'll think of Monmouthshire.

Happy with our wives and children,
  We on our native land might be.
If the length of our misfortunes,
  We could only once foresee,
Oh for those we left behind us,
  From our eyes runs floods of tears,
Altho' from death the have reprieved us,
  We think our sentence too severe.

Many a heart will beat in sorrow,
  Many an eye will shed a tear,
Many an orphan and it's mother
  Will lament in Monmouthshire;
For the third of last November,
  When their fathers went astray,
Tens of thousands will remember
  The sad disasters of the day.

We will conclude our mournful ditty,
  Which tills our aching hearts with pain
Shed for us a tear of pity—
  We never shall return again;
And when we've reach'd our destination,
  O'er the seas through storms and gales,
O may you live at home in comfort,
  While we lament in New South Wales.

J. FRANCE, Printer, Shrewsbury.

Plate 8

might be a fairly unusual metre, or a well-known chorus, such as 'Derry down' (not applicable here); to take the tune of an analogous song, which happens to fit (for example, a poaching or crime tune could well be used for 'The Last Farewell' (Plate 8)); to take any suitable tune which happens to fit; to make up a tune in traditional style. Only the first of these alternatives is perhaps totally satisfactory, but all the others were used by traditional and street singers as a matter of course, which is sufficient justification.

It is obvious that the historian will have to allow for bias in these songs, as indeed he would have to do with any source. Many of the broadsides were deliberately propagandist, and not solely from one side. In the election of 1784, for example, when Pitt was campaigning against Fox, 'Ballads were weapons on both sides, and not only in London', writes James Wardroper (*Kings, Lords and Wicked Libellers* (John Murray, 1973), p. 101). '*The Morning Herald* reported that "ministers have actually sent down three coach-loads of *ballad-singers* to Yorkshire. They are hired at a fixed salary." A covered waggon full of ballads and pamphlets went with them.' Pitt at least must have been pleased with the results because ten years later, William Gardiner tells us, 'Ballad-singers were paid and stationed at the ends of streets, to chant the downfall of the Jacobins, and the glorious administration of Mr Pitt' (*Music and Friends* (3 vols., 1838–53), vol. I, 1838, p. 222).

Even greater use of the form was made by ordinary people, particularly during the nineteenth century. In Wiltshire on 2 September 1826 Cobbett met 'weavers from the North, singing about the towns ballads of Distress' (*Rural Rides*, ed. G. Woodcock (Penguin, 1967), p. 341). The practice was so widespread that professional beggars cottoned on to it, singing in London 'the well-known ditty of

> We are all the way from Manchester
> And we've got no work to do!

set to the tune of "Oh, let us be joyful" ', writes Henry Mayhew, and he adds that when these 'starved-out manufacturers' made an oration it was not 'in the Lancashire or Yorkshire dialects, but in a cockney voice, of a strong Whitechapel flavour' (*London Labour and the London Poor*, vol. 4, 1862, in selections edited by Peter Quennell as *London's Underworld* (Spring Books, 1950), p. 423).

The genuinely distressed sometimes made up their own songs and then went round with the hat after singing, sometimes having their songs printed for sale. Strikes often gave rise to ballads of distress because of the hardship caused, but often the strikers' case was argued. Indeed, ballads were frequently used as a major means of propaganda by the strikers. During the Preston strike of 1853–4 scores of ballads were circulated. Even a much smaller dispute, such as the Kidderminster carpet weavers' strike of 1828, produced its small crop. *The Times* tartly commented (2 April 1828):

In the address circulated by the Weavers' Committee, they profess a determination to be peaceable, but this profession ill accords with one of the songs published under their sanction. We give a verse as a specimen:

> See our masters how they bind us
> In the midst of slavery;
> See the tyrants how they drive us
> To death or liberty.
> Then rise like men in bravery,
> To join the cause or die;
> We will be free from slavery,
> And have our liberty.

Such language as this cannot be too strongly reprobated.

Disasters and accidents also stimulated ballads, which commented on the circumstances and sought money to help the dependants of the victims. This practice continued until well into the twentieth century — indeed, the latest example I know dates from the disaster at Auchengeich, Lanarkshire, in 1959. (A version can be heard on *The Bonny Pit Laddie* (Topic 12TS 271—2), issued in 1975.) However, it seems that the most recent practice is to put the songs not onto a ballad sheet, but onto an extended-play record, which is then sold to raise money and to make a case. An example of this stems not from an accident, but from a dispute over the closure of a steelworks at Shotton, in North Wales. The record was released by the Steelworks Action Committee in 1973 (Plate 9).

Plate 9

The folk songs and street ballads which I have been considering were produced in order to communicate. We hear in them voices from the past, speaking in a popular idiom, with strength, passion, and, at times, humour. They are surely worth a place in schools, as human documents of historical value.

A vast amount of this material is available, some recently reprinted or recorded, more still waiting to be turned up in archives or taken down from living informants. In other words, there are opportunities for teachers and pupils to do their own research in this field. Even small events and small towns produced material which can be found in local newspapers, memoirs, libraries, and archive collections. Collecting from living informants is a different matter. While they often have excellent personal reminiscences and sometimes memories from the past which have been handed down by oral tradition, they are less likely to know songs. The effort of asking is nevertheless worthwhile, and even if songs are not found people's recollections are nearly always of some value.

These local sources illustrate and supplement national history, and sometimes modify it. Songs with local relevance often mention specific places, people, or events, and can connect with landscapes, buildings, or artefacts. For example, the opening of a canal might have been celebrated in song, depicted on a token, described in the press and, if not buildings, then the canal itself is still there to be seen. Songs can therefore be used to illuminate certain topics, or to provide a starting-point for investigating a local industry or event.

The extent to which songs are used will vary with the degree of interest of the teacher. A single song can be thrown in to arouse initial interest, to underline a point, or to make a memorable conclusion. Certain themes, studied over a period of time — transport, poverty, or crime, for example — could feature a number of songs, introduced at intervals.

The language of songs is often economical and memorable, with rhyme and tune helping. The illumination which a song gives has a good chance of being retained, even when it is heard in isolation. It is possible, of course, for songs to be used as essential landmarks in a teaching scheme. Keith Gregson, for example, Head of History at Brierton Comprehensive School, Hartlepool, has developed a Mode 3 CSE course consisting of a series of units each of which has a song as a central element. He believes that it is the human element in the songs 'which appeals to the below-average child much more than political history'. This is not merely a soft option, either. Gregson expects a detailed knowledge of the meaning and implications of the songs in his examinations.

Ideally, songs are sung, but by no means all teachers of history are confident singers. If they cannot bring themselves to have a go — and pupils are normally remarkably tolerant of the activities of 'sir' in this field — then recordings might be used. Some are commercially available; others might be made by interested friends or colleagues. Even the local folk-song club might be willing to help, if approached. In some cases groups of pupils in the school might be interested and proficient enough to be able to make recordings for class use. A history teacher could always approach a music colleague to ask for assistance in teaching a song or two.

The great strength of songs and ballads lies in their ability to express the views, reactions, and emotions of ordinary people, in a distinctive and memorable idiom. They are uniquely capable of giving the feel of history and of bringing the past to life.

7 *Folk music and drama*
Folk dance

ROBERT LEACH

Plate 10 The midsummer festival at Burford, Oxfordshire, has music, drama and dance as inseparable and complementary parts.

Music in the drama lesson needs no justification. Mime and movement to pieces such as Mussorgsky's *Night on the Bare Mountain* or *Pictures at an Exhibition* or Stravinsky's *Rite of Spring* are the rule in the drama room rather than the exception. And many teachers go beyond this, using records of sound effects, electronic music and so on as stimulus.

But the huge popular culture of the folk world still seems to have been tapped surprisingly little by drama teachers. This is a pity, as the wealth and variety of material makes it suitable for almost any taste. The natural closeness of much in folk song to the experience of most of our pupils means they find little difficulty in adjusting to the idiom — less difficulty often than in responding to Stravinsky or Mussorgsky.

Take, for instance, the 'Droylsden Wakes', recorded by Ewan MacColl on *Steam Whistle Ballads* (Topic 12T 104), and published in *The Penguin Book of English Folk Songs*, edited by Ralph Vaughan Williams and A.L. Lloyd (1959). Here is a dialogue song between a man and his wife, who argue in traditional fashion about who does the most work. But when the wife suggests she is being worked to death, the husband turns their common discontent outwards and suggests that 'we fight for our rights 'stead of fighting at home!' Let two pupils learn this song, dress up as the characters, and sing it, and its power will quickly be apparent. It is in fact an excellent way into much 'social' drama, being on one level purely comic but on another raising fundamental questions about husband—wife (mum—dad) relation-ships and the connection between home and work. An improvisation on these themes can be greatly enriched in both form and content by earlier work on the 'Droylsden Wakes'.

The song itself is almost certainly left over from some old Lancashire custom, and there are many such customs which are dramatic and which include song or music. It suggests what we know from other sources — that to the 'folk', drama and music are almost inseparable. The traditional mumming plays show this most clearly. Many of these are now published, and they are becoming recognised as excellent vehicles for acting in the first three or four years of the secondary school. The point to be made here is that nearly all these plays include song and dance. A good example is the 'Pace Egg Song', from the traditional *Pace Egg Play* performed every Easter in the streets of Midgley in Yorkshire; the song is sung by all the performers as they process in a circle at the end of the play. Folk actors are folk singers as well, and the one activity is as natural as the other.

This is seen even more clearly in other types of folk play. *Folk Plays*, edited by Robert Leach (Theatre Workshop Series, Harrap, 1978), includes both *The Plough Play*, which has four separate songs as well as a dance, and *The Sword Dance Play*, which has almost as much song as speech in addition to the sword dance itself. This play ends, significantly, with the instruction 'Then they dance and afterwards sing any popular songs.' Tunes for all the songs are printed with the texts in this collection, but performers are certainly under no obligation to use the given tunes. In the first instance, at least, it may be better to use any tunes the performers know which will fit the words, nursery-rhyme tunes, tunes of football songs, music-hall songs or hymn tunes — all are grist to the mill provided the pupils sing! The singing may really be only shouting, but it is still worth insisting on to convey the flavour of the folk play, and to suggest the inseparability of drama and song. The same is true of the music. Any sort of instrument — bells, combs with tissue paper, desk tops or upturned wastepaper baskets banged with rulers for drums — will do initially so long as there is some feeling of musical excitement. Moreover, many of our pupils will be shy of singing, and accompaniment even of the crudest sort will probably be a help to them. So it, too, is worth insisting on.

The folk play gives one sort of key to the use of folk music in drama. It uses an archetypal story — St George, the hero, challenged to mortal combat by the Bold Slasher or the Turkish Knight, a high theme which is set into a homely framework with characters such as Father Christmas and the comic devil Beelzebub:

> In comes I, old Beelzebub,
> And over my shoulder I carries my club,
> And in my hand my dripping pan —
> Now don't you think I'm a jolly old man?

At a deeper level, the folk play re-enacts the age-old theme of death and rebirth; it is a remnant of an ancient fertility rite. The manner in which this is carried out — the chivalric boasts of the champions echoed in the absurd and nonsensical boasts of the Doctor who is actually performing the magic of bringing life back to the dead hero — makes the folk play uniquely valuable for drama with young people, and suggests the extraordinary richness to be found within the folk tradition.

Folk songs and ballads are ideal raw material for acting. The old definition of a ballad — a song or poem that 'tells a story' — suggests the reason. The first and most important aspect of playmaking with young people is the narrative element, and the ballad or folk song supplies this in an exceptionally vivid and evocative form. The ballad deals in incident, it moves quickly by a technique somewhat akin to film montage, and it leaves enough unsaid to require the prospective playmaker to enter into it imaginatively.

It is worth suggesting that to introduce work on a specific song, playing a record of the song, and inviting pupils to join in with it, is more effective than a mere reading of the words would be. Folk music frequently has a peculiarly spontaneous 'feel' to it, which is at once accessible and atmospheric. The tunes of many songs are quite easy to pick up, and I would always encourage pupils to sing with the record at the second or third playing. Apart from being an enjoyable exercise in itself, this is a quick way for them to get under the story's skin, to experience at first hand what I have called its 'feel'. There is no doubt in my mind that the drama work is improved after an introduction which includes this kind of participation, and it also helps to make singing a natural activity in drama work.

A good example of this which I have often used with groups of pupils is 'The Devil and the Ploughman', sung by A.L. Lloyd on *A Selection from the Penguin Book of English Folk Songs* (Collector JGB 5001; now deleted, but see text and tune in *The Penguin Book of English Folk Songs*). Nothing could be simpler than joining in the whistled refrain after the second line of each verse and the final 'To my fal-de-ral little law-day'; the sense of fun which the song generates is swiftly conveyed. The song contains three clearly defined scenes for acting: first, the Devil, encouraged perhaps by the ploughman, takes the wife; second, the Devil reaches his 'front gate' where the thirteen imps are dancing in chains (a marvellous theatrical set-piece, this), and the wife beats them with her pattens; and third, the Devil returns the wife to the ploughman. This outline will do for a story, but obliquely in the song other issues are raised which pupils working at any depth dramatically will want to explore. For instance, when the Devil takes the wife, what is the attitude of the son? And what are the attitudes of the various characters when the Devil brings the wife back? How is the humorous ending translated into drama? These are specifically dramatic questions of the sort our pupils ought to be tackling, though they are left deliberately sketchy in the song.

There is also the problem of how to act the two journeys which a good dramatisation of this song will include. We are told that the Devil 'lugged her along like a pedlar's pack', he 'trudged' along, and, after the wife had assaulted the thirteen imps, the Devil 'bundled her up on his back amain'. The version which A.L. Lloyd uses in *The Penguin Book of English Folk Songs* is full of such dynamic language, challenging any actor to interpret the words originally. A journey is often a crucial element in drama and epic (we think of the *Odyssey*, *Peer Gynt*, *The Caucasian Chalk Circle* and many more), and here the pupil is forced to face it at an appropriate level. The fact that it is comic helps, though a hint of menace may also be there.

A song like this has many layers which can be explored by pupils, though of course for many pupils too much detail, too many problems set, will obscure the value of the work. Some groups, however, would want to take up a line like 'He'd a bad wife as many knew well' and invent a scene to explain the ploughman's desire to be rid of his wife and the fact that 'many knew well' that she was 'bad', a scene in which perhaps she publicly humiliates him. Similarly, a relationship between the Devil himself and the imps is implied by their use of the word 'father'. Perhaps this relationship forms an ironic contrast with the relationships within the human family, and here again a scene might be devised to illustrate this. A different approach to more detailed work might be through the making of masks and costumes, and there is scope for this, too, in 'The Devil and the Ploughman'.

There are plenty of other ballads and songs which provide this kind of open-ended opportunity. For a group who have an interest in crime — and many secondary pupils do — the folk ballads provide almost limitless openings. 'In Newry Town', recorded by the Critics' Group on *A Merry Progress to London*, is an excellent example, telling the story of a highwayman with — perhaps unusually — an attempt to explain his turning to crime in terms of his childhood and his love of a woman. It is in the convention of the gallows confession, so perhaps these reflections, which provide the song with its main point of reference, are merely conventional, yet that is no reason why they should not lead into a discussion among interested pupils as to what effect the hero's early experience and his relationship with his father and mother might have had on his subsequent turning to highway robbery. He is evidently a sort of latter-day Robin Hood:

> I never robbed no poor man yet,
> Nor any tradesman caused I to fret;

and his daring in going 'to Covent Garden to see the play' is somewhat akin to the daring shown by Robin Hood in his visits to Nottingham. At any rate, a dramatisation of this song contains a series of exciting possibilities. There are, first, the robberies themselves, followed each time by his 'carrying home the gold to my heart's delight'. The scene at Covent Garden playhouse, where he is chased and arrested, should provide plenty of scope, as well as the possibility of research into the eighteenth-century theatre or the eighteenth-century police force. And finally the funeral makes a suitably grand ending to the story, though whether it is a real funeral or merely a vision which passes before the highwayman's eyes as he stands under the gallows with the rope round his neck is best left for the performers themselves to decide.

A single record such as *A Merry Progress to London* (Argo ZDA 46) yields more than one dramatisable story. For instance, on this record there is also a version of 'Georgie Barnell', the story which provided the eighteenth century with one of its most popular plays, *The London Merchant*. There is also the gruesomely comic 'Jarvis the Coachman', the story of a group of revellers who hire a coach and make the coachman drive to the gibbet. There, he is forced to stand under it while they tie a rope round him and then haul him up and leave him there. 'I whooped, I bawled, I hollered', but the sight is so frightening that the horse of a would-be helper, a butcher, bolts, and it is not until a brickmaker, presumably going to work the next morning, passes that the unfortunate coachman is freed.

In a quite different vein, 'The Gresford Disaster', recorded by Ewan MacColl on *Steam Whistle Ballads* and published in *Poverty Knock*, edited by Roy Palmer (Cambridge University Press, 1974), tells the story of the negligence of the colliery manager, the fireman and the shotfirer, and how their combined inefficiency, or, in the words of the song, their 'criminal ways' led to the loss of about 250 men.

> The owners have sent some white lilies
> To pay for the colliers' lives,

the song says grimly. 'The Donibristle Moss Moran Disaster', recorded on *The Iron Muse* (Topic 12T 86), is another song of a pit disaster which I have used with many classes. It suggests a further line of work which is often worth pursuing. One of my classes, having worked on this song, were encouraged to write their own ballad, and the following is one fourteen-year-old boy's work:

Factory Disaster

> Every day we go to work
> With our packs on our backs.

I can't help thinking I'm flogging a dead horse
'Cause I'm very careless.

(Chorus) Oh, I'm sorry I'm alive,
            I wish I could flee
            Away from the work
            That's the death of me.
            I wish I'd worked at school
            And got a degree,
            Instead I'm just a fool
            In society.

Maybe I'm nervous, I don't know,
But I find it hard to cope.
Everything I do seems to work out wrong,
To me it's just a joke.
(Chorus) Oh, I'm sorry I'm alive, etc.

One day I was playing around
With a working lathe.
I pushed my mate accidentally to its grip,
Now the whole floor's crying.
(Chorus) Oh, I'm sorry I'm alive, etc.

I was the leader of the factory gang
And the organized fights.
I saw my best friend wrapped round a lathe,
Now I'm sorry I'm alive.
(Chorus) Oh, I'm sorry I'm alive, etc.

Everybody is screaming out loud
And I'm the centre of guilt.
Never before have I seen such a disaster,
It's the end of the world.
(Chorus) Oh, I'm sorry I'm alive, etc.

Interestingly, the boy who wrote this song made up his own tune for it and, though no singer in the conventional sense, recorded it on the tape recorder. He had become so immersed in it by then that he persuaded a group of his friends to join him in converting it into a radio play which they then recorded. It is worth noting in passing here that sometimes it is better to use the pupil's own work as the stimulus for drama, rather than a recorded ballad. The method of work may be the same, but the take-off point is — or appears to be — different.

More important, the work that this boy did shows how the tape recorder can often be a vital link between song and drama, particularly for a boy like this one, who was shy of drama, or for pupils unused to acting. A model to consider for use in the classroom is the radio ballad, a form devised by Ewan MacColl, Peggy Seeger and Charles Parker. Six of their radio ballads are now available on record, on the Decca Argo label, and among best of them is *Singing the Fishing*:

Fisherman: If you fish for the herring, they rule your life. They swim at night, you've got to be out there at night waiting for them to swim.

Singer: With our nets and gear we're faring —
Fisherman: Of course, it's a wonder, too, you see, you pick one of them little fish up, and it's vibrant with life, brrrr, like that.
Singer: On the wild and wasteful ocean —
Fisherman: Numbers — you realise it's only one of millions and millions and millions — when the little people swim up properly, they really do it.
Singer: It's there on the deep
                 That we harvest and reap
                 Our bread —
Fisherman: There's no lazy men when herring about.
Singer: As we hunt the bonny shoals of herring.
Fisherman: When you're doing well and catching fish, they talk to them all the time, 'Come on, spin up, my darlings, come on', and they absolutely cajole them into the nets.

Here we are at the very root of folk song, whose language and rhythms are the language and rhythms of vernacular speech. The juxtaposing of authentic speech — 'actuality' — and song which has grown from that speech is a hallmark of the radio ballad. Charles Parker defined the form in these terms in his notes to *The Ballad of John Axon*:

The radio ballad is a form of narrative documentary in which the story is told entirely in the words of the actual participants themselves as recorded in real life; in sound effects which are also recorded on the spot; and in songs which are based upon these recordings, and which utilize traditional or 'folk-song' modes of expression. By dispensing with conventional continuity devices of studio narrator, caption voice, dramatic vignette, and so on, the radio ballad makes something of the same demands on its audience as does the traditional ballad (insistently drawing the listener to participate imaginatively in the action by having, himself, to work and fill out the deliberately spare and open-ended form). While the radio form is much more complex, it retains that quality of authenticity, of concrete and direct utterance, which the ballad proper shares with the best of documentary.

An examination of *Singing the Fishing* amplifies this definition. It tells the story of the herring fishermen from the 1890s to the present day through the experiences of the men themselves, and particularly through the experiences of Sam Larner and Ronnie Balls. The use of the word 'story' here might at first listening to the work seem strange — there is no plot in the conventional sense, no dénouements, no characters even, except the people of the fishing communities, who simply talk of their own lives. Yet the piece is a story in a deeper sense than this, in that it unfolds in a logical way, one speech or song or section leading on from the last, till we find ourselves deep into the lives of these remarkable men.

The introductory section, some of which is quoted above, sets the tempo and the method. There is something about the sea, it suggests. Fishing acquires a hold over the fishermen. 'When we came on shore to find another job, somehow or other the sea always took you on', says one fisherman, and another, Sam Larner, says, 'When we left school, it was the sea or gaol for us.' Thrown into the situation thus (just as we are with the traditional ballad — for example, 'Oh, where have you been to, Lord Randal, my son?') we want to know why. What is there about the sea that makes it the only alternative to gaol for these men? The ballad takes us back to Sam Larner's boyhood in the 1890s, how he was the cabinboy who had to 'find his sea legs', 'watch and learn' and whose 'Uncle Jimmy used to flog me — then he'd cry.' 'Real old bulldog breed, they were', he tells us; 'they didn't care for nothing, neither God nor man, they didn't.' When he left home, he experienced 'a dread', and out at sea, 'when she began to lift, you began to think of mother at home then'.

Sam Larner's youth was tough but good. It is picked out through the subtle selection of telling detail which gives us a rare insight into the life of the man and, through him, other fishermen. When he slept on duty, they'd chuck a bucket of cold water over him. When he returned to shore, with the money from the voyage in his pocket, he went to South Shields and there visited the playhouse to see a piece entitled *The Wages of Sin*. The title is explained to Sam when the hero enters near the end of the play and says, ' "The wages of sin is death" — and he shot 'im, he shot 'im in the last act.' As Sam grows to manhood and becomes a deckhand on the *Snowflake*, we suddenly hear him burst into song:

> Oh, sailing over the Dogger Bank,
> Wasn't it a treat . . .

And this points to the other ingredient of the radio ballad — the use of song. It is introduced even while the BBC announcer is telling us what the programme is. As his dry voice soberly reads the credits, he is interrupted by the sprightly voice of the old man, Sam Larner, singing with gaiety and energy:

> Up jumped the herring, the king of the sea,
> Said he to the skipper, 'Look under your lee',
> Singing, windy old weather, boys,
> Stormy old weather, boys,
> When the wind blows, we'll all go together.

Apart from amusingly puncturing the bubble of the BBC's gravity, this suggests the absolute centrality of music and song in the radio ballad. The songs in this first section bind together the fragmentary utterances of the fishermen, giving them artistic unity and a new kind of significance. There is the harsh simplicity of the song which accompanies Sam Larner's first experiences of the sea, heightening the effect of what he is telling by its pinpointing of the reality of his situation — keep your stove clean, peel the spuds, scrub the table. The language of this song is deceptively ordinary (notice the single-syllable concreteness of 'keep', 'stove', 'clean', 'peel', 'spuds', etc.); it has the kind of spareness we associate on the one hand with the old ballads and on the other hand with orders given to a newcomer to a job. Furthermore, in a phrase such as 'the old slop bucket and the frying pan', Ewan MacColl has been able to use a rhythm which is at once appealing and poetically and musically interesting.

The next song, 'The Shoals of Herring', has an air of nostalgia which captures Sam Larner's feelings about his early manhood; but at the same time it contains a potential excitement which carries the hope of good times ahead, and promise of youth which will be fulfilled when they catch the shoals of herring. And indeed this is precisely what does happen, for almost as soon as Sam Larner became a deckhand, the steam drifters were introduced — 'the steam drifter . . . the loveliest ship for the job that ever was built'. The years between 1899 and the First World War were, we are told, 'a bonanza, a gold rush'. The men were 'masters of the sea' and the herring fleet blossomed as never before.

And never since, for the story goes on to tell of the hard times between the wars. Sam Larner's herring, which jumped up at the beginning of the ballad, now has a different cry:

> Up jumped the herring, the king of the sea,
> And he sang out, 'Old skipper, now you can't sell me.'
>
> Up jumped the herring, the king of the shoal,
> And he cried, 'You'd do better to be on the dole!'
> In this windy old weather.
>
> Up jumped the herring, all broken and spent,
> And he cried, 'Drifting's finished, so who'll pay the rent?'
> In this windy old weather,
> Stormy old weather.
>
> Up jumped the herring right under our lee,
> And he cried, 'Skipper, dump me right back in the sea.'
> In this windy old weather,
> Stormy old weather,
> When the fleet's scrapped, we'll all rot together.

Notice the use of the traditional device of cumulation — each verse adds another line to the chorus. But when we reach the last line, it has been unexpectedly changed to a pungent and bitter comment. During the Second World War, when the herring-fishing industry was needed again, the import of the song changes again:

> Up jumped the herring, and he looked to the shore,
> And he cried, 'There's a war on, they need us once more.'
> In this windy old weather,
> Stormy old weather,
> When the wind blows, we'll all pull together.

And so we are brought to today, when the fishing fleet is guided by technology, particularly the depth sounder, which can find the fish far more easily than ever was possible in the old days: 'If you're playing blind man's buff, it's like lifting up the handkerchief.' And the theme song for this third section has a jaunty purposefulness:

With our diesel engines, nylon nets,
RT and echo-sounding sets,
With a crew of ten to toil and sweat,
We're away to fish for the herring-o.

It is only after we have followed the changing fortunes of the herring fishermen through seventy years that we can reach any valid understanding of the hold the sea has on them, why it is the only alternative to gaol for them. The understanding is tentative, not dogmatic: man is a hunter, consequently he fishes; once you have sailed the sea, 'the things ashore don't seem big enough to worry about'. The last song sums up something of the fisherman's outlook and experience in a sombre chorus:

Our ships are small and the sea is deep,
And many a fisherman lies asleep
In the salt sea water.

But still there's a hungry world to feed,
So we go where the shoals of herring breed
In the salt sea water.

This brief summary of *Singing the Fishing* does scant justice to the depth and integrity of its texture. The speech patterns of the fishermen themselves, for instance, the inflection, accent, rhythm and control of imagery could never come out on the printed page: the ballad must be listened to with an ear ready for the richness of vernacular speech. The significance of *Singing the Fishing* is that it has grown from a team who have immersed themselves in the folk tradition and used it to create a new dramatic form.

Ewan MacColl, whose extensive work in theatre and radio as well as in the world of folk song led him towards this form of creation, wrote the songs quoted here. Obviously he is a highly gifted artist as well as an experienced writer of plays and songs. Yet he would be the last person to suggest that the making of songs in the folk tradition is an esoteric activity, beyond the scope of our pupils. The 'Factory Disaster', quoted earlier in this chapter, suggests precisely the opposite, and we know that primary-school children are steeped in songs, rhymes, rituals and catches which are in one sense the bedrock of our folk tradition. What we have to do is to nourish that tradition and give it the opportunity to continue. The fact that so many children who are not apparently artistically gifted can write poetry, particularly free verse, so convincingly, suggests that there is no good reason why they should not write songs in a folk idiom.

The storm sequence from *Singing the Fishing* demonstrates that effectiveness of expression is not incompatible with simplicity. The storm is created by a simple montage effect, cutting between song, speech and sound effect. The basic sound effect used is the voice of the auctioneer selling off the fish on the quay, an effect earlier introduced to suggest the prosperity of the good fishing times and used again later when the men come home and can see the profits of their work. In this sequence, however, the auctioneer's urgent tone conjures up both the lashing of the rain and the fear of the men. Set against his tense gabble is the prediction of the storm – the shipping forecast from the BBC and an old saying from Sam Larner:

> Quick rise after low
> Indicates the stronger blow.

The speeches describing being at sea in a storm are serious, engaged but not excited, estranging in the Brechtian sense, and they are counterpointed by the 'Beaufort Scale' song, the performance of which demonstrates the men's growing terror:

> Gale Force nine, Gale Force nine,
> Fighting for the nets and lines,
> Water black and white and gray,
> Now the air is full of spray.
> Gale Force ten in the Beaufort Scale,
> Now it blows a living gale.
> Force eleven, Force eleven,
> Close your eyes and pray to heaven.

The song is built on the same principle as 'Green Grow the Rushes-o' ('I'll sing you one, O') or 'Old Joe Braddlum' ('Number one, number one, Now my song has just begun'), and these songs are models which are accessible to every pupil.

There are of course many songs about the sea, and in this radio ballad Ewan MacColl was able to lean on our immediate associations with sea shanties, songs of lovers who went over the sea, songs of pirates and sea fights. Yet, as we now know, practically every human activity has a good body of songs, and new ones can be made to fit exactly what seems appropriate in the making of a radio ballad or other drama using the folk tradition. It is often a good idea with young people who begin to write songs to start with a known tune and make up words to fit it. There is no need to use rhyme, though this may come later. The making up of tunes – usually variants of known tunes, at first – can come later, too. Making up the words can sometimes present the greatest problems, but here Ewan MacColl's practice of using actual speech as a base to work from is extremely valuable. If the subject of the song can be recorded, as the fishermen were recorded by the makers of *Singing the Fishing*, it is likely that his speech will be rich enough to provide much of the material, with some adaptation.

An example of such songmaking for dramatic purposes will show how this can work. A play I was recently involved in making was a documentary drama concerning the closure of the Birmingham Fairs in 1875. It was called *Fair Play* and deliberately used a good deal of folk material, since it seemed to us that this reflected best the fair as a popular recreation. Song and music formed a basic structuring device, binding the various elements of the play somewhat in the manner of the radio ballads, though because we were using the stage, a visual medium, rather than the radio, there were differences.

When the *Fair Play* audience arrived in the foyer, they were met by a living fair, stalls set up and manned by the young actors themselves. Among the gingerbread and toy stalls, the boxing booth, the beggars and thimble-riggers, were ballad-sellers, one with ballads pasted on the wall for sale, and one walking about with ballads

Plan of theatre for *Fair Play*

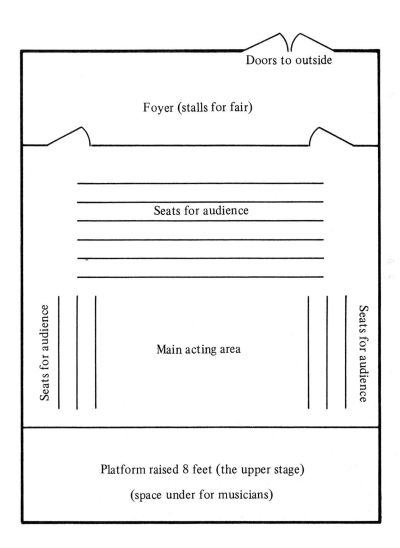

Doors to outside

Foyer (stalls for fair)

Seats for audience

Seats for audience

Seats for audience

Main acting area

Platform raised 8 feet (the upper stage)

(space under for musicians)

stuck on a placard board and in his hat. Amid the cacophony of the show people shouting their wares, these sang — or shouted — the ballads they were hawking. Their presence and their activity was authenticated by the accounts of the Birmingham Fairs of the nineteenth century we had unearthed in our researches. At this point in the evening, the theatre doors were locked: the audience had to experience the fair whose closure was the subject of the play.

Finally, at a minute or two after the advertised curtain-up time, the doors were opened and a barker appeared, exhorting the crowds to roll up to the theatre booth to see *The Brave Sailor's Bride*. The audience moved into the theatre and the show proper began with a ten-minute melodrama, a piece that was actually performed at the Birmingham Fair of 1874. At the end of this, the first song was introduced and became a theme song running through the play. It was slightly adapted from the song 'The Rawtenstall Annual Fair', recorded by the Oldham Tinkers on *Deep Lancashire* (Topic 12T 188):

> Down behind the gasworks, down in Birmingham —
> That's a little town in Warwickshire —
> Last Saturday night, me and the lads,
> Ooh, our kid, we had some right good cheer:
> There were ice cream, switchbacks, coconuts and waxworks,
> Figure eights and roundabouts,
> Weren't we all delighted when we heard the showman shout:
>
> 'Roll up, roll up, come and see the fat girl,
> Forty stone of loveliness and every bit her own';
> Ooh, she were a big 'un, with accent on the big,
> And all the fellers with walking sticks kept giving her a dig.
> She were a great big lassie as didn't know her chassis
> Were blown up with air, I do declare.
> Well, everything were champion until some silly clown
> Stabbed 'er with a pin. Said the showman with a frown:
> 'All hands to the pump, lads, me vessel's going down!'
> At the Birmingham Annual Fair.
>
> 'Roll up, roll up, see the 'ouse of Myst'ry,
> Ladies pay a tanner to be tickled in the dark.'
> In went the lads, just for a peep,
> The showman pulled a lever and we landed in a heap;
> Down he shot 'em, right to the bottom,
> Frills and bows for everyone to see,
> There were shouting, screaming, everything were rife,
> I saw some funny things I'd never seen in all me life;
> I even saw some things I'd never seen upon me wife;
> At the Birmingham Annual Fair.
>
> 'Roll up, roll up, come and see the mermaid,
> See the lovely lady, half a woman, half a fish.'
> In went the lads, to show it wasn't swank,
> When little Tommy 'Iggins put some whisky in the tank;
> Well, she got frisky, swimming in the whisky,

And when she come up for air,
She bowed to the audience, gave her tail a swish,
Her tail it come off and she really looked delish,
She says, 'What do you want, lads, a bit o' meat or fish?'
At the Birmingham Annual Fair.

The song was illustrated with actions. The first introductory verse was sung as a solo. At the end of it, 'Roll up, roll up, come and see the fat girl' was sung straight to the audience by the whole cast, who entered at this point. The fat girl was carried in by two boys, and at the appropriate moment her balloons were popped with a pin carried by one of the actors. The showman's line — 'All hands to the pump, lads, me vessel's going down' — was sung solo by the showman, and everyone joined in again on the last line. For the next verse, the lights were dimmed and the action mimed with squeals and giggles. The third verse was similarly mimed, in green 'underwater' light this time. The mermaid was wheeled in on a trolley and Tommy Higgins gave her a swig out of a whisky bottle.

At the end of the song, the cast froze and the curtains were drawn back on an upper stage (where the melodrama had been performed) to reveal the council chamber. Three of the crowd below read out petitions which were handed up to the Mayor above. After the third petitioner had finished, the crowd sang, slowly and quietly:

Down behind the gasworks, down in Birmingham —
That's a little town in Warwickshire —
Last Saturday night, me and the lads,
Ooh, our kid, we had some right good cheer.

The tune then continued through the verse on penny-whistle and guitar, under the Mayor's opening speech:

Mayor (*music continues*): Motion — that the Markets and Fairs committee be, and they are hereby, instructed not to let in future any land belonging to the Corporation for the purposes of shows or exhibitions of any kind whatsoever at the Whitsuntide or Michaelmas Fairs or permit or suffer any of the public streets or thoroughfares within the borough to be used or occupied at such fairs for the same or similar purposes. (*Music stops.*) Alderman Osborne to move.

At the end of Alderman Osborne's speech, during which the whole cast had been a silent audience on the main stage area below, a further verse of the 'Annual Fair' theme song was sung and mimed.

The use of music and song as an integral part of the play, illustrating and commenting on the action on the one hand and binding its disparate elements together structurally on the other, will be apparent from this description. It became even more central in the middle section of the play dealing with the showmen themselves. It seemed to us that an important consequence of closing a fair, as the Birmingham

City Council had done in 1875, was the effect this action would have on the lives of the showmen. Because of this we had quite a long section in the play in which we attempted to get underneath the gaudy candy floss of the showmen's public lives to discover the other, private side, and give that some expression. The structure of this section of the play was deliberately schematic and depended on the use of song. It worked like this:

Scene	Song	Subject of scene
1	Song 1 ('Come all you young people')	The fair begins
2	Showmen's patter	
3	Song 2 ('Come all you bold showmen')	The showman's job
4	Song 3 ('Oh dear, what can the matter be?') } Song 4 ('Wallflowers') }	The showman's childhood
5	Song 2 ('Come all you bold showmen')	The showmen as people
6	Mountebank's patter	
7	Song 1 ('Come all you young people')	The end of the fair

Song 1 in this scheme was from a nineteenth-century broadside. We had to invent a couple of verses for it so that it fitted exactly what we wanted, but basically it captured precisely the feeling we wished to convey of the beginning of the fair:

> Come all you young people, wherever you be,
> And give your attention and listen to me.
> The song that I sing, oh, the truth you shall hear,
> All the fun and diversion of this famous fair.

> With great preparation this fair is begun,
> For most of the people like seeing the fun.
> Some on foot, some on horse, some in chaise will repair,
> Some loading in wagons to ride to the fair.

> They'll tipple like fishes and prattle like parrots,
> And gobble down cakes like a sow would do carrots,
> While some with their sausages here will regale;
> Give me beef and ham and a pot of good ale.

> There's the big and the little, the lusty and tall,
> Some with plenty of money, some got none at all;
> Some diverting of others with a number of rigs,
> Some dancing to fiddles and squealing like pigs.

> . . .

This song was sung as a solo, and during it people entered the stage, with lines indicating various reactions to the beginning of the fair. For instance, two women entered thus:

1st Woman: As I was coming up the Bull Ring this morning, I see many of the war chariots that the travelling people that come to the fair live in.

2nd Woman: Women sucking short clay pipes peer through the windows of their caravans as they jolt slowly towards their destination.

These two lines were culled from contemporary newspaper accounts, very slightly adapted. The bigger shows in the fair advertised in the press, so early in the scene we used one such advertisement:

Man: Day's Crystal Palace Menagerie will arrive this day from Walsall, and will march in procession through the principal streets en route to their well-known ground, Moat Row, facing Bromsgrove Street.

And, near the end of the scene:

Man: Day's Crystal Palace Menagerie has arrived and will exhibit in Moat Row during the fair. Its latest arrivals are the crying crocodiles, monster blue and red gorilla, two Indian elephants landed in Liverpool on Monday last, the baby elephant (the smallest one in Europe), performing lions, etcetera, making it the best collection travelling. Admission — ladies and gentlemen, one shilling; working classes, sixpence.

By the end of the introductory song, the whole cast was on stage and they mimed the alehouse scene during the last two verses, while the lights dimmed down:

> The alehouse is crowded, you can scarcely get in,
> Some calling for beer, some for cider and gin;
> The landlord laughs in his sleeve and his shoulders he shrugs:
> He sells off his bad beer in short-measured mugs.

> So now to conclude the diversion and fun,
> All the people are crowding and the fair has begun;
> And the shouts and the patter ring out on the air,
> And we're in the middle of Birmingham Fair.

The last of these two verses was composed by us. We needed to focus closely on the subject of our play, and the broadside song's text understandably gave us no opportunity to do this. So we made a verse up for ourselves. At the end of the song, the stage was in blackout, through which came the showman's patter:

1st Patterer: Rollo-bowlo-pitch,
Three shies a penny at your old Aunt Sally
For a coconut or a good cigar,
For a good cigar or a coconut,
Come rollo-bowlo-pitch.

2nd Patterer: Tuppence the basin. All English pudding basin for anybody's beefsteak and kidney pudding; come — tuppence, or I'll smash it, tuppence or I smash it. What, you won't pay tuppence? You shan't have it cheaper. The all-English pudding basin as used in our Royal Queen Victoria's kitchen at Windsor

Palace. Windsor! Who says tuppence? Well, if you won't, then . . . (*Sound effect – SMASH.*)

3rd Patterer (*a thin voice*): 'Alf a pint, penny winks!

4th Patterer: Walk up, walk up, ladies and gentlemen. Just a-going to begin. Only one penny to the gallery. So be in time. Walk up, walk up.

These lines, all taken from genuine sources, were spoken in darkness. When the lights came up again, we went straight into the scene about the showman's job:

1st Singer: Come all you bold showmen who live by the fairground,
Come listen, I'll tell you of the travelling life,
For fair lights are shining and barkers are shouting,
And fun and diversion are everywhere rife.

1st Speaker (*music continues*): Such plausible knaves.

2nd Speaker: A picturesque army of Bohemians who seem to spring up in our streets with their tents and shows in a single night and stay among us for two or three days until they vanish.

3rd Speaker: Many persons look upon van-dwellers and showmen quite as the 'rogues and vagabonds' they were dubbed in earlier days, and treat them accordingly.

2nd Singer: There's some people say that we're all rogues and vagabonds,
That we are a nuisance and must be moved on;
We're gypsies and tinkers, we're vagrants and beggars –

1st Speaker: Such plausible knaves.

2nd Singer: But we live to please you, and we please you to live.

The song 'Come all you bold showmen' was wholly composed by the group performing the play. The necessity to make our own song arose partly at least because we could not find an extant song which attempted to say anything about life from the showman's point of view. Such a song may exist, but if so we never found it. If we were going to structure the scene by the use of music, this section clearly demanded a song. So we took a known and appropriate tune, 'Spencer the Rover' (published in *Love Is Pleasing*, edited by Roy Palmer, (Cambridge University Press, 1974)), and fitted words to it. It will be seen from the second verse quoted above that we did not always rhyme the verses. I do not think that this particularly matters. One of the great advantages of using folk music as far as the playmaker is concerned is that, probably more than any other kind of music, folk music carries the words in such a way that they can be heard and understood quite easily. The words, in fact, are as important in this idiom as the music, and provided they are sung clearly the lack of rhyme does not greatly matter. Besides, young people often find rhyming extremely difficult, and I have seen promising work turned into rubbish by the writer's attempts to rhyme.

During this section of the play, the actors were putting up their various booths, turning to speak to the audience whenever they had a line. It was this section of the play, which aimed to express the showman's life view and experience, that required detailed and laborious research. This was vital, however, because it was from the results of the research that the songs were built up. (For a full discussion of this subject, see Robert Leach, *How to Make a Documentary Play* (Blackie, 1975).) A first and obvious source for material of relevance was the press of the time. Luckily, our public library had microfilm copies of local newspapers going back beyond 1850, and this provided much useful material of all sorts – the councillors' speeches, for instance, were reported verbatim; the advertisements and descriptions were usable, only rarely needing adaptation; and of course the correspondence columns provided a wide variety of contemporary views. Ransacking the newspapers was done by a group of about ten or a dozen and began some months before the date of the production. We found the best way to do this was to take a cassette tape recorder to the library and simply to read the relevant article aloud onto tape. This had to be done very quietly so that other library users were not disturbed, but copying down enormous articles, particularly from microfilm, was daunting to say the least. Besides, when the cassette was played back, the whole group could listen to it at once. Writers of the period also provided useful source material. We used, for instance, Mayhew's interviews with mid nineteenth-century street entertainers in *London Labour and the London Poor* (1851; for a more recent edition, see a selection, *Mayhew's London*, ed. Peter Quennell (Spring Books, 1969)), 'Lord' George Sanger's *Seventy Years a Showman* (1926; reprinted by MacGibbon and Kee, 1966), Charles Dickens, and many others. They were useful, too, as a check against our most interesting and probably most educationally valuable research activity. This was the interviewing of showmen themselves (and, incidently, fair-goers). Through the local Showmen's Guild, we traced a number of old showmen who were happy to talk about their lives, and give their opinions:

I think anyone that closes a fair, they're not only closing a fair, they're stopping a lot of people from getting a living, which is their heritages and their birthright.

When we compared the attitudes of the modern showman with those of his grand-fathers or great-grandfathers of a hundred years ago, we found an extraordinary similarity. Here is a modern showman speaking on tape:

They're not only sacrificing somebody's livelihood and birthright, but they're giving the people nothing. The people must have enjoyment.

Compare this with the lisping Mr Sleary's comments in *Hard Times* by Charles Dickens:

Thquire, thake handth, firtht and latht! Don't be croth with uth poor vagabondth. People mutht be amuthed. They can't be alwayth a learning, nor yet they can't be alwayth a working, they an't made for it. You *mutht* have uth, Thquire. Do the withe thing and the kind thing, too, and make the betht of uth – not the wortht!

It was during one of our taped interviews that a showman said:

We are pleased to live and we live to please. You see there's a lot in that, and I mean it's sense, there's nothing silly about it. We get our living by pleasing people and if we don't please 'em, we don't get a living.

A strikingly expressed thought, and one which the showman in question, Jake Messham, had obviously considered deeply. Consequently, it finds its way into our song quoted earlier: 'But we live to please you, and we please you to live.' It is from the speech of the people involved that the song grows. A boy who had worked as a gaff lad on the dodgems described in great detail how the dodgem booth was set up:

Each plate weighs about over a hundredweight, and there were sixty of them to fix. We carried them in pairs, one on each side. The job was easy to start with 'cause we started near the tyre and worked outwards. Towards the end your forearms were aching and your shirt was soaked with sweat . . .

This found its way into a verse of the song:

> Your shirt's soaked with sweat and your forearms are aching,
> You're slaving to get your gaff fitted up right . . .

Later in the same interview, the boy remarked:

I used to help put up other stalls, especially the easy ones like the coconut shies and rifle ranges.

Jake Messham said:

If you go back and you think, well, who was they? – well, we had some of the brains of the country in show business – electrical engineering – because they had to learn it the hard way, and when they'd got it they had to mend it themselves.

The people we interviewed, like those interviewed by Henry Mayhew and his assistants over a century earlier, all stressed the need for the showman to be able to turn his hand to anything. This is expressed in the song, using as far as possible the words of the interviewees:

> I've played parts at mumming, I've shown off my freak shows,
> I've put up a coconut shy on the side;
> I've mended the gallopers and I've worked swings and roundabouts,
> And still I'm the showman who's known far and wide.

To return to the making of *Fair Play*, we found that once the showman being interviewed had talked about his job, he began to talk about himself, usually includ-

ing details of his childhood. Consequently, this was how we developed the play.
The section was introduced by a group of children running in, singing 'Oh dear,
what can the matter be?' They then faded into the background, playing a singing
game, 'Wallflowers', while the showmen spoke of their experiences of childhood
from the main stage area where their booths were. At the end of the sequence, the
children ran out singing:

> Off to the dungeons you must go,
> You must go, you must go,
> Off to the dungeons you must go,
> My fair lady!

The childhood experiences led naturally to the adult experiences of the showmen,
and this was signalled by a return to the home-made song, 'Come all you bold showmen'. As the earlier section using this song had been begun by the use of the barker's
patter, so this section was ended now by the appearance of a mountebank selling a
quack remedy to the audience – his speech we found verbatim in a newspaper contemporary with the closure. This made a convenient bridge to the last section, the
end of the fair. The first speech in this section was again from a contemporary newspaper, the second from an interview about the Stratford Mop Fair with a Stratford
policeman. The song, sung by the soloist who had sung 'Come all you young people',
is the true ending of the broadside; its mention of the 'new song . . . bought at the
fair' suggests the important place song had in the nineteenth-century fairground,
and helped to justify (if justification were needed) our use of the idiom:

Woman: Now – late at night – groups are dotting the usually quiet streets, strolling
homeward in the clear moonlight, sated with the hum of drums and the noisy
verbosity of clamorous showmen shouting their 'walk-ups'.

Singer: When the fair it is over then homeward they throng,
And the lads and the lasses they trip it along.
Men, wives, likewise children then homewards repair
And read the new song that they bought at the fair.

Policeman: It was a happy do, but it usually ended up with the cells all full.

Singer: So now to conclude the diversion and fun,
Which may be revived when the next fair doth come,
Some I doubt will repent they took no better care,
For in less than nine months they'll remember the fair.

This description of *Fair Play* gives some idea of how music can be an integral
part of a full-length, home-made, documentary play. The method, obviously owing
much to Ewan MacColl's method in creating the Radio Ballads, is certainly accessible to teachers and pupils. At its lowest level it is a sort of dramatic collage. But
more radically I would argue that MacColl has developed an artistic form which is
at once relevant to the needs of many of our pupils and rooted in the folk tradition.

Its particular significance is that it uses that tradition creatively rather than passively and thus suggests its real vitality.

A complete documentary of the kind described here is a major undertaking — the school play, perhaps, or a large project for integrated studies. The exercise is undoubtedly tremendously exciting and a particularly valuable way for pupils to become involved in what they are doing. A central feature of the work is the use of folk song for the reasons adduced earlier, and it is worth noticing that in many documentaries made in recent years, such as those by the company of the Victoria Theatre, Stoke-on-Trent, folk song has been a noteworthy element. Published scripts which are worth looking at in the school context include Peter Cheseman's Stoke documentary, *The Knotty* (Methuen, 1970), Alan Plater's *Close the Coalhouse Door* (Methuen, 1969), John Hipkin's *The Massacre of Peterloo* (Heinemann Educational, 1968), Robert Leach's *The Wellesbourne Tree* (Blackie, 1975), and Jon Raven and Malcolm Totten's *The Nailmakers* (published by The Black Country Society, 1975).

Folk music and folk song can thus be used in drama in a wide variety of ways, from the single-lesson dramatisation of a short song to the complex integration of a big documentary play. Sometimes, it may be merely a starting-point. Pupils might listen to a song, then make up a different adventure involving the same central character. Or they might listen to an old song which they could then rework into a modern idiom. The work might be used primarily as an exercise in making masks or costumes, or it might provide opportunities for exploring ideas through mime and movement. At one end, the work shades off into dance, at the other into English, both of which areas are covered in other chapters of this book.

I believe the most important notion we gain from using folk song in drama is the inseparability of singing and acting. The mumming play shows us their unity in the folk tradition, and if that is not enough let us look at the primary-school playground:

All (as they circle one girl who sits on the ground):
  Poor Mary sits a-weeping,
  A-weeping, a-weeping,
  Poor Mary sits a-weeping
  On a bright summer's day.

  Oh, Mary, what you weeping for,
  What you weeping for, what you weeping for,
  Oh, Mary, what you weeping for
  On a bright summer's day?

Girl in centre: I'm weeping for my true love,
  My true love, my true love,
  I'm weeping for my true love
  On a bright summer's day.

All: Stand up and choose your true love,
  Your true love, your true love,
  Stand up and choose your true love
  On a bright summer's day.

(*Girl in centre stands, points to one girl, shouts, 'You!' These two now break out of the circle, as the other girls sing*):

All: They've gone to get married,
         Get married, get married,
         They've gone to get married
         On a bright summer's day.

(*The other two return to outside the circle.*)

The Two: Open the gates and let us in.
All: Not before you bow and kiss.
1st Girl: Here's a bow (*bows*), and here's a kiss (*kisses*),
The Two: Open the gates and let us in.

(*The circle breaks to let them in. The first girl joins the circle, the second sits in the middle — she is now poor Mary, and the game begins again.*)

FOLK DANCE

Folk dancing has unfortunately acquired a prettified, whimsical image which bears no relation to what it actually is but which understandably repels teenagers. Like most prejudices, this one springs from ignorance, and a simple way of breaking the prejudice down is to find something out about the subject. For instance, Hugh Rippon's *Discovering English Folk Dance* (Shire Publications, 1975) is simple, direct and informative. If the vitality of the folk dance is to be enjoyed by young people, however, it may still be necessary to disguise it as drama or physical education or some other subject.

One good way of introducing folk dance is to invite a good Morris side to perform in the school playground, and let the pupils watch. They will soon realise how demanding, and how far from prettified, it is. Another method is to use skipping games, round games, even games like conkers, to introduce the idea of dance. This can be related to drama games, in which the main point is concentration and self-consciousness is minimised. A third way is to begin from simple rituals and build these up through the use of masks and movement to the point where dance is introduced. A combination of these approaches is probably best with reluctant groups.

The Sword Dance is of course basically ritualistic (Plate 11). Work on it can begin with the formation of the 'lock' — a piece of communal legerdemain which is bound to fascinate young secondary pupils — and continue with the mock decapitation of the person in the centre of the circle. Complications of dance can be introduced at the same time as appropriate speech from the *Sword Dance Play*, so that learning is painless and the enjoyment is increased.

A vital characteristic of folk dance is its energy. The Broom Dance, from E.M. Leather's *Folklore of Herefordshire* (1912; reprinted by EP Publishing, 1970), is a good example of a noisy, exhausting dance, using brooms to jump and hop round, to bang on the floor and to leap over. Since it requires more energy than skill, and does not require a partner or even a particular formation, it may be a good dance to start this type of work with. In a surprisingly short time, a line of broom dancers, impressive to watch and enjoyable to be part of, will be able to display their skill.

The traditional Morris dance also required energy and stamina. The dancers leap high, whack each other's sticks and stamp vigorously on the ground (Plate 12). Sticks are better than handkerchiefs to start with, being more exciting to use, and the addition of costume — flowery hats, bells on the knees, and so on — helps some young people to enjoy these dances, though for others they may prove an embarrassment. Most important with Morris dancing for teenagers is not that they execute intricate steps with total accuracy but that they enter the spirit of the dance with gusto. There is no reason why they should not invent their own dance figures if this keeps them going, and for those who want to improve their technique an after-school club may be the answer.

A form of Morris dance which some teenagers will take to is the Nutters Dance from Bacup, Lancashire (Plate 13). (The name is certain to appeal!) Here the dancers beat the rhythm with discs of wood fastened to the hands and knees. Again, it is not necessary for a class to acquire the actual steps which the Britannia Coconut Dancers use — let them process round the hall trying to keep time with their 'nuts' while walking, then running, then skipping. Then introduce a figure of eight and more complicated figures. Always keep introducing new variations so that the interest is kept and skill developed without fuss.

Rather like the Nutters Dance, perhaps, is clog dancing, where the clogs keep the rhythm. Some pupils at least will probably be interested in acquiring skills here, since clog dancing is initially an individual dance. Nevertheless, teams of clog dancers are often more impressive than individuals, and the basic steps are quite easy to learn.

Finally, an example of more dramatic dance is the Horn Dance from Abbots Bromley in Staffordshire (Plate 14). Here the dancers dance a figure of eight and then form into two lines to charge each other with their antlers. At the third change, the lines pass through each other and the figure is repeated.

It is unlikely that a school will have six or eight sets of antlers, and this suggests a related but important adjunct to any folk dancing done in secondary schools. Let the pupils make their own imitation antlers out of papier-mâché and chicken-wire or out of wood. This link with art and craft is useful, and certainly adds to the experience of the dance work. Many folk-dance teams include a hobby horse or a dragon or an 'old tup'. These can also be made by the pupils. Add, too, a fool with a pig's bladder (a balloon on a stick is a simple way of creating this, but pupils will not accept this for long and will think of better ways of making it.)

In all this, the emphasis is on doing, on active participation which throws the whole self into the activity. Whether the music is made by a gramophone record or — better — by one or more pupils on guitar or comb-and-paper or ruler and dustbin lid, the point is primarily to experience the exhilaration of the folk dance.

The work is probably most successful, in the early stages at least, when carried on in short courses, say, three or four consecutive forty-minute drama or physical education lessons, when a great deal of energy will be expended before the particular dance is dropped, and more usual work taken up again. But come back to folk dancing half a term later so that it acquires a natural place in the syllabus, and gradually build up a repertoire. The after-school club, continuing all the time and giving displays frequently, keeps folk dance present in the minds of pupils. It helps, too, in the creation of an atmosphere in the school sympathetic to folk dancing, and such an atmosphere is three-quarters of the battle against ignorance. Once it is accepted that everybody does folk dance, boys as well as girls, just as it is accepted that everybody does P.E. or drama or writes poetry or does woodwork, then we are well on the way to breaking through old prejudices.

I have suggested that the first appeal of folk dance is its vitality. This should not be taken to mean, however, that there is no skill involved. Good Morris dancing or clog dancing, for instance, requires a great deal of practice in often intricate steps and a high degree of physical control. The good dancer is at least as skilful in his way as the singer is in his, and pupils should certainly be encouraged to develop their skill. The greater a dancer's mastery in his art, the more he is able to express and the richer his audience's response. Moreover, a good dancer can explore solo jigs, complex Morrises and the whole area of country dancing which has not been touched on here. Folk dancing offers a unique kind of physical exhilaration, while demanding great control and a surprising degree of stamina.

Note

This article deliberately sets out general ideas and gives no references to specific steps, figures, etc. The interested reader is referred in the first place to:

F. Kidson and M. Neal, *English Folk Song and Dance*, Cambridge University Press, 1915; reprinted EP Publishing, 1972

R. Nettel, *Folk-Dancing*, Arco Publications, 1962

C. Sharp, *The Morris Book*, 5 parts, Novello, 1907—14; reprinted EP Publishing, 1973

The Country Dance Book, 6 parts, Novello, 1902—22; reprinted EP Publishing, 1972

The Sword Dances of Northern England, Novello, 1911—13.

Plate 11 The climax of the Grenoside Sword Dance.

Plate 12 A Morris dance with sticks, Headington Quarry, Oxfordshire.

Plate 13 The Nutters Dance, Bacup, Lancashire.

Plate 14 The Horn Dance, Abbots Bromley, Staffordshire.

8 *Singing style and accompaniment*

SANDRA KERR

'Traditional music, instrumental and vocal, is a system of music in its own right. It has its own rules, and by these it must be judged.' (Breandán Breathnach, *Folk Music and Dances of Ireland* (Talbot Press, Dublin, 1971), p. 92). In the late 1950s and early 1960s the free and easy 'it belongs to everybody and everybody can do it' philosophy of many of the American minstrels, who contributed a great deal to the dissemination of folk song, made the question of singing seem very simple. Over-simple, some might say. But as the present revival has progressed, the realisation of the extent of both the folk repertoire and its attendant disciplines and skills has given rise to much debate on how the music should be performed. What follows in this chapter is not a neatly packaged formula guaranteed to give perfect results every time but advice on what to listen to from the vast amount of available recorded material, and suggestions on singing folk songs in a reasonably authentic style, and accompanying them in a way that will complement and enhance them.

It is only necessary to look at the traditional singers of the songs — farm labourers, fishermen, miners, and of course the countless women, workers themselves both inside and outside the home — to realise that the songs they would produce would not be the same as those of a singer trained in a conservatory. The music we are concerned with is in many ways a functional music in its natural setting. A singer from Nova Scotia tells us:

I was born into a house where someone was singing most of the time, and when song was the only entertainment. The women made their labour sweeter by singing the old songs as they worked at spinning, weaving, knitting, piecing patchwork and hooking rugs. Father did some work as a cooper, and I remember he had a special song he always sang when he was finishing an axe handle. And every night he sang, excepting once a week when his newspaper came. That night, he read the paper aloud to us, every word of it.
(Evelyn Kendrick Wells, *The Ballad Tree* (Ronald Press, 1950), p. 306)

The songs arose out of the reality of life, and the way in which they are sung reflects that reality, although as A.L. Lloyd comments in *Folk Song in England* (Lawrence and Wishart, 1967), p. 180), 'generally the folk-song makers chose to express their longings by transposing the world onto an imaginative plane, not trying to escape from it, but colouring it with fantasy, turning bitter, even brutal, facts of life into something beautiful, tragic, honourable, so that when singer and listeners return to reality at the end of the song, the environment is not changed but they are better fitted to grapple with it'.

Many teachers, while inspired by such songs, are loath to tackle the task of learning to sing themselves, feeling that their basic equipment is not good enough; that their voices are not 'beautiful'. E.K. Wells has this to say on voice quality:

A folk singer has a peculiar quality of voice that makes the music itself sound different: one is not sure of the intervals, or even the notes, and is puzzled by the frequent breaks of rhythm. Since the singer does not recognize his tune as existing apart from the story of his song – asked to hum the tune, or to recite the words, he is often at a loss – and since he considers the tune merely as a medium and not an end in itself, a background to enhance the beauty of the speech, his natural delivery sometimes does not sound like a tune at all. His curious tonal production often defies musical scoring, and his half-chant is more like speech than melody. And if he is old, toothless, and crackvoiced, the problem is increased. These are some of the reasons why the inexpert writing down of a folk song is often the means of killing it. Its essential quality goes out of it unless all the fine distinctions can be caught. The nuances of tone and rhythm, inaudible or baffling to the amateur, become the concern of the expert.
(Wells, op. cit., p. 270)

The main aim of the folk singer is to communicate a story, not to make beautiful noises. The resulting performance may be arresting, for in the course of telling the tale the singer might employ all kinds of melodic and rhythmic variations or employ a striking tone of voice. But these skills are all devices which the singer uses to *interpret* the song.

Tone

The term 'open tone' has been used to describe clean sound, free of vibrato, that is characteristic of much of the singing of these islands. Listen to the women of Barra, for example, on *Waulking Songs from Barra*, Tangent TNGM 111, as they improvise in couplet and refrain songs to accompany the work of waulking cloth. The feeling of lightness and space that many singers get into their voices may well be the result of the functional nature of some songs, but also of how the songs were learnt. An old singer from Wiltshire, Bill Whiting, told me how he had learnt his first song by repeating line after line as it was sung to him across a field by the labourer with whom he was ploughing.

Sam Larner from Winterton in Norfolk (who can be heard on *Now is the Time for Fishing*, Folkways FG 3507), though he sang in the intimate environment of the local pub, managed to achieve this same openness, possibly from his background as a herring fisherman, but also from the fact that his obvious enjoyment of songs like 'Butter and Cheese and All' caused him to smile and thus broaden the tone. Try it. Sing a verse of a song, say a shanty, or a humorous song, first with the muscles of the face very relaxed and without much mouth movement; then repeat it with the muscles gently but not exaggeratedly tensed into a slight smile. Listen to how the tone is brightened.

I am not suggesting that this is *the* sound for all songs or that every note you sing should be accompanied by a fixed grin. For instance, Joe Heaney of Galway (*Joe Heaney*, Topic 12T 91) makes great use of nasal tones and humming notes on *m*s and *n*s particularly in his singing of lyrical songs and ballads. He learned his singing from Colm Keane, his uncle, and tells how for years he never sang in his uncle's presence, but listened and assimilated and, in the initial stages, imitated what he had learned as exactly as he could. Later he made the songs his own by experience, by thought and by relating his own life to the events and emotions expressed. No finer advice could be given to someone wishing to sing folk songs. Imitation is the means by which we initially learn speech and all manner of social skills, so try and imitate what you hear in the singing of traditional singers. However, care is important if we are not to fall into the trap of adopting merely the idiosyncracies of others.

Traditional singers do not sing in a different accent from the one in which they speak. Your own accent will make the song much more credible to the listener and may even dictate that a certain tone be used. There are many instances in traditional singing where both accent and occupation have affected style. For instance, John Strachan, an Aberdeenshire farm labourer singing 'bothy' songs, demonstrates what has been called the 'plooman' style, characterised by a rhythmic approach developed from the pace of walking behind a plough, a sonorous tone with the consonants hit heavily and the vowels 'chewed', and the use of many 'conversational' or speaking cadences. Distinctive as this style is, the phrasing of the words is still natural, that is to say, as in speaking.

On phrasing, there is really not much more to be said than this. Approach the pronunciation as if you were speaking the words. As a basic rule — to which there are exceptions — the traditional singer would do so, because, as has already been stated, the singer wants to tell the story. Since the words are of prime importance, singers tend to extend the musical line to fit the words rather than trying, as in the limerick, to 'cram as many words into the line as ever they possibly can'! Furthermore, the use of dynamic effects is absolutely foreign to the traditional manner. The singer will not soften or swell the tone for dramatic effect, but maintain an evenness to the end of the song.

Before we move on, let me describe a few voice-production exercises you might find helpful. Standing with the feet about a foot apart, your weight evenly distributed and the upper torso, particularly the neck and shoulders, relaxed, find a pitch in the middle of your range and, projecting the sound to a fixed spot about ten feet from you and at eye level, sing the note to the sound of *a* as in 'hat'. Do not force the sound and beware of tension creeping into the face and neck. Let the sound last as long as you continue to expel air and consciously try to maintain the evenness that has been described and that you have identified by listening to traditional singers. Try the same exercise with different vowel sounds: *o* as in 'hot'; *u* as in 'shoe'; *e* as in 'feet'; *a* as in 'faction'. Take the same vowels but this time project them in short bursts of sound, using short breaths making use of the muscles in the diaphragm to direct the sound at your target, as it were. Try these exercises at different pitches and constantly remind yourself that you want clean, open sounds in the front of the mouth. To develop humming and nasal tones, keeping the same relaxed position and choosing a comfortable pitch, gently produce the consonant *m* alternating with *n* and feel the vibrations in the lips, the roof of the mouth, behind the teeth and around the nose. Combine this exercise with the vowel exercises. They are not difficult, neither are they a substitute for actually singing the songs and listening to traditional singers, but if you do them regularly and with some concentration they will help you to listen critically to your own singing.

Decoration

Decoration, or embellishment, when applied to traditional singing, means the improvised addition to and changing of the basic melody of a song in order to enhance it or to point out an important phrase or a new direction in the story. Joe Heaney gives the lie to the myth that it is an unconscious and natural ability that all traditional singers have. He has described how he can see in his mind's eye the shape of the decoration he is about to use; he is absolutely clear about when and how he can decorate a song. For instance, he says that if there are lots of syllables in a line there is no room for embellishment, but that shorter lines give him scope for either suspending notes for effect or adding grace notes. Listen to him singing 'The trees they grow tall' (*Joe Heaney*, Topic 12T 91) and the effectiveness of his approach will be apparent, though the terms 'suspension' and 'gracing' will prove inadequate as descriptions of the multiplicity of vocal ornamentation he employs.

At this point it is important to note that much remains to be written on both the analysis of decoration and the establishment of a common terminology of description. A lecture on ornamentation given by Peggy Seeger provides a much fuller and more detailed guide (*Ornamentation and Variation for the Folk Revival Singer*; duplicated booklet available from Pam Bishop, 39 Ashfield Avenue, Kings Heath, Birmingham B14 7AT). This section will confine itself to descriptions and notations of a few of the most common decorations, mainly with reference to the song 'George Collins'.

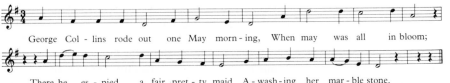

George Collins rode out one May morning,
When may was all in bloom,
There he espied a fair pretty maid
A-washing her marble stone.

She whooped, she hollered, she highered her voice,
Held up her lily-white hand,
'Come hither to me, George Collins', said she,
'And thy life shall not last thee long.'

He put his foot to the broad waters' side,
Over the lea sprung he,
He embraced her around her middle so small,
And kissed her red rosy cheeks.

George Collins rode home to his father's house;
'Arise, my dear mother, and make my bed,
Arise, my dear sister, and get me a napkin,
A napkin to tie round my head.

'For if I should chance to die this night,
As I suppose I shall,
You bury me under the marble stone,
That joins the fair Eleanor's hall.'

Fair Eleanor sat in her room so fine,
A-working the silver twine,
She saw the fairest corpse a-coming
As ever the sun shone on.

She said unto her serving maid,
'Whose corpse is this so fine?'
'This is George Collins's corpse a-coming,
Who was a true lover of thine.'

'Come, put him down, my six pretty lads,
And open his coffin so fine,
That I might kiss his lily-white lips,
For ten thousand time he has kissed mine.'

The news was carried to London town,
And wrote on London gate,
And six pretty maidens died all of that night,
All for George Collins's sake.

Bearing in mind what has been said about speech patterns in singing, let us look
at the use of rhythmic variation as a basic aspect of decoration:

She whooped, she hol-lered, she highered her voice, Held up her lil - y - white hand, etc.

The effect here is to make the words of the song more natural and to prevent the singing from being too four-square. It could be helpful when songs are learnt from books, which tend to give the tune as it would be sung to the first verse only. If the singer feels that the song requires a completely arhythmic approach there is enormous scope for extending notes, speeding up phrases and otherwise disregarding bar-lines and other tempo indications. Robert Cinnamond of County Tyrone is a superb singer in the free style. He can be heard on *You Rambling Boys of Pleasure* (Topic 12T 269). To hear that what he does can be learnt by an urban singer to whom the style was initially quite foreign, listen to John Faulkner on *John and Sandra* (Argo ZFB 2), singing 'The Grand Conversation on Napoleon', which he learnt from Cinnamond's recording.

For songs with a marked rhythm, a very useful and common form of decoration is the use of 'anticipation'. This is executed by singing the melody note, then, whilst still on the same syllable, singing the next note in the melody:

George Col-lins rode out   one May   morn - ing,   when etc.

If combined with a 'slide' (in which the voice evenly moves from one melody note through the intermediate pitches to the next melody note) the effect can be to smooth the line of the tune, making the rhythm less marked.

The 'mordent', a decoration which is sung at speed and therefore written as having no time value, is sung before the melody note, starting on that note and going to another above or below before returning again:

George Col-lins rode out   one May   morn-ing,   when etc.

Brigid Tunney displays a brilliant range of variations in her singing of 'As I roved out', particularly in her use of mordents which vary in pitch from a tone to a fifth away from the melody note (*A Soldier's Life for Me*, Topic 12T 196). (This can best be heard by slowing down the recording.)

There are many more decorations which come under the general description of 'gracing', and others which can be described as 'impulse' decorations such as trills, glottal stops, shakes and so on — many of which, with careful listening, can be isolated and imitated. This applies also to the differing ways in which one can come off a note, by using falling or dying tones or casting the voice upwards in a kind of yelp — both of which techniques are used in work songs. A final word, however, from Peggy Seeger.

There is obviously more scope for external decoration in the melismatic melody [one with more than one melody note per syllable]. Apart from this, each song has a different requirement, according to speed, rhythm, and subject matter. Each singer has to take into account his own interpretation of the song, with regard to tone, effort and general style.

It is useful to develop a personal style, by using certain ornaments consistently, and many field singers have in fact done this. But a singer should always interpret a song and should not impose an unsuitable style of decoration on it. Above all, be consistent within each song and don't throw all the decorations you know into the one piece.
(op. cit.)

Interpretation

Harry Cox once talked about a song he had known from his youth, 'Betsy, the Servant Maid' (*Harry Cox*, EFDSS Folk Classics LP 100). In the song, the young master of the house has fallen in love with Betsy, who is sold into slavery in the colonies by the young man's mother, who disapproves of his choice. Harry ended his account of the story with a sudden and uncharacteristic burst of emotion' 'You see', he said, 'she didn't want him to marry one of *us*!' Harry learnt many of his songs from broadsides, yet no one listening to him singing a song like 'Van Diemen's Land' could doubt his identification with the subject nor deny that he had made the songs his own. He had overcome the problem of 'getting songs off the page'. There are some ways in which this can be done, which can, at the risk of seeming mechanistic, be set out as a list of procedures.

1. Know your song: not simply the text and tune, but the background, too. In 'George Collins', for instance, what is the significance of the marble stone? Why should George become ill after crossing over water and kissing the beckoning girl? And what about the may being in bloom? In some parts of Britain may is called 'mother-die' and it is an ill omen when brought into the house.
2. Find out if there is an extant traditional performance of the song on which you might base your own interpretation.
3. In what kind of situation might the song have been sung? Might it have accompanied work? (Don't forget that caring for children is work: one Kentucky singer whose mother was recorded by Cecil Sharp, said as she picked up the baby before she began to sing, 'I always feel more like it when I'm holding a young 'un.')
4. Read the text aloud. This will give a good indication of how to phrase the song.
5. Tell the story. Often this will reveal aspects of the song which might have escaped you. A group of eleven-year-old girls had heard the ballad 'The Two Sisters'. In retelling the story to the teacher one girl became very involved at the point where the drowning sister begs the older sister to help her out, saying that she will give her everything she has. 'You have beauty: you can't give me that', said the young story-teller. The line does not occur in the ballad, but by its use the story-teller showed her understanding.

6. Try to relate the events in the song to your own experiences, to what you have read and heard from other people. Yet another Nova Scotian singer, Mrs Grover, whose repertoire includes classic Scots ballads, broadsides, local ballads about sea-captains and wrecks, folk hymns and nursery songs, sums up this feeling: 'When I sing these songs, it seems like I'm the fellow they're all happening to.'

Of course the time comes when it is necessary to concentrate on the purely vocal aspect of performing the song. The right pitch for the song must be found according to one's own vocal range and the feeling and mood of the song. One might approach the singing by deciding what kind of 'vocal effort' would achieve the desired effect. Here, it might be useful to explain that Ewan MacColl with Theatre Workshop extended Rudolf Laban's theory of effort, which had been used before specifically in the field of dance, and applied it to voice production. The basis of the idea is that every vocal effort has three elements – time, weight and direction; for example, a 'thrusting' effort (and it can be demonstrated physically) is fast, heavy and direct (like a thrust in fencing). A change in these elements results in a different effort; for instance, if we change the time element of the thrust it becomes slow, heavy and direct, resulting in a 'press'. A simplified scale of efforts which it might be useful to try to apply vocally is set out here.

Scale of efforts

Time	*Weight*	*Direction*	*Effort name*
fast	heavy	direct	thrust
slow	heavy	direct	press
fast	light	direct	dab
fast	light	indirect	flick
slow	light	indirect	float
fast	heavy	indirect	slash
slow	heavy	indirect	wring
slow	light	direct	glide

You will find that the application of the theory of efforts to voice production will provide a method of achieving tonal variety.

Accompaniment

Before even thinking of what instrumentation to use, know your song well and be able to sing it unaccompanied. The song still comes first, even if several instruments are added to the performance, and all the basic work on tone, phrasing, decoration and interpretation should be done first. You are then in a position to say what the basic feeling of the song is, and whether it needs instrumentation to enhance the melodic line or to point up the rhythm. In other words, know why you want an accompaniment and let the song dictate the nature of it.

Rhythmic/percussive accompaniment

Particularly effective for recruiting songs and many of the satirical broadsides of the nineteenth century is the use of instruments such as spoons and various kinds of drums. Staverton Bridge, a group of revival singers and musicians from Devon, use percussion very tastefully (in combination with other instruments) even in traditional ballads (*Staverton Bridge*, Saydisc SDL 266). In effect the melodic line is left free and the words are heard clearly, even starkly, while the accompaniment provides a commentary on the narrative. A good example of this can be heard with the singing of 'I should like to be a policeman' by Terry Yarnell (*Waterloo–Peterloo*, Argo ZFB 68). The American magazine *Sing Out* publishes very good instructions on the playing of all kinds of instruments, including a tear-out record of examples.

Linear and parallel accompaniment

In this kind of accompaniment the instrument is playing in absolute unison with the singer. The instrument can also be said to provide a parallel accompaniment when it plays the same tune and decorations but an interval of a fifth away from the key of the singer. For instance, the singer might begin his song on 'doh', which might be the note C if he is in that key, whilst the accompanist starts on 'soh', or the note G, which is the tonic of the key in which he will play. It sets up an edgy feeling, very good for many of the transportation songs, which need, both in the singing and the playing, a sense of foreboding.

Obviously in this style of accompaniment the player needs to know the singing of the song well enough to mirror exactly all the phrasing and decoration. Terry Yarnell sings 'The Press Gang' with a parallel accompaniment, using the whistle (once called the 'penny-whistle', but this is now obviously a misnomer) and the English concertina (*As We Were A-Sailing*, Argo ZDA 137).

The whistle can be bought in most music shops, and a tutor is available (Michael O Halmhain and Seamus MacMathuna, *Tutor for the Feadóg Stáin* (Litho Press, Dublin, 1971), with accompanying cassette or reel-to-reel tape). It is an instrument which is learned first by many musicians, particularly in Ireland, being relatively simple to master and easily portable. The concertina, on the other hand, is a virtuoso instrument – played in its Anglo-German form as it is by John Kelly (*John Kelly: Fiddle and Concertina Player*, Topic 12TFRS 504), or in its English form by Alastair Anderson (*Concertina Workshop*, Topic Free Reed 12TFRS 501). It is an excellent accompanying instrument, since it can produce a melodic line, harmony, chords, and drone. A concertina newsletter, *Free Reed* (available free from Neil Wayne, Duffield, Derby), provides up-to-date information on all aspects of the instrument.

Linear and parallel accompaniments can of course be played on many other instruments such as the fiddle and the mandolin. The latter, producing notes of short duration, is double-strung and tuned and fingered as a fiddle. (The tuning is G—D—A—E.) It is struck with a plectrum. The effect is light and tinkling. A good example of its use in parallel accompaniment, combined with percussion, can be heard on the song 'Gossip Joan' sung by Frankie Armstrong (*The World of the Countryside*, Argo SPA 304). The fiddle (violin) is an instrument which demands a great deal of skill, but fortunately there is now a vast amount of fiddle music on record, both instrumental music from Scotland and Ireland and an increasing amount of fiddle accompaniment. When used alone with the voice its possibilities are endless, and it can accomplish many of the nuances of which the human voice is capable. It has been said by many expert players that someone wishing to play can do worse than take formal violin lessons to learn the basic techniques, then begin to assimilate traditional styles by listening to and observing traditional players at work. Many examples of fiddle accompaniments will be found on records already referred to.

Drone and linear accompaniment

A drone — a continuous note usually on the tonic ('doh') and/or the fifth ('soh'), can be very satisfying to sing against. It provides a firm base — a strength which can particularly well point up the modal character of many of the tunes. Although a drone and melodic line can be produced on some of the instruments already referred to, such as the concertina and fiddle, the only drone instruments indigenous to these islands are various forms of bagpipe. Small varieties, such as Uillean or Northumbrian small pipes, are increasingly being used in accompaniments, often with good results (e.g. *Cut and Dry Dolly*, Topic 12TS 278). There are tutors for both kinds of small pipes: E. and J. Vallely, *Learn to Play the Uillean Bagpipes* (Armagh Pipers' Club, n.d.); J.W. Fenwick, *Instruction Book for the Northumbrian Small-Pipes* (Northumbrian Pipers' Society, 1974). On these instruments see also Anthony Baines, *Woodwind Instruments and Their History* (Faber, 1967).

However, there is another drone instrument more widely available, and that is the Appalachian dulcimer (see Jean Ritchie, *The Dulcimer Book* (Oak Publications, 1963)). It is a delightful instrument, and can provide a delicate accompaniment for lyrical songs and ballads. It is played, on a table or across the lap, by fretting the melody string with a piece of dowelling or the fingers, and picking with the fingers of the right hand or striking with a plectrum across the melody string and the two drone strings. It is fretted, not chromatically, but modally, and is relatively easy to learn. One excellent example of its use is in the song 'The Furze Field', sung by Ewan MacColl on *The Wanton Muse* (Argo DA 85). By simply using a parallel-drone accompaniment, yet at the same time approaching the tune as a circular one, Peggy Seeger plays the tune two bars behind the singing and the effect is of a round between voice and instrument, a weaving and meshing which is absolutely in keeping with the eroticism of the song.

This approach owes much to the technique of 'follow-up' accompaniment traditionally associated with American Negro blues, in which the singer repeats on his instrument the melody of the phrase he has just sung. A remnant of this form has become fairly standard in revival accompaniments in which the last half or even the whole of the final line of the melody is played as a kind of 'tag', giving a breathing space before a verse in which a new development takes place in the song. It is well worth experimenting with this idea inside verses too, since another dimension can be added by repeating small phrases in pauses in the verses and even discreetly underneath another, harmonically compatible, phrase of the song.

Chords and intervals

One of the most common forms of accompaniment, associated mostly with the guitar and concertina, is the playing of single bass notes followed by chords. In a duple-time piece the effect would be a kind of '*um*-cha' sound — or '*um*-cha-cha' in triple-time tunes. For those wishing to learn the guitar any of the folk-style tutors available give diagrams of chord shapes and some illustrations of right-hand finger styles. These can be adapted to needs and taste. Another form of accompaniment is the addition of a series of single notes which harmonise with the melody. The effect is more spare than the use of full chords, which can sometimes swamp a tune. 'Interval accompaniment', as it might be called, is skilfully used by Peter Hall (*Beware of the Aberdonian*, Topic 12TS 84).

Compound accompaniment

It is often effective, and always enjoyable, to use more than one instrument in an accompaniment. Bearing in mind that the song comes first and that the instruments are to complement the singing, it is a good idea to build from one instrument and then add only what is missing from what that instrument is doing. For instance, one might begin with a simple bass-note and block-chord accompaniment on guitar, and, feeling that the melody needs pointing up, add a melody line on a whistle, combined with a sustained interval accompaniment played on the concertina. There are any number of permutations, of course, but if each instrument has a clearly defined role in the accompaniment, the effect will never be cluttered. Some of the most exciting accompaniments come about by letting instruments assume a role with which they are not usually associated; for instance, by playing the melody only in absolute parallel on the guitar without chords, or by playing long smoothly held intervals on the fiddle, and so on. Some of the worst accompaniments (and this has nothing to do with instrumental skill) come about by allowing the instrument to become a crutch for limp singing, or a substitute for understanding or caring for the songs.

9 *Resources*

MICHAEL GROSVENOR MYER

RECORDS

Since the folk revival of the early to middle fifties, the record industry has, of course, co-operated in catering for public interest in folk music and song. Innumerable records relevant to the contents of this book have been issued. The commercial labels (EMI, Fontana, Pye, Polydor, etc.) have, naturally enough, recorded folk artists like the Dubliners, the Spinners, the Clancy Brothers (and, latterly, the electric groups – Steeleye Span and such); and have also produced many albums, often at budget prices, with such titles as *Irish Folk Hits* and *Favourite Folk Songs*. In common with all the popular issues of such companies, these have a relatively short catalogue life – a new record by any artist or group replaces the previous one, and titles are deleted when their commercial appeal diminishes. I shall not, therefore, concern myself much with such folk-pop products; enquiry through catalogues, dealers, or periodicals is necessary to establish what, of this type, is available, at any given moment.

The specialised folk labels are in an entirely different category. They rarely delete (though they may, of course, occasionally run out of stock), so their issues may be regarded as a sort of folk archive.

The leading labels of this type are Topic (originally a branch of the Workers' Music Association, with all that that implies politically, but now independent); Argo (the 'educational and cultural' branch of Decca); and Leader – though, since this company's production and distribution have been taken over by the Transatlantic company (now called Logo Records), there has been a tendency to delete items less widely in demand. On the other hand, Transatlantic themselves specialise to a considerable extent in folk music, having issues the famous Young Tradition in the late sixties, for instance, and being responsible for British reissues of such American singers as Jean Ritchie; so their products are worth keeping an eye on.

In addition there are many American labels specialising in folk (Folkways, Riverside, etc.), and overseas labels from nearer home like Claddagh of Dublin and Outlet of Belfast, available through specialist shops like Dobell's Folk Shop of Charing Cross Road, Collett's of Shaftesbury Avenue, the Folk Shop at the English Folk Dance and Song Society (EFDSS), Cecil Sharp House, 2 Regent's Park Road, London NW1 7AY, and various shops throughout the provinces. These are listed in the annual Folk Directory, published by, and available through, the EFDSS – a publication which any reader of the present book will find invaluable in many ways (fuller details in the 'Books' section below).

Through such shops, too, as well as through folk clubs, may often be obtained the output of that host of small, specialist, privately owned labels (Broadside, Westwood, Folk Heritage, Tradition, Sweet Folk and Country, etc.) which put out records of fairly popular folk-club performers in small numbers. These come and go for reasons different from (in fact opposite to) those which govern the products of the big companies noted above.

Information as to what becomes available on both the 'pop' and the small labels, and indeed news of all new folk issues, can best be obtained through the Record Reviews section of *Folk Review*, a monthly magazine which I shall deal with more fully under periodicals.

Topic have always been conscious of the educational value of their records. At different times, they have produced a series of pamphlets on the use of folk records in the teaching of various subjects; a periodical teachers' bulletin; and most recently, currently available free on application, a select 'educational catalogue'. Both this and their general catalogue of recorded folk music are informative documents, giving full details of the contents of each record and notes on the artists.

Both traditional 'source' singers and the best of 'revival' singers are among Topic's stable of artists. Traditional singers include – among many others – Willie Scott, the Border shepherd, Fred Jordan of Shropshire, Paddy Tunney of Donegal, all of whom have solo albums; and, most important of all perhaps, the singers on the Folk Songs of Britain series. This is a ten-record collection of field recordings of English, Scottish, Welsh, Cornish, Shetland, and Irish traditional singers and musicians, originally issued by Caedmon Records of New York, and reissued in Britain by Topic. The editors of the series are Peter Kennedy and Alan Lomax.

The ten records are arranged by subject, as follows: vol. 1 – *Songs of Courtship* (12T 157); vol. 2 – *Songs of Seduction* (12T 158); vol. 3 – *Jack of All Trades* (12T 159); vols. 4 and 5 – *The Child Ballads I* and *II* (12T 160–1) (i.e. versions of ballads included in Francis J. Child's definitive collection, *The English and Scottish Popular Ballads*, 1882–96); vol. 6 – *Sailormen and Serving Maids* (12T 194); vol. 7 – *Fair Game and Foul* (12T 195); vol. 8 – *A Soldier's Life for Me* (12T 196); vol. 9 – *Songs of Ceremony* (12T 197); vol. 10 – *Songs of Animals and Other Marvels* (12T 198).

Each record in the set is accompanied by a booklet which goes into exhaustive detail about each song's provenance, variants, analogues, broadside and other printed versions, other archive recordings, etc.

Such thorough documentation is typical of the approach of Topic (and, indeed, of all the good specialist folk-recording companies). A Topic issue, for instance, *The Bonny Pit Laddie: A Miner's Life in Music and Song* (12TS 271–2), featuring the well-known Tyneside group the High Level Ranters, has a twenty-four-page insert.

This goes comprehensively into techniques of mining, with sketches of bell pits, drift/shaft systems, split shafts, etc.; lists of mine jobs; a glossary; and a history of mining – in addition, naturally, to full notes on all the songs, and their words. It is indispensable for any project or topic work on coal-mining, heavy industry, Tyneside, and so on.

Even those records without insert booklets have full and informative sleeve notes. Topic's notes are of notably high standard, being either the work, or written under the influence and direction, of their artistic adviser A.L. Lloyd.

A recent Topic project has been a series issued in co-operation with *Free Reed* magazine, aimed at devotees of the concertina and related free reed instruments, in which there has been a strong revival of interest. Some of the best of folk instrumentation can be heard on these records, which can be identified by the prefix 12TFRS to their catalogue numbers. Topic's usual prefixes for their twelve-inch long-play records are 12T (mono) or 12TS (stereo); extended-plays have TOP, and samplers TPS.

'Impact' records, formerly Topic's specifically 'educational' label, have been discontinued, and any reissues will be integrated with the main catalogue. However, *The Valiant Sailor* (12TS 232) on the Topic label, issued to tie up with the school songbooks by Roy Palmer (see 'Books' below), should still be available.

Mention should also be made here of Topic's sampler no. 6, *Ballads and Broadsides* (TPS 201), a selection of songs from various of the company's records, intended to complement Michael Pollard's Pergamon book of the same name, and accompanied also by a separate set of teachers' notes by Michael Pollard, available direct from Topic.

Some other Topic issues of particular educational interest are:

– *The Iron Muse: A Panorama of Industrial Folksong* (12T 86) (various artists) and *Steam Whistle Ballads* (12T 104) (Ewan MacColl); classics of folk-music recording, of particular interest to teachers of social studies, history, etc.
– *Frost and Fire* (12T 136) (The Watersons) and *All Bells in Paradise: Carols for All Seasons* (12T 192) (The Valley Folk); two records of ritual songs, for religious education, history, social studies, English, etc.
– *Farewell Nancy* (12T 110), *Sea Shanties* (12TS 234), *Sea Songs and Shanties* (sampler no. 7, TPS 205), *The Valiant Sailor* (12TS 232), *Liverpool Packet* (TOP 27), *Blow the Man Down* (TOP 98), *A Hundred Years Ago* (TOP 99); for project work connected with the sea and sailors, history, geography, etc.
– *The Jacobite Rebellions* (12T 79) (Ewan MacColl); history.

Topic's samplers – cheap records, giving thematic selections by a sort of cannibalising process from albums in the main catalogue – are excellent value.

Topic's regional series should be mentioned too: *Deep Lancashire* (12T 188) and *Owdham Edge* (12T 204), *Transpennine* (12TS 215), *Canny Newcassel* (12TS 219), *The Wide Midlands* (12TS 210); particularly interesting, I should think, to schools in the areas concerned.

Topic's address is Topic Records Ltd, 27 Nassington Road, London NW3 2TX (telephone 01 435 9983).

Like Topic, **Leader Records** issue both traditional and revival singers and musicians. There is, in fact, a pun involved in the name. The company was founded by Bill Leader, an experienced recording engineer with a particular interest in folk recording. He adopted the practice of putting out traditional records on the Leader label, and called the related revival label 'Trailer'.

Particularly noteworthy is *Unto Brigg Fair* (Leader LEA 4050), an invaluable remastering of some recordings made on wax cylinders by Percy Grainger in Lincolnshire in the first decade of the century, and originally issued by the Gramophone Company — a pioneer instance of the use of modern electronic techniques in folk collecting. Among the singers to be heard is the great Joseph Taylor, singer of the famous song which gives the record its title, and which, when Grainger played it to his friend Delius, inspired his famous concert rhapsody. There is a story that Mr Taylor, invited to attend the first performance, joined in vigorously from the audience; but a glance at the photographs in the extremely informative booklet attached to the record sleeve will show this tale to be almost certainly apocryphal. Mr Taylor was, by that time, a septuagenarian retired farm bailiff, prosperous and highly respected. No one could be farther from the patronising stereotype of the unlettered and clownish yokel who wouldn't know how to behave in a concert hall. And his singing, of such famous songs of which he was the original source as 'Brigg Fair', 'Creeping Jane', 'Maria Marten', was superb.

Among the glories of English folk song, and another important source of many of our best-known traditional songs, are the Copper family of Rottingdean, Sussex. They have a tradition of family glee- and harmony-singing going back to the seventeenth century at least. The Folk Song Society (forerunner of the present English Folk Dance and Song Society) owes its existence largely to Mrs Kate Lee's having noted some songs in 1898 from Messrs James and Thomas Copper. They were made honorary members of the Society, and their famous 'Here's Adieu, Sweet Lovely Nancy' was the first song published in the Society's journal.

The present head of the family, Bob Copper, stands in a unique and interesting relationship to the folk revival. He is both a conscious and sophisticated folklorist, collector, and author, and heir to, and living embodiment of, a great folk-song tradition — the two sides of folk studies present in one man. *A Song for Every Season* (Leader LEAB 404), a four-record set of the family's songs, edited and annotated by Bob Copper, and sung by himself, his cousin Ron, and his son and daughter, John and Jill, is thus one of the most important of traditional recordings. A one-record selection has recently been issued (Leader LED 2067).

Many other important traditional singers and musicians will be found in Leader's catalogue. Mention may be made of their memorial album to the late Billy Pigg, virtuoso of the Northumbrian small pipes (Leader LEA 4006); to the Masters of Irish Music series; and to records of an important Norfolk singer, Walter Pardon,

A Proper Sort (LED 2083) and *Our Side of the Baulk* (LED 2111).

Trailer are less oriented towards school use than are Topic. Their only attempt at a record meant explicitly for school use, *Songs of a Changing World* (Trailer LER 2083) was not very successful. However, *The Fate o' Charlie: Songs of the Jacobite Rebellion* (Trailer LER 3002) is of obvious historical interest (and, incidentally, features Barbara Dickson, in the days before her appearance in a satirical musical about the Beatles rocketed her into the top twenty).

Martyn Wyndham-Read's *Ned Kelly and That Gang* (Trailer LER 2009) is another 'concept album', about early Australian history. Here may be mentioned also, out of turn but in the same connection, Topic's *The Great Australian Legend* (12TS 203).

Projects on such subjects as magic and witchcraft would find useful Dave and Toni Arthur's collection of magic ballads, *Hearken to the Witch's Rune* (Trailer LER 2017). The cycle of the seasons is the theme of *Maypoles to Mistletoe* (Trailer LER 2092), though I don't find this as impressive as Topic's *Frost and Fire* and *All Bells in Paradise*, previously mentioned.

Trailer don't do anything quite comparable to Topic's 'regional' series, but the North-east is well represented by three albums by the High Level Ranters of Newcastle: *The Lads of Northumbria* (LER 2007), *High Level* (LER 2030), and *A Mile to Ride* (LER 2037).

The address for enquiries regarding Leader and Trailer records is Leader Sound, 209 Rochdale Road, Greetland, Halifax HX4 8JE (telephone: 04227 6161).

Decca are, of course, one of the oldest, largest, and most respected of record companies. There have been folk issues on several of their labels — on the Decca label itself; and recently Deram, in association with a company called Gama, have put out good records by Shirley Collins and Martin Carthy.

In the main, though, their folk music appears on **Argo**. This shows that Decca take folk seriously, and are aware of its importance as an educational medium as well as of its entertainment value. Argo also have probably the widest range of poetry and spoken-word records of any label.

Over the last ten years or so, the Anglo-Scots folk singer and folklorist Ewan MacColl, together with his American wife, Peggy Seeger, also both singer and scholar, has been associated with Argo in four important series of records. MacColl is probably responsible more than any other single individual for the postwar revival of interest in folk music.

In collaboration with BBC producer Charles Parker, and with Peggy Seeger as musical director, he brought out the series of Radio Ballads in the 1950s and 1960s — a series of programmes each dealing with a particular industry or aspect of working-class life. By means of recorded interviews, interpolated with traditional and folk-style music and song and sound effects, a total picture was built up in each programme — one of the most successful and consummate examples ever of the 'project' or 'topic', to put it into educational terms. These programmes are presentable, therefore, to any class doing topic work as an exemplar of what can be done, and are, of course, essential in turn as stimulus for topic work on any of the industries or subjects they deal with. The six Ballads to have been reissued by Argo in record form are: *The Ballad of John Axon* (DA 139), first of the series, the true story of a driver posthumously decorated by the Queen for gallantry in a rail crash, and hence a study of the railway industry in the late days of steam; *The Big Hewer* (DA 140) — coal-mining; *Singing the Fishing* (DA 142) — the herring fleet; *The Travelling People* (DA 133) — the lives of, and the attitudes of others to, gypsies, tinkers, and other 'travellers'; *The Fight Game* (DA 141) — the life of the professional boxer; and *On the Edge* (DA 136) — a study of the opinions and aspirations of young people. Songs from the Radio Ballads can be heard on *The World of Ewan MacColl and Peggy Seeger* (SPA-A 102 and 216).

MacColl and Seeger are responsible also for *The Long Harvest* (ZDA 66–75), a ten-record set on which they compare British and American variants of forty-four ballads and songs, each of which is sung by both of them in anything from two to eight versions, English, Scottish, Irish, and American. Each variant is, of course, printed in an extensive insert, together with notes on the ballad's provenance; variants; social, ritual and historical background; discography; bibliography, alternative titles, etc. *The Long Harvest* is undoubtedly one of the most important direct contributions on disc to folkloric studies. Teachers of music, history, English, social studies, and humanities will all find it of use, interest — and entertainment.

The Paper Stage (DA 98–9), a two-record set, brings a similar format and apparatus to broadside versions of Elizabethan plays. The ballads sung are 'The Taming of a Shrew', 'King Lear and His Three Daughters', 'Arden of Faversham', 'The Frolicksome Duke, or the Tinker's Good Fortune' (on which is based the Introduction to *The Taming of the Shrew*), 'Titus Andronicus's Complaint', 'Gernutus, the Jew of Venice', 'The Spanish Tragedy', and 'A Warning Piece to England against Pride and Wickedness' (the source of George Peele's *King Edward I*).

Taking their inspiration from the MacColls, the Critics' Group has produced an interesting and varied set of thematic records including *As We Were A-Sailing* (ZDA 137) and *Ye Mariners All* (ZDA 138). *Waterloo–Peterloo* (ZDA 86) — the Napoleonic Wars and the Industrial Revolution in song — and *A Merry Progress to London* (ZDA 46) — London through the ages — are both of interest to historians, and teachers of related subjects.

Other performers on the Argo label are Jon Raven and Peter Bellamy. Raven is an expert on and an indefatigable researcher in the industrial history of the Midlands — an interest represented in records like his *Kate of Coalbrookdale* (ZFB 29). His *Canal Navigation* radio programmes, using songs, readings, etc., have been reissued on cassette, incidentally, by his own Broadside record company, of 68 Limes Road, Tettenhall, Wolverhampton. Peter Bellamy is a talented singer who has set a number of Kipling poems to music in the folk idiom on Argo: *Oak, Ash and Thorn* (ZFB 11) and *Merlin's Isle of Gramarye* (ZFB 81), both of which consist entirely of settings of the interpolated verses in *Puck of Pook's Hill* and *Rewards and Fairies.* A record of settings of the *Barrack-Room Ballads* (FRR 014) is available on the Free Reed label (for which see below, p. 158).

Some other Argo issues to note: Cyril Tawney's *Children's Songs from Devon and Cornwall* (ZFB 4), for primary schools particularly; *Songs and Music of the Redcoats*, various artists (ZDA 187).

Argo's address is 115 Fulham Road, London SW3 (telephone 01 589 5293).

Of particular interest in Scotland will be **Tangent Records'** Scottish Tradition series of field recordings made for the School of Scottish Studies of Edinburgh University, under the direction of such leading folklorists as Hamish Henderson. Titles issued to date are: I. *Bothy Ballads* (TNGM 109); II. *Music from the Western Isles* (TNGM 110); III. *Waulking Songs from Barra* (TNGM 111); IV. *Shetland Fiddle Music* (TNGM 117); V. *The Muckle Sangs* (TNGM 119/D); VI. *Gaelic Psalms from Lewis* (TNGM 120).

The interest of nos. II, III, and VI, sung entirely in Gaelic, may be restricted; but the other three should be of side interest, especially no. V, a beautiful double album of Child ballads in sung versions which are still extant.

The accompanying documentation to all these records is as good and full as may be found. A.L. Lloyd has written of this series, 'I take these to be among the most important folk music recordings ever issued in Britain.'

Tangent's address in Tangent Records, 52 Shaftesbury Avenue, London W1V 7DE.

BOOKS

For libraries

Francis J. Child's *The English and Scottish Popular Ballads*, the standard variorum collection whose numbers and nomenclatures both scholars and singers still append to their versions of what are called 'the great ballads', is available in a five-volume paperback edition, published by Dover (New York, 1966). Child printed few tunes, but the deficiency has been admirably remedied by B.H. Bronson in *The Singing Tradition of Child's Popular Ballads* (Princeton, 1976). Other recommended standard ballad collections are *The Oxford Book of Ballads* edited by James Kinsley (Oxford University Press, 1969) and a great improvement on Q's collection of 1910, and Matthew Hodgart's *Faber Book of Ballads* (1971).

EP Publishing Ltd, of East Ardsley, Wakefield, Yorkshire, are engaged on a useful series of reprints of standard early works of folkloric scholarship, including F. Kidson's *Traditional Tunes* (reprinted 1970) and F. Kidson and M. Neal's *English Folk Song and Dance* (facsimile reprint, 1972), Cecil Sharp's *English Folk Song: Some Conclusions* (reprinted 1972), Joe Wilson's *Tyneside Songs and Drolleries* (reprinted 1970), and Alfred Williams's *Folk Songs of the Upper Thames* (facsimile reprint 1970).

Sharp's *English Folksongs from the Southern Appalachians*, famous and fascinating fruits of his forays into American mountain country in the second decade of the century, is published in two volumes by Oxford University Press (1917); Faber have a useful paperback selection, somewhat misleadingly entitled *Eighty English Folk Songs* (1968), edited by Sharp's colleague on the expeditions, Dr Maud Karpeles. Dr Karpeles has also edited an extensive selection under the title of *Cecil Sharp's Collection of English Folk Songs*, in two large volumes (Oxford, 1974), together with a much briefer version of the same work, *The Crystal Spring* (2 vols., 1975).

The Copper family has already been mentioned in the 'Records' section above. Bob Copper has published two books with Heinemann. *A Song for Every Season* (1971; also Paladin, 1975) tells of his family's tradition and their place in their community. *Songs and Southern Breezes* (1973) is an account of the people Mr Copper met in the course of his folk-song collecting for the BBC in the 1950s. Both books have excellent supplements of songs mentioned in the texts.

Stan Hugill is probably the last man living actually to have worked under sail as a shantyman. His *Shanties of the Seven Seas* (Routledge and Kegan Paul, 1961) is an exhaustive, knowledgeable, and informative collection and exposition; and *Shanties and Sailors' Songs* (Herbert Jenkins, 1969), as well as containing many fine songs, is a mine of information on the conditions in which they were first sung. Lewis Winstock's *Songs and Music of the Redcoats, 1642–1902* (Leo Cooper, 1970) does as much for the Army — its associated Argo record has already been mentioned. The name of A.L. Lloyd, leading folklorist, has already cropped up several times in this chapter. His *Folk Song in England* (Lawrence and Wishart, 1967, Panther, 1969, or Paladin, 1975) is essential. Recent fine additions to the field are Peter Kennedy, *Folksongs of Britain and Ireland* (Cassell, 1975) and Ewan MacColl and Peggy Seeger, *Travellers' Songs from England and Scotland* (Routledge and Kegan Paul, 1977).

Songbooks

The books listed in this section are not the familiar type of school songbook, intended to be bought in sets for the use of music departments for the singing lesson, and containing a few 'folk' songs, often in bowdlerised and/or prettified versions, among all sorts of other material. Rather, they are books compiled by people with specialist knowledge of folk song and its nature, not necessarily in every case with schools in mind. This is not, of course, to suggest that music teachers will not find some if not all of them useful for the singing lesson.

Penguin have some excellent folk-song books. *The Penguin Book of English Folk Songs*, edited by Ralph Vaughan Williams and A.L. Lloyd, is not a mere reprinting of previously known variants; the policy followed by its editors was to disseminate more widely versions formerly published only in the scholarly and not very accessible columns of the old *Journal of the English Folk Dance and Song Society*. Since its first appearance in 1959, the Penguin book has come to be regarded as a standard classic of folkloric scholarship.

Penguin also have books of folk songs American (edited by Alan Lomax, (1968)), Australian (edited by J.S. Manifold (1964)), and Canadian (collected and edited by Edith Fowke (1974)). In association with the last of these, Leader have recently issued an LP of some of Dr Fowke's field recordings on which the book was based, under the title of *Far Canadian Fields* (LEE 4057).

The English Folk Dance and Song Society publishes a vast number of song books, far too many to list here. Details are available from the Society. Stephen Sedley's *The Seeds of Love* (Essex Music, in association with the EFDSS, 1967) is an admirable and useful collection of love songs (many of them, it should be noted, are songs of most explicit sexual content: the warning that teachers of lower age-groups may wish to vet the book first may be taken, of course, to apply to many books and records).

Frank Purslow has done a magnificent job in editing into singable form the vast corpus of manuscripts in the possession of the EFDSS which resulted from the collecting in southern England early this century of the Hammond brothers and George Gardiner. The results of his work are contained in four excellent EFDSS paperbacks, *Marrow Bones* (1965), *The Wanton Seed* (1969), *The Constant Lovers* (1972), and *The Foggy Dew* (1974).

The Singing Island (Mills Music, 1960) is an attractive collection of English and Scots folksongs compiled by Peggy Seeger and Ewan MacColl; plenty of good notes. Roy Palmer is responsible for an admirable collection of *Songs of the Midlands* (EP Publishing, 1972).

Roy Palmer has also published with Cambridge University Press two books more explicitly intended for school singing: *Room for Company* (1971), and *Love Is Pleasing* (1974). These are available both in a piano and a melody edition; the latter gives recommended guitar chords.

Textbooks

More and more, as this present volume demonstrates, folk song is coming to be regarded as resource material in various aspects of the curriculum. Naturally enough, more and more books are appearing to make the necessary connections thus implied. In the Cambridge University Press Resources of Music series are four books edited by Roy Palmer. In them folk songs, complete with music, appear alongside contemporary letters, documents, accounts, etc., to illustrate various aspects of social history. There are helpful, though unobtrusive, editorial commentaries, and full notes on the origins, collations, etc., of the song versions used. Titles so far available are *The Painful Plough* (1972) (about the agricultural labourer in the nineteenth century), *The Valiant Sailor* (1973) (lower-deck life in Nelson's navy), *Poverty*

Knock (1974) (nineteenth-century industrial life) and, in collaboration with Jon Raven, *The Rigs of the Fair* (1976) (popular sports and entertainments). *The Valiant Sailor* (Topic 12TS 232) was issued by Topic in association with the book of that title.

Roy Palmer's *A Touch on the Times, Songs of Social Change 1770–1914* (Penguin, 1974), as well as dealing with the social history of the period, is illustrated by a wealth of old photographs and other graphic material which make it a valuable stimulus book. Roy Palmer approaches life in the army in the same way in *The Rambling Soldier: Life in the Lower Ranks, 1750–1900, Through Soldiers' Songs and Writings* (Kestrel Books and Peacock, 1977).

Michael Pollard's *Ballads and Broadsides* (Pergamon, 1969), associated with Topic's sampler record no. 6 (TPS 201), gives us folk song for the English lesson – a special sort of poetry book, as Michael Pollard himself has described it.

Of course, poetry books have always included the words of a few traditional ballads and lyrics. Increasingly, though, the poetic significance of these *as songs* is coming to be stressed; so that there may be a record of reading and singing issued alongside the book, or some of the tunes may be printed, as in David Holbrook's Iron, Honey, Gold series (4 vols., Cambridge University Press, 1965), and Geoffrey Summerfield's *Voices* (Penguin, 1970).

Periodicals

Each year, the English Folk Dance and Song Society publishes a Folk Directory. This invaluable work of reference contains details of all folk clubs, folk artists, folk films available, records of the year, companies producing folk records, university courses in folklore, etc., etc., etc. It is available (as, incidentally, in case of difficulty, should be practically any record or book mentioned in this chapter) from the Folk Shop, Cecil Sharp House, 2 Regent's Park Road, London NW1 7AY (telephone: 01 485 2206).

All members of the EFDSS receive, three times a year, the society's magazine, *English Dance and Song*; and, once a year, the more scholarly *Folk Music Journal*, successor to the celebrated *Journal of the English Folk Dance and Song Society*.

Several of the popular music papers cover folk events mainly from the pop point of view, give news of goings-on on the folk scene, review folk records, and publish articles on and interviews with folk musicians. *Melody Maker* probably provides the best coverage of this type.

Any teacher interested in folk music in education, or any librarian in a school where folk is used, would do well to take out a subscription to the monthly *Folk Review*, the only professionally produced national-circulation magazine entirely devoted to the subject. Apart from all other considerations of interest and enjoyment, its record and book reviews are the best way of keeping up to date with what is available as folk resource material. At the time of writing, an annual subscription costs £4.00. Write to *Folk Review*, Austin House, Hospital Street, Nantwich, Cheshire.

The American journal *Sing Out* is also of great value to the enthusiast. It is published at 595 Broadway, New York, NY 10012 and can be obtained in Britain through the EFDSS.

POSTSCRIPT

Since this chapter was written, Free Reed, mentioned in the section on Topic Records, has re-formed as an independent record company. They run a mail order service from Free Reed Records, Duffield, Derby, and have a shop at 13 Chalk Farm Road, London NW1 (telephone 01 267 0296).

Their material is not confined to the music of the concertina and related instruments, although this does, of course, represent a good proportion of their output. Of particular interest to schools is *The Transports* (FRRD 021/022), a superb ballad opera by Peter Bellamy, telling the true story of the tribulations of an East Anglian couple sent to Australia as convicts on the first fleet to the new colony, where they eventually prospered and founded a commercial dynasty. It is particularly to be recommended to teachers of history and English; and of music, in view of its ingenious use of folk-song variants in its original tunes, and in the care taken to make the music sound authentically of the period. Dolly Collins, the musical director, has used only instruments known to have been in use in the church-loft bands of the 1780s, the period of the narrative.

There is also a lot of interesting sociological information in *The Tale of Ale: The Story of the Englishman and His Beer* (FRRD 023/024); though the appeal may be to the teacher rather than to the pupil.

December 1977

Index

INDEX OF SONGS AND BALLADS

(Entries for quotations are in italics)

159

SELECTIVE GENERAL INDEX